Gnostic Secrets
of the
Naassenes

This image, created by Christopher Hills, is described by him as the symbol
of "nuclear evolution," and appears in his book
Nuclear Evolution: Discovery of the Rainbow Body.
It is also a symbol of the Sacred Jordan.

Gnostic Secrets of the Naassenes

The Initiatory Teachings of the Last Supper

MARK H. GAFFNEY

Inner Traditions
Rochester, Vermont

Inner Traditions
One Park Street
Rochester, Vermont 05767
www.InnerTraditions.com

LIBRARY OF CONGRESS CATALOGING-IN-PUBLICATION DATA

Gaffney, Mark.
  Gnostic secrets of the Naassenes : the initiatory teachings of the Last Supper / Mark H.
Gaffney.
      p. c.m.
  Includes bibliographical references and index.
  ISBN 0-89281-697-X (pbk.)
  1. Naassenes I. Title
  BT1437.G34 2004
  273'.1—dc22

                                                                    2004004033

Printed and bound in the United States at Lake Book Manufacturing, Inc.

10   9   8   7   6   5   4   3   2

Text design and layout by Virginia Scott Bowman
This book was typeset in Sabon with Tagliente and Myriad as the display typefaces

Illustration credits

Frontispiece: from Christopher Hills, *Nuclear Evolution: Discovery of the Rainbow Body*
(Boulder Creek, Calif.: University of the Trees Press, 1977); figure 11.1 from J. E. Circlot,
A Dictionary of Symbols (London: Routledge and Keegan Paul, 1971); fig. 12.1 from Joseph
Campbell, ed., *The Mysteries: Papers from the Eranos Yearbooks.* Copyright © 1955 by
Princeton University Press. Reprinted by permission of Princeton University Press; fig. 12.2
from Erich Neumann, *The Great Mother: Analysis of the Archetype.* Copyright © 1963 by
Princeton University Press. Reprinted by permission of Princeton University Press; fig. 12.4
is a photograph by the author, courtesy of the Siddha Yoga Ashram in Oakland, California;
fig. 12.5 from Kieran Kavanaugh and Otilio Rodriguez, trans. *The Collected Works of
St. John of the Cross.* Copyright © 1964, 1979, 1991 by Washington Province of Discalced
Carmelites, ICS Publications, 2131 Lincoln Road, N.E., Washington, DC 20002-1199, U.S.A.,
www.icspublishing.org; figure 13.1 © Erich Lessing/Art Resource.

*To the many victims of Christian intolerance,
past and present.*

*If they ask you "What is the sign of your Father in you?"
tell them "It is movement, and rest."*
THE GOSPEL ACCORDING TO THOMAS (SAYING 50)

The Guru principle moves, and moves not.
VERSE 62, THE GURU GITA (SRI SKANDA PURANA)

The mover of all things is itself unmoved.
THE REFUTATION OF ALL HERESIES 5.7.25
(THE NAASSENE SERMON)

Contents

Introduction

DESPITE THE MILLIONS OF WORDS WRITTEN and the hundreds of books published every year on the subject of Christianity, the origins of our Western religious tradition are imperfectly understood. Of course, the official representatives of the various orthodox churches would probably dispute this in the strongest terms. They generally hold that the New Testament is a completed work of revelation, a done deal. According to them, the duly vested Church authorities long ago resolved whatever few loose ends remained to be tidied up from the early period of revelatory scripture, and because the important matters of faith have not changed over the many centuries, all that modern-day Christians need do to be saved is believe, obey, and, ultimately, reap faith's reward in the hereafter.

Today, however, increasing numbers of Christians are disenchanted with the standard salvation formula. They find the liturgy tiresome and the rituals and sacraments empty exercises. They are distrustful of doctrines and are not persuaded by pat answers to profound questions. They find neither comfort nor inspiration in tedious sermons and they resent ministers who lay guilt trips on members of the congregation. Indeed, many are angry because they believe they have been deceived or lied to by the Church. As a result, they tend to regard not only Church corruption but all of the above as symptomatic of a deeper malady: the failure of institutional religion. Some, despite their misgivings, choose to remain within the Church. Others have voted with their feet and have left. Yet all crave devotion and all are in

1

search of deeper answers about their faith. These Christians should read on. This book has been written with them in mind, which brings us back to the matter of origins . . .

Scholars generally agree that during its first centuries Christianity faced serious competition from numerous rivals, including Mithraism, Judaism, the official cults of Rome, various other pagan Mystery religions, and Gnostic Christianity. But among these rivals, the last was viewed as by far the most pernicious threat—and why were Gnostic Christians considered so dangerous? Because, as one Church patriarch named Irenaeus wrote late in the second century, "[T]heir language resembles ours, while their sentiments are very different." The Gnostics, in other words, masqueraded as Christians! Irenaeus went on: "[Their] error is craftily decked out in an attractive dress . . . to make it appear to the inexperienced . . . more true than truth itself."[1]

In fact, so closely did Gnostic Christians mimic the genuine article that even priests could not always discern the subtle differences between the true and the false. For which reason, we are informed, many were led into error. Bishop Irenaeus was one of the first to warn his fellow Christians about the insidious danger. He was also the first to use the term Gnostic, based on *gnosis,* the Greek word for knowledge. The crux of the problem was that these Gnostics claimed to be in possession of an advanced form of Christianity involving secret teachings, a claim the orthodox bishops flatly denied.

Around 180 C.E. Irenaeus penned a lengthy treatise to unmask the hoax, and about forty years later another Church father, Bishop Hippolytus, compiled a ten-volume opus of his own. These antiheretical writings earned Irenaeus and Hippolytus a reputation as authorities on the matter of heresy, and their views exerted an enormous influence on the subsequent development of Christianity. The orthodox bishops who came after them followed in their footsteps, which is how tradition works. Even today Irenaeus and Hippolytus hold a special place of respect among orthodox scholars and are studied by each new generation of Christian theologians.

The orthodox view is that the Christian faith owes nothing to

Gnosticism.² Gnostic Christianity was a later development, an errant stepchild of the second and third centuries C.E. According to this view, it played no part in the formative period of Christianity, nor was it a tradition in itself. Indeed, it borrowed (or stole) everything from orthodox Christianity. In 1967 the scholar G. van Groningen went so far as to claim that Gnosticism "became a real threat . . . as a parasitic religion feeding on Christianity."³ Kurt Rudolph, author of *Gnosis: The Nature and History of Gnosticism,* agreed. Rudolph wrote that because "Gnosticism prospered on the soil of its host religion . . . [it] should rightly be described as parasitic."⁴ Numerous other scholars have espoused similar ideas.

No wonder that nearly all Christian scholars and theologians have ratified the Church's long-standing campaign to stamp out Gnosticism, generally regarded as a scourge. Such was the view of W. F. Albright, one of the leading biblical scholars of the twentieth century. Albright was a brilliant linguist and a pioneering archaeologist, and in one of his last books, *History, Archaeology, and Christian Humanism,* he wrote, "Their belief[s] . . . stand in direct opposition to the Gospel. No wonder that the orthodox . . . reacted violently against the ideas of the Gnostics . . ."⁵ Most Christian scholars have agreed with Albright. Indeed, the unanimity of support for the Church's suppression of Gnostic writings and teachings has been remarkable and the variety of apologetics almost endless.

Even those scholars who have struck a more sympathetic tone have usually imputed a negative value to Gnosticism, suggesting, for example, that it was a form of escapism. James M. Robinson exemplified this trend. Robinson headed up the team of scholars who prepared an important compendium on Gnostic Christianity, *The Nag Hammadi Library,* first published in 1977 and to which we will make frequent reference.⁶ Robinson was genuinely enthusiastic about Gnosticism, but he also believed it " . . . was the religion that expressed most clearly the mood of defeatism and despair that swept the ancient world in the early centuries of the Christian era."⁷ In other words, whoever they were, the Gnostics were dreamers and escapists.

This encompasses the mainstream of opinion—and, we note, is exclusively pejorative.

Scholarship's dismissive attitude raises an important question: How, then, do we account for the remarkable resurgence of interest in Gnosticism over the past two centuries? It appears that we Christians have been drawn to it, despite ourselves, like moths to the flame. Our fatal attraction to a notorious creed is no fluke; it is a real phenomenon, well attested to by the many papers and books that scholars grind out each year on the subject.

The interest in Gnosticism is genuine enough, yet there is also something irksome about the scholarship to date. Such has been my experience. I have read many of the studies, and in every single case they have failed to persuade me that the authors have done more than scratch the surface. Given the negative impression that these studies almost always generate, their typically dismissive conclusions are not surprising. If the scholars are to be believed, Gnosticism was a very strange religion. While I am the first to agree that some of the Gnostics were more than a little strange, in the following pages I hope to show that the general negative impression is a false one, a mere artifact. The problem, as we shall see, has nothing to do with Gnosticism—it has everything to do with the adequacy of scholarship itself.

In the following chapters we will break new ground by entering into the world of the Gnostics. We are going to try to understand their spiritual world as they themselves understood it—indeed, as they experienced it—an unprecedented leap for scholarship. In the process of allowing the Gnostics to speak for themselves and tell their own very different story, we will arrive at conclusions that are utterly subversive to orthodox Christianity and which, I predict, will eventually stand tradition on its head.

We are going to examine powerful evidence that the Gnostic element was present in Christianity from the beginning, and was, in fact, the very heart of the teachings of Jesus. We will discover that the Gnostic controversy that developed in the second century C.E.—the issue that obsessed Church leaders such as Irenaeus—occurred not because pristine Christianity became polluted by Gnostic heresy, as the Church argued and still contends, but because the bishops of the fledgling Church so rearranged their priorities in their attempts to consolidate institutional Christianity that they lost contact with their own spiritual (Gnostic) roots.

This historic watershed has come within reach thanks to a serendipitous confluence of events. During the same period that witnessed the modern revival of interest in Gnosticism, archaeologists, meanwhile, were busy amassing an enormous amount of documentary evidence about the ancient world, and this included sensational discoveries. One of the most important breakthroughs occurred in 1945, when an entire Gnostic library, which had been stashed inside a clay jar, was unearthed at Nag Hammadi, Egypt. After many frustrating delays, the trove was finally published in its entirety in 1977.[8] Another stupendous discovery occurred in 1929 on the coast of Syria at a place called Ra's Shamra: an entire cuneiform library from the ancient city of Ugarit.

In addition to these sources, we will draw upon the English translation of the Jerusalem Bible Reader's Edition (New York: Doubleday, 1968) and also upon apocryphal scriptures such as the Book of Jasher (meaning the Upright) and pseudoepigraphic scriptures such as the Book of Enoch, both of which came to light after having been lost for many centuries. Our primary source document, however, is the most important of all from the standpoint of illuminating Christian origins: the *Refutation of All Heresies*, penned in the third century C.E. by Bishop Hippolytus, one of the two heresiologists already mentioned here.

The *Refutation* disappeared for many centuries after it was written and was not discovered until 1842. The first English translation appeared in 1868 and stirred a brief flurry of interest, but unfortunately other archaeological discoveries at the turn of the twentieth century overshadowed it. An adequate commentary did not appear until 1984. Now, at long last, thanks to the corroborating scriptures unearthed at Nag Hammadi, its true importance can finally be established, because a portion of the *Refutation*, found in Book 5, is one of the keys to early Christianity.

I shall never forget the first time I opened this part of the *Refutation,* known as the Naassene Sermon, a remarkable polemic aimed at one of the Gnostic groups, the Naassenes. Even though I knew almost nothing about Gnosticism and even less about Hippolytus, I was captivated from the start, but it took years of further study before I penetrated the document.

It is important to realize that Gnosticism was not a religion. Many competent scholars have erred in this regard. It was an inclination—mystical, existential, and experiential—that was present to some degree in nearly all of the ancient religions. It took numerous forms; even within Christianity there were different Gnostic sects—Hippolytus mentions a number of these in his *Refutation.* While I do not dispute his judgment that many, perhaps most, were divergent, one of the Gnostic communities stood out: the Naassenes, so named, according to Hippolytus, because they "presumed to celebrate a serpent" (*Refutation* 5.6.3). The bishop derived the name from *naas,* which, he tells us, is the Hebrew word for "snake" or "serpent." This was an error on his part.[9] The actual Hebrew word for snake is *nahash.* The Naassenes were more generally known as Ophites, from *ophis,* the Greek word for "serpent."

These Naassenes were among the first Christians to be declared heretical. Hippolytus placed them squarely at the head of his index and devoted five substantial chapters to refute them, more space by far than he allotted to any other heterodox group. This is the surest indication of the odious importance he attached to them. Indeed, Hippolytus leaves no doubt: He refers to their beliefs as "the silly and crazy notions of fools" (*Refutation* 5.10.1) and emphatically describes Naassene heresy as the root error from which all other heresies had sprung (*Refutation* 5.11.1). Likening heresy to a many-headed hydra, his intention in refuting the Naassenes is to lop off "the heads of this delusion" once and for all and to "exterminate the monster" (*Refutation* 5.11.1).

Whether Hippolytus believed that he had succeeded we cannot know. Too many centuries stand between then and now. We have no information about when the Naassenes were finally dispersed; Hippolytus is our only source. Indeed, we have no information about the sect at all except what he preserved in his *Refutation*. Fortunately, as we shall see, this is sufficient, because Book 5 of his treatise includes a long, rambling monologue that Hippolytus himself surely did not compose. Rather, it appears to have been recorded verbatim. This text, known as the Naassene Sermon, will serve as the main focus of our study, and it has a great deal to teach us about our Christian origins. (See the appendix for the text of the Sermon.)

Over years of study, as I delved deeper into the Naassene Sermon and explored its many scriptural citations, my first intuition was confirmed. I was amazed to discover that its unknown author(s) wielded an encyclopedic command of scripture, a fact that is not necessarily evident from a superficial reading. I also found buried in the text a wealth of thematic connections and, by implication, a coherent body of teachings. I was no less impressed by the clarity, insight, integrity, and originality of the Naassene interpretation of the evolving Judaic tradition that had reached its culmination in the birth and life of Jesus. I was persuaded that several scholars were right to conclude that Hippolytus had stumbled onto one or more mystical writings that were never intended for public consumption and had embedded them in his *Refutation*.[10] This material was surely intended for the eyes of select individuals, those who were ready to receive more advanced spiritual instruction.

The Naassenes claimed to have acquired their mystical teachings from James the Just, the brother of Jesus (*Refutation* 5.7.1). Were they lying? Evidence that we shall examine in the chapters that follow suggests that they were not. In the process of compiling for posterity the false beliefs of the sect he most despised, Hippolytus may have unwittingly preserved a vital link to the original Nazarene community in Jerusalem—hence to Jesus himself! This is why the Naassene Sermon is so important to us. The bishop's achievement is all the more remarkable because, as we shall see, judging from his own transparent statements, he clearly failed to understand the Gnostic material that had passed into his hands. It is ironic that his very ignorance enhances his credibility as a witness: His acerbic attempts to discredit Naassene belief are plainly refuted by the very material he compiled and recorded.

In reading the Naassene Sermon, what becomes strikingly obvious about the sect is its syncretism. Unlike the institutional Church, which sought to sever every link with antiquity, this group insisted on maintaining continuity with the past. In this respect, strangely enough, the Sermon finds strong support in archaeology, which has amply demonstrated that Christianity did not arise in a vacuum. It is an interesting bonus that in the process of rediscovering those old links we gain a deeper appreciation of what makes Christianity unique—an appreciation the Naassenes plainly shared more than 1,700 years ago.

I should mention, at this point, my disenchantment with the term Gnostic. I hesitate to use the word both because of its negative associations and because I believe that the Naassenes never referred to themselves as such, except, perhaps, in a general sense. If asked, they probably would have described themselves as disciples of Jesus. The term, however, has no suitable alternative, so I will use it throughout the following chapters with this caveat.

As I continued to delve into the text of the Sermon, I discovered a stunning attempt—insofar as I know, unprecedented in the Judeo-Christian tradition—to describe firsthand, using symbolic and figurative language, an elevated spiritual experience. I am not referring to a momentary epiphany or a flash of insight *(satori);* I mean the ultimate experience. In the following pages we will present this evidence and go even further by showing the precise points of correspondence between Gnostic Christianity and the spiritual traditions of India and Tibet—thus mapping out the common ground between East and West.

I am aware that this is an ambitious book. It should be read in sequence, beginning to end, with a couple of exceptions: The curious are invited to peek ahead at any time to chapters 5 and 10 for more about the *Refutation of All Heresies* and the Naassene Sermon. These chapters include detailed background information, an account of the rediscovery of the *Refutation,* a review of past scholarship, and commentary. Those who wish to follow the discussion point by point can read and refer to the complete text of the Naassene Sermon found in the appendix. Throughout the book I have included citations pertaining to the Sermon—(*Refutation* 5.7.1), for example—to help in this regard. Also included is a glossary of obscure terms.

In the course of my research for this book I found myself ineluctably drawn backward in time as I pursued various loose ends and antecedents. While I found that most traces played out in fuzzy lacunae—in the dangling thoughts of long-forgotten scholars or the silent ruins of dead cities—my efforts did not go entirely unrewarded. To those who persist, the ancient world occasionally does yield up its secrets. The book's final chapters will discuss anomalous clues that hearken back and hint at remarkable events at or before the dawn of history. Because the evidence of these is still thin, we shall have less to say of them. The greatest archaeological discoveries belong to the future.

In the introduction to his landmark 1977 book, *The Nag Hammadi Library,* which made available for the first time in English an entire corpus of Gnostic scripture, the editor James M. Robinson, whom I have cited already, wrote:

> Now the time has come for a concentrated effort, with the whole Nag Hammadi library accessible, to rewrite the history of Gnosticism, to understand what it was really about, and, of course, to pose new questions. Rarely has a generation . . . had such an opportunity!

I can only second the words of James Robinson. Were he with us today, I know he would welcome this book about the Naassenes, the purpose of which is to announce that the "concentrated effort" of which he spoke with such obvious excitement has finally borne fruit. The good news is herein, awaiting the reader.

PART ONE

At the Jordan

1

The Parting of the Waters

IS IT CHANCE ALONE THAT RULES THE WORLD-AS-STAGE, determining when great spiritual figures will appear on earth? Or does a higher law govern such things? With regard to Jesus the Nazarene, the question is not answerable by scholarship alone, yet it is no less intriguing. Certainly Palestine in the first century C.E. was ripe for religious upheaval. Social unrest was on the rise and revolution was in the air. The same messianic flame that had fired the successful Maccabean revolt against the Greek Seleucid rulers during the second century B.C.E. was smoldering again. In 6 C.E. the zealot Judas of Galilee organized the first guerrilla campaign against the Roman military occupation and, for a time, stirred up considerable trouble for the heirs of Herod the Great. The outlaw from Galilee violently opposed Roman taxation and preached his own sectarian brand of messianism. From that time until the general revolt of 66–70 C.E., the Roman rulers of Palestine faced continuous unrest and periodic insurrection. To the Romans, their unruly Jewish subjects must at times have seemed ungovernable.

Jewish hatred of Rome was as old as the conquest. Roman rule dated to 63 B.C.E., when the general Pompey triumphantly entered Jerusalem at the head of his legions. The general achieved instant infamy by forcing his way into the great temple and ripping aside the veil before the holy of holies, thereby defiling Judaism's most sacred precinct. The deed was neither forgotten nor forgiven. Years later the occasion of Pompey's ignominious death in Egypt—the general was assassinated when he ran afoul of Julius Caesar—was cause for celebration among Jews.

Relations with Rome never improved. The situation was not helped by a succession of incompetent and brutal Roman administrators. The historian Josephus tells us that in 45–46 C.E., when Fadus was procurator of Judea, a zealot named Theudas gathered a large band of supporters and led them down to the Jordan River.[1] The zealot claimed to be a prophet and boasted that he could divide the waters. Josephus describes this man Theudas as a magician who deluded the people with wild ideas. But wild or not, the Roman procurator was taking no chances; Fadus moved quickly to crush the incipient rebellion. A troop of horse soldiers was dispatched. The self-proclaimed prophet was captured and summarily executed. The head of Theudas was prominently displayed for weeks in Jerusalem, a sober reminder to passersby that Rome meant business when it came to insurrection.

And there were other, similar cases. Josephus informs us that "impostors and deceivers persuaded the multitudes to follow them into the wilderness," pretending "that they would exhibit manifest wonders and signs." Some claimed to be the much anticipated Messiah. The Egyptian mentioned in the Lukan Acts (21:38) was apparently one of these. He led a large crowd of followers to the Mount of Olives, where he invoked the prophecy of Zechariah 14:4–6, calling on Yahweh to come down from heaven and save the nation.[2] For many years the Books of Zechariah and Daniel had fueled the apocalyptic belief that the end of days was near at hand. In that hour God himself would appear and save the righteous few while punishing Israel's enemies. The case of the Egyptian shows that at least some Jews also believed that the final judgment could be hastened by "storming heaven"—that is, by invoking prophecy (Matthew 11:11–15).

Despite the passage of nineteen centuries and the advent of modern science, biblical prophecy has never entirely surrendered its hold on the Christian mind. Each year millions of words are penned on the subject and dozens (if not hundreds) of books are published. Yet, incredibly—

as we are about to discover—some of the richest scriptural gold has completely eluded Christian writers and scholars. The claim of Theudas is a prime example. What did it mean—to divide the waters? The idea sounds peculiar to us in the modern age. Whether the Roman rulers of the first century C.E. understood the words we cannot say. They may have needed a bit of coaching by their Jewish quislings. But ordinary Jews understood; the meaning was portentous. It was taken for granted that the true Messiah would command the waters. Such a display of mastery would be a certain sign of his legitimacy and authority.

The concept of the waters may seem strange to us moderns, but it had a universal currency in the ancient world. The idea did not arise within Judaism, however. The waters theme long predated Moses and even Abraham and was assimilated into Judaism only much later. From there it found its way into early Christianity. The waters turn up in the New Testament in the familiar passages that describe how Jesus calmed the storm and walked upon the Sea of Galilee (Mark 4:35–41, 6:45–52, John 6:19, Luke 8:22–25). Crucially, other New Testament passages, such as John 3:5—"Unless a man is born through water and the Spirit he cannot enter the kingdom of God"—and various Gnostic Christian sources we shall explore in this study show that the concept's meaning was not limited to brute mastery over the elements. The waters had mystical significance as well, and this is reflected in the link—emphasized by Jesus—with Spirit. This association did not originate with Jesus, however. The link between water and Spirit was ancient even in Jesus' day—which is not to say that its mystical significance was widely understood. On the contrary, it was not. In every age the vast majority have not understood the deeper meaning of the waters, and this probably includes hotheads like Theudas, most Jews of the time, and even the majority of early Christians. So perhaps we should not be surprised that within the short span of three centuries after the crucifixion, the mystical connection had been wholly expunged from the teachings of the Church. No wonder the concept of the waters is so foreign to us, today—we have been cut off from our own roots. Fortunately, our loss is not irrecoverable. In subsequent chapters we shall explore the theme of the waters: its evolution, its meaning, and, especially, its deeper significance. As we are going to discover, the idea traces to the dawn of history and thus is a part of our collective human heritage.

THE WATERS

Every child knows the tale, whether from church and Sunday school or from Hollywood, Cecil B. DeMille, and Charlton Heston: how the bearded patriarch Moses lifts up his serpent staff and commands the mighty waters of the Red Sea, whence the waters part and the Israelites cross over a dry seabed flanked by towering walls of water. And Pharaoh's troops, following in relentless pursuit, are swamped and destroyed, allowing the Israelites to make good their escape into the wilderness of Sinai, where, according to tradition, they wander for forty years.

Whatever its factual basis in history, the parting of the waters by Moses and the Hebrew Exodus from Egypt is one of the defining episodes in Judeo-Christian tradition. It is a pity that the tale of Joshua's subsequent crossing of the Jordan is less well known. According to the Book of Joshua, this second crossing occurred near Jericho, probably not far south of Adamah, which lies at the confluence of the Jabbock River and the Jordan. Today a mound known as Tell Damiela, the ruin of some ancient city, lies near the site. Joshua 3:1–17 recounts the event in considerable detail. The Jordan is normally a pacific stream, narrow and easily forded. But we are told that on this occasion, at harvesttime, the river is in full flood—impassable. Following Yahweh's instructions, Joshua bids his men carry the Ark of the Covenant down to the riverbank a half-mile above where the Israelites have gathered. No sooner do the men step into the swollen river with the ark than the waters recede in a solid mass and remain suspended, as if held behind an invisible dam. The Hebrews watch, no doubt in utter amazement, and then simply stroll en masse across the dry bed into the Promised Land.

This second repetition of the parting of the waters in the Book of Joshua is noteworthy. The fact that the motif recurs a third time in

II Kings 2:8 is even more remarkable. The Books of I Kings and II Kings are attributed to the Deuteronomist, the same seventh-century B.C. Judean scribe responsible for the Book of Joshua and—scholars agree—Deuteronomy, Judges, and Samuel.[3] This story of the third crossing occurs in the context of the final return of the prophet Elijah to his hometown of Gilead in Transjordan. The Deuteronomist tells us that on this occasion the great prophet is accompanied by his chief disciple, Elisha, and also by an entourage of some fifty members of the "brotherhood of the prophets" ("sons of the prophets," in the King James Bible). While there is no mention of a flood or a swollen river, the scribe takes pains to mention the others in attendance, even though they play no part in the events that are about to ensue. Their importance is in their capacity as eyewitnesses. Indeed, we are left to ponder whether the story would have found its way into scripture at all if corroborating observers had not been present. By explicitly mentioning them the scribe is informing us that real history, not legend, is being recounted. Of course, given that Elijah and Elisha lived in the ninth century, some two hundred years before the Deuteronomist himself, the scribe must have relied on written records and perhaps on oral tradition, so even if we assume his integrity as a historian, we still must judge the extent to which others had already embellished real events before the Deuteronomist compiled the various accounts. The Deuteronomist describes in detail the circumstances of the crossing and how Elijah is subsequently translated—in other words, taken up bodily into heaven:

> And they went on together. Fifty of the brotherhood of prophets followed them, halting some distance away as the two of them stood beside the Jordan. Elijah took his cloak, rolled it up and struck the water; and the water divided to left and right, and the two of them crossed over dry-shod. When they had crossed, Elijah said to Elisha "Make your request. What can I do for you before I am taken from you?" Elisha answered, "Let me inherit a double-share of your spirit." "Your request is a difficult one," Elijah said. "If you see me while I am being taken from you, it shall be as you

ask; if not, it will not be so." Now, as they walked on, talking as they went, a chariot of fire appeared and horses of fire, coming between the two of them; and Elijah went up to heaven in the whirlwind.

It is one of the most extraordinary and peculiar scenes in the Bible. We are left to wonder at the meaning of the expression "a double-share of your spirit." Biblical scholars have long interpreted the phrase as referring to the inheritance of a double share of the paternal estate by the firstborn son (Deuteronomy 21:17). There is a problem, however, with this standard interpretation: The circumstances of the story do not fit the purview of the scriptural principle.[4] The law of double inheritance of the firstborn applied in cases where a man had two wives but loved only one of them. Naturally, he might tend to favor the son born of the preferred wife. The law, instituted to protect the rights of the unloved wife and her son, stipulated that the father could not bequeath the majority of his wealth to the favored son if the favored son was second born. Instead, he was required to honor the less-favored first-born son by providing him with a *double* share of inheritance.

Clearly, however, the rule has nothing to do with the events at the Jordan recounted in II Kings. Therefore, the reference to the "double-share" of Elijah's spirit must have some other unexplained significance. Nor does the mystery end there. In the same episode, the theme of the parting of the waters repeats yet again; however, now it is the disciple Elisha who commands the waters. The text continues:

Elisha saw it [the chariot] and shouted "My father! My father! Chariot of Israel and its chargers!" Then he lost sight of him [Elijah], and taking hold of his clothes he tore them in half. He picked up the cloak of Elijah, which had fallen, and went back and stood on the bank of the Jordan. He took the cloak of Elijah and struck the water. "Where is Yahweh the God of Elijah?" he cried. He struck the water, and it divided to right and left, and Elisha crossed over.

Apparently the cloak drops at the very moment when Elijah disappears into the whirlwind. The Deuteronomist further informs us that "[t]he spirit of Elijah came down upon Elisha" (II Kings, 2:13–15). We are immediately reminded of the baptism of Jesus at the Jordan, when, according to scripture, the Spirit similarly descends upon Jesus. The passage in II Kings also recalls the first appearance of Spirit in the Bible, in Numbers (11:24–30), an episode that occurs during the wanderings in the desert. Moses gathers seventy elders of the people to the tent of Yahweh, the early forerunner of the temple, whence "Yahweh came down in the Cloud. He spoke with him [Moses], but took some of the spirit that was on him and put it on the seventy elders. When the spirit came on them they prophesied . . ."

How, then, are we to explain these biblical episodes involving the parting of the waters? The fact that the pattern repeats multiple times is a certain indication of its importance. Are these events a record of divine revelation or some natural occurrence on which legend was later based? Not surprisingly in our scientific age, scholars have preferred naturalistic explanations. One of these, Hans Goedicke from Johns Hopkins University, pointed out that the famous description in Exodus of a sudden receding of the waters followed by a flood bears a striking resemblance to the behavior of a tsunami. Goedicke proposed such an event as the basis of the Exodus story, theorizing that the tsunami had been caused by the serendipitous eruption of the volcano Thera in the Aegean Sea.[5] The maverick thinker Immanuel Velikovsky had a different explanation. Velikovsky opted for a near miss by a comet, the cataclysmic effects of which would have been no less dramatic.[6] Nature-based theories have even been advanced to account for Joshua's parting of the waters at the Jordan. Ian Wilson, a writer better known for his research on the Shroud of Turin, proposed in 1985 that the event described in Joshua was the result of a major earthquake. He theorized that the quake temporarily dammed up the Jordan River, which conveniently enabled the Hebrews to cross it and sack Jericho, whose walls were destroyed by the same temblor.[7]

But even if we assume that some reasonable explanation based on a natural event might account for the Red Sea parting for Moses and possibly even the Jordan parting for Joshua, I doubt if even the most richly endowed imagination could conceive of a suitable nature-based explanation in the cases of Elijah and Elisha. These repetitions seem perversely designed to frustrate every attempt in this direction. We intuitively sense that in II Kings we are in the presence of something "other," what the writer Rudolf Otto called the "numinous" or, in other words, "the holy."[8] In the story of Elijah and Elisha it becomes impossible to ignore the likelihood that what begins as a straightforward demonstration of power mechanics—mastery over nature—is transformed into something very different that can only be described as *sublime.* After all, the parting of great waters shows a brute hand, however impressive. But a spiritual ascension is another matter entirely, a conundrum that is beyond the realm of nature and will not be explained unless we fathom both the ancient link between water and Spirit and the mind of the Deuteronomist. The facts of scripture suggest an evolution of meaning and a gradual maturation of the Judaic tradition. According to W. F. Albright, one of the greatest biblical scholars of the twentieth century, II Kings was written in "the purest classical Hebrew, of a type that can hardly be later than the eighth century [B.C.E.]."[9] Albright's protégé, Frank Moore Cross, adjusted his teacher's estimate and settled on a seventh-century B.C.E. composition date, which has found general acceptance.[10]

There seems no way to avoid the conclusion that in the story of Elijah and Elisha we are presented with a spiritual lesson without parallel in the Old Testament, the sole possible exceptions being the ascension of Enoch briefly mentioned in Genesis 5:21–24[11] and the ascension of Noah, which is not found in the Bible and is known only from old Hebrew legends. That the episode at the Jordan described in II Kings involves both the parting of waters and spiritual ascension is significant enough, but that it also incorporates the relationship of master (Elijah) and disciple (Elisha) is even more extraordinary—not simply because both of these inspired prophets were great Yahwist reformers, but also because of their incontrovertible links to the New Testament, links that we shall now explore.

2
The Mind of the Deuteronomist

THE KEY TO THE MIND OF THE DEUTERONOMIST is a scripture known as the Gospel of Thomas, one of a trove of Gnostic gospels found near Nag Hammadi, Egypt, in 1945, and collectively known as the Nag Hammadi library (see the introduction).[1] While several fragments of the text of Thomas were known before this date, the 1945 find represented the first complete copy.[2]

Many parts of the Gospel of Thomas are nearly identical to passages in the gospels of the New Testament, but Thomas is not derivative: Form critical analysis shows it to be an original "sayings source" of Jesus. Further, the material in Thomas is not assembled in a historical narrative in the manner of the New Testament Gospels. The text's 114 sayings and parables are numbered and presented sequentially, but loosely so and in no apparent order.

According to Helmut Koester, one of the scholars who helped translate and prepare the Nag Hammadi library for publication, recent studies of Thomas have failed to show *any* dependence on the New Testament. In fact, they show just the opposite: Koester writes, "In many cases the sayings from Thomas are preserved in a form that is more original than any of its canonical parallels."[3] This suggests that the Gospel of Thomas predates the New Testament and may even have been one of the original sources for the canonical scriptures. Although the manuscript of Thomas found at Nag Hammadi was written in

20

Coptic (the native language of Egypt in the first centuries C.E.), paleographic analysis confirms that the Coptic version was based on an older Greek original. Helmut Koester thinks the Gospel of Thomas dates to the earliest period of Christianity.[4] If this dating is correct, it refutes the standard view of a sharp divide between early Christianity and Gnosticism. Until very recently, most scholars regarded Gnostic Christianity as a second-century C.E. aberration.[5] The early dates associated with Thomas and his Gospel's thoroughly Gnostic tone challenge this view, and strongly suggest that a mystical Gnostic element was present in Christianity from the beginning. As we shall see, analysis of the Naassene Sermon, the primary source document for this book, also supports this conclusion.

AT THE JORDAN

We have already mentioned in chapter 1 the striking similarity between the events at the Jordan recorded in II Kings and the event, more than eight centuries later, of Jesus' arrival at the Jordan to be baptized by John the Baptist. On the first occasion we have the pairing of Elijah and Elisha, and subsequently the pairing of Jesus and John the Baptist. Both episodes occur at streamside and both involve a spiritual initiation, easily identifiable as such by the descent of the Spirit. We have already discussed the Old Testament account (II Kings 2). With regard to the baptism of Jesus described in the New Testament, all of the synoptics (Mark, Matthew, and Luke) agree that after John baptizes him the heavens open and the Spirit, in the form of a dove, descends upon Jesus. A passage in John (3:3) also confirms this: Jesus tells Nicodemus and several other pharisees, "Unless a man is born from *above*, he cannot see the Kingdom of God" [italics mine].

This quote from John is taken from the New Jerusalem Bible, which adheres more closely to the original Greek. In other editions the passage is translated as: "I tell you solemnly, unless a man is born *again*, he cannot see the Kingdom of Heaven" [italics mine]. Here, translating the Greek as "again" rather than "above" reduces spiritual initiation to a ritualized immersion in water, thus obscuring the vital transformative role of the Spirit. (See John 16:13.) Nor is this translation merely an honest mistake. It served (and serves) the intended purpose, which was (and is) to elevate the corporal authority of institutional Christianity. Although there is no scriptural evidence that Jesus baptized his disciples or even advocated the practice, during the second century C.E. baptism became one of the Church's main sacramental prerogatives.

THE DOUBLE DYAD: SCRIPTURAL EVIDENCE

Surprisingly, the obvious parallels between these two remarkable episodes at the Jordan River, one from the Old Testament, one from the New, have not been discussed or even noted by orthodox scholars, insofar as I am aware, despite the fact that the double dyad of Elijah/Elisha and Jesus/John is easily established from the Bible itself—it certainly does not require resorting to Gnostic material. We know that Jews living in the first century C.E. widely anticipated the return of the prophet Elijah based on the prophecy of the fifth-century B.C.E. prophet Malachi (3:24), whose foretelling constitutes the final line of the Old Testament: "I will send you Elijah before the coming of the Lord." The words of Malachi explain the many questions put to John the Baptist in the New Testament Gospels. So impressed are the people by John that they quite naturally wonder if he is the returned Elijah, or possibly the Messiah. Of course, John emphatically denies that he is either (John 1:20–23). Citing Isaiah 40:3, he asserts that he has come to prepare the way for another, one far greater than he, who will baptize with Spirit instead of water (John 1:24–34). The Baptist further states that he is not fit even to loosen the sandal of this great teacher to come. But even John's denials appear to affirm the prophecy of Malachi, as does his physical description, which is strikingly similar to that of Elijah in the Old Testament: According to Mark 1:6, "John wore a garment of camel skin, and he lived on locusts and wild honey." Compare this with II Kings 1:8, where Elijah is described as wearing "a hair cloak . . . and a leather loincloth."

Notwithstanding the Baptist's disclaimers, Matthew, Mark, and Luke unanimously identify John as the reincarnated soul of Elijah. Consider, for example, the following passage from Matthew 16:10–13, which relates an incident that occurs immediately after the Transfiguration, when the apostles question Jesus:

> And the apostles put this question to him "Why do the scribes say, then, that Elijah has to come first?" "True," he replied, "Elijah is to come to see that everything is once more as it should be; however, I tell you that *Elijah has come already* [italics mine] and they did not recognize him but treated him as they pleased; and the Son of Man will suffer similarly at their hands." The disciples understood then that he had been speaking of John the Baptist.

Here, Matthew even adds an extra line of explanation, lest there be any doubt about the intended meaning. In another instance that occurs after John the Baptist's imprisonment (Matthew 11:10–15), several of John's disciples visit Jesus and question him about John. Jesus replies:

> I tell you solemnly, of all the children born of women, a greater than John the Baptist has never been seen; yet the least in the Kingdom of Heaven is greater than he is. Since John the Baptist came, up to this present time, the Kingdom of Heaven has been subjected to violence and the violent are taking it by storm. Because it was toward John that all of the prophecies of the prophets and of the Law were leading, and he, if you will believe me, is the Elijah who was to return. If anyone has ears to hear, let him listen!

As mentioned in chapter 1, in the first century C.E. numerous zealots and false prophets attempted to hasten the final apocalypse through rash acts and by invoking prophecy—hence the reference by Jesus to the violent who are "taking it [heaven] by storm."

These passages from Matthew—and similar ones in Mark (9:9–13) and Luke (7:26–30)—appear to be a ringing affirmation of the reincarnation (or transmigration) of the soul of the Old Testament prophet Elijah as the New Testament John the Baptist. This leads us to a conclusion that is absolutely stunning:[6] If John is Elijah, who then is Jesus if not the reincarnated soul of the Old Testament prophet Elisha? The difference, of course, is the dramatic reversal of roles: He who was formerly the disciple returns as the master and the former teacher reappears as the "voice crying in the wilderness whose function is to prepare a way for the Lord" (Matthew 3:3–4, Isaiah 40:3). The Hindu saint Paramahansa Yogananda pointed out these important relationships many years ago in his famous *Autobiography of a Yogi.* It is both curious and revealing that it took the unique perspective of an Easterner—a non-Christian—to prod us Christians into awareness of this important idea.[7] Of course, Christian scholars have chosen to ignore Yogananda. They find such a reversal of roles simply incomprehensible, probably due to their overly rigid beliefs about Jesus. Yet, as we shall see, compelling scriptural evidence supports Yogananda's powerful insight.

This brings us back once again to the account of the Deuteronomist, the scribe who compiled II Kings some 2,700 years ago, and to a crucial piece of evidence in his story of Elijah's ascension into the whirlwind. We recall that when Elijah bids his disciple to make a final wish, Elisha requests "a double-share" of his teacher's spirit. We have already determined that in the context of the story this phrase cannot refer to the law of double inheritance. Yet the Deuteronomist surely had some purpose in mind when he crafted this phraseology. I believe I stumbled upon that purpose quite by chance while reading an Old Testament study by the scholar George Wesley Buchanan. In his exhaustive comparative analysis of the miracles of Elijah and Elisha, Buchanan observed that the Deuteronomist attributed seven miracles in all to Elijah and fourteen to Elisha.[8] Amazingly, the number of Elisha's miracles was precisely double that of Elijah! In my view this was no accident. It strongly suggested to me that the Deuteronomist's purpose was historical: to inform his reader that from a spiritual standpoint, the disciple Elisha greatly surpassed his teacher. This would also account for the dramatic reversal of roles in the New Testament, the overshadowing of the teacher (Elijah—now John the Baptist) by his former disciple (Elisha—now Jesus).

An affirmation of this stunning interpretation can be found in Saying 4 of the Gospel of Thomas, in which Jesus states: "The man old in days will not hesitate to ask a small child seven days old about the place of life. For many who are first will become last, and they will become one and the same . . ." The passage is an amplification of Matthew 19:30: "Many who are first will be last, and the last first." (See also Mark 10:31 and Luke 13:30.)

The clue we have identified illuminates the meaning of this otherwise obscure passage. I suggest that the first line refers to an ancient soul (the man old in days = Elisha = Jesus) who incarnates to complete his spiritual journey. Like ordinary men, this old soul is born into the world ignorant of his divinity and his true destiny. Yet as he begins to awaken spiritually, perhaps from an early age, he seeks out a prophet (Elijah) who, though not an ancient soul, is nevertheless capable of serving as his spiritual guide (or teacher or guru). The last line, "and they will become one and the same," refers to the culmination of this teacher–disciple relationship. In spiritual traditions the role of the teacher is to facilitate the awakening of spiritual energy within the disciple, then to lead him to the well and induce him to drink deeply. In the moment when the disciple experiences the full flowering of his innate divinity, disciple and teacher become "one and the same." At this point the teacher's job is done. Just as one candle lights another, so the teacher kindles the flame of spiritual knowledge in the disciple. But even a teacher can be outshone by an old soul who is destined from birth to become an avatar—that is, a great spiritual being.

The cryptic phrase "For many who are first will become last" suggests the phenomenal switch we have just described: the eclipse of Elijah (John the Baptist) by his disciple. He who was first has been surpassed. It is notable that Saying 4 from the Gospel of Thomas also mentions the number seven—a child seven days old—seven being the signature of Elijah, referring to the prophet's seven miracles as recounted in scripture.

Confirmation of this interpretation can be found in the Naassene Sermon, the primary source document for this book (*Refutation* 5.7.20–21). Bishop Hippolytus not only tells us that the Naassenes, a Gnostic Christian sect based in Alexandria, made heavy use of the Gospel of Thomas, but he actually cites the very passage (Saying 4) that we have been investigating! Here, however, it appears in an amplified form. Although a number of scholars have made note of its presence in the Naassene Sermon, none has explained the amplified meaning.[9] Hippolytus writes:

> They [the Naassenes] hand down an explicit passage from the Gospel according to Thomas, as follows: "He who seeks me will find me in children from seven years old; for there concealed shall I be made manifest in the fourteenth age." But this is not [the teaching] of Christ, but of Hippocrates, who uses these words: "A child of seven years is half a father." And so it is that these [heretics] . . . say that in fourteen years, according to Thomas, he is manifested. This, with them, is the ineffable and mystical λογος (logos). (*Refutation*, 5.7.20–21)

To understand a layered manuscript such as the Naassene Sermon, it is essential to know at all times who is saying what. In the above passage Bishop Hippolytus demonstrates that he does not understand the mystical material that has passed into his hands. In the process of offering his own explanation, he alters the word *days* to *years* so that it conforms to a known saying of Hippocrates, the father of Greek medicine. Nevertheless, the bishop unwittingly succeeds in confirming our interpretation: He states that the Naassene heretics regarded the number fourteen as the number of the logos, which in this context can refer only to Jesus. In fact, several pages later the Sermon explicitly identifies the logos with Jesus: "He is the Christ, the Son of Man who takes form . . . and comes from the unformed logos" (*Refutation*, 5.7.33). Thus, the "fourteenth age" mentioned in the passage affirms our previous discovery, the number fourteen being a defining mark, the "fingerprint" of

Elisha, referring to the number of his miracles recounted in II Kings. This meaning was probably encrypted to conceal the details about Jesus' identity from all except those deemed worthy to know. Similar cases of veiled language can be found in the New Testament. For example, in Matthew (13:10–5) an inner circle of disciples ask Jesus, "Why do you talk to them in parables?" The teacher replies:

> Because the mysteries of heaven are revealed to you, but they are not revealed to them. The reason I talk to them in parables is that they look without seeing and listen without hearing or understanding. So in their case this prophecy of Isaiah is being fulfilled.

Jesus then recites from Isaiah 42:1–4:

> You will listen and listen again, but not understand,
> see and see again, but not perceive.
> For the heart of this nation has grown coarse,
> their ears are dull of hearing, and they have shut their eyes,
> for fear they should see with their eyes,
> hear with their ears,
> understand with their heart,
> and be converted and be healed by me.

The Naassene Sermon is sometimes fragmentary and often obscure, but there can no longer be any doubt that its author incorporated within it secret teachings intended for spiritually mature Christians. In this case the Sermon illuminates Elisha's request for a "double-share" of Elijah's spirit. Here, the key to its meaning is the number fourteen, which has no significance apart from its relation to seven. As the great linguist Cyrus Gordon pointed out in his milestone study *The Common Background of Greek and Hebrew Civilizations*, the ancients—the Babylonians, the Greeks, and even the Hebrews—often expressed the number fourteen as "twice seven."[10] In the context of the Naassene Sermon, the number fourteen (twice seven) recalls the ratio discovered by George Wesley Buchanan, the doubling of Spirit cast in veiled language to establish the mystical equivalence of Elisha and Jesus. Surely this was the Naassene understanding.

OTHER EVIDENCE

Other scriptural evidence supports this conclusion. In II Kings 2–8 the ascension of Elijah is closely followed by the Elisha Cycle, which describes in detail the fourteen miracles performed by Elisha. What is striking about these miracle stories is that they seem strangely out of place in the Old Testament, reading more like the Gospel of Matthew, Mark, or Luke. What is more, the miracles attributed to Elisha anticipate those later performed by Jesus, including the multiplication of loaves, the healing of the sick, the foretelling of the future, and even the raising of the dead (II Kings 4:42–44, 5:1–27, 8:7–15, 5:1–19).

Additional evidence of this equivalence can be found in the New Testament. Luke 4:25–30 describes a curious episode at the start of Jesus' public ministry: While teaching in the synagogue, Jesus demonstrates an uncanny knowledge of the miracles of Elijah and Elisha. Indeed, the Jews in attendance are so nonplussed by the extent of his knowledge—which includes intimate details—that they become enraged. According to Luke, they hustle Jesus outside for the purpose of killing him, although he escapes.

Matthew 3:14–15 presents another curious piece of evidence. Here, the scene is the Jordan River, where a puzzling exchange occurs between Jesus and John the Baptist. Jesus has come to be baptized, but John demurs. When Jesus insists upon it, John says, "It is I who need baptism from you. And yet you come to me!" Jesus then gives a reply so cryptic that it has never been explained by scholars: "Leave it like this for the time being; it is fitting that we should, in this way, do all that righteousness demands," at which point John acquiesces. Based on everything we have discovered, the meaning of this puzzling exchange becomes clear. Although the spiritual attainment of Jesus (Elisha) has far surpassed that of his former teacher (Elijah), out of love and respect

Jesus deems it fitting to be baptized by him. It would appear that the deep and mysterious teacher–disciple relationship survives even death and reincarnation.

Last, let us examine the words spoken by the crucified Jesus shortly before drawing his final breath: *"Eli, Eli, lama sabachthani?"* The expression, drawn from the first line of Psalm 22, is usually translated as "My God, my God, why have you forsaken me?" Yet Matthew's account of this final moment suggests a very different interpretation, one that confirms the relationships we have discovered:

> When some of those who stood there heard this, they said, "The man is calling on Elijah." And one of them quickly ran to get a sponge, which he dipped in vinegar and, putting it on a reed, gave it to him to drink. "Wait!" said the rest of them, "and see if Elijah will come to save him." (Matthew 27:47–50)

The name Elijah, which contains within it the old Canaanite and Hebrew word for God (El), means "whose God is Yahweh." This accounts for the orthodox translation that Jesus *in extremis* called upon the Father (Yahweh). But the eyewitnesses to the crucifixion heard it differently. According to Matthew, they believed that Jesus was calling out not to God, but to Elijah. But why would Jesus do so, unless he was the reincarnated soul of Elisha? In that case, Jesus was crying out the name of his beloved teacher.

Let us now briefly review what we have learned: The words of Jesus as recorded in the New Testament appear to strongly affirm the reality of the transmigration of souls (reincarnation). Moreover, there is powerful scriptural evidence that the great soul known as Jesus likely studied with the prophet Elijah in a previous incarnation or, in other words, at an earlier stage of his spiritual journey. Of course, these insights fly squarely in the face of orthodox Christianity. Although the Church never specifically repudiated the equivalence of Jesus and Elisha, as early as the third century C.E. Bishop Hippolytus denounced a Jewish Christian sect known as the Elchasaites for teaching that Jesus had reappeared on earth more than once (*Refutation* 9.8–12). It may well be that in the heresy of the Elchasaites we can perceive the more specific contours of the Naassene teaching. Like the Naassenes, the Elchasaites and other Jewish Christian groups such as the Ebionites probably descended from the original Nazarene community in Jerusalem, which was dispersed far and wide during the Jewish War (66–70 C.E.). In the war's aftermath, the survivors no doubt attempted to reconstitute the former flourishing Jesus movement, but unfortunately the outcome was not a unified success. It seems that a number of Jewish Christian sects did emerge, each with similar but slightly differing beliefs. The Gentile Church of Rome eventually denounced most of these communities as heterodox, and Rome prevailed because by this time it had defined what it meant to be a Christian. The general issue of reincarnation continued to be controversial, but the Church did not formally declare the transmigration of souls anathema until the Fifth General Council convened by Justinian in 553 C.E.[11]

ON CHRISTIAN APOLOGETICS

Christian scholars typically defend the Church's holy war against heresy as necessary to preserve a hard-pressed Christian faith in the dangerous times of the first centuries C.E. Besieged from without by a host of pagan cults and proselytizing Jews and from within by heretics of every stripe, Christianity—we are told—had to fight for its survival. On this basis, scholars insist, the Church was correct to throw out dubious gospels and winnow down Christianity to the essentials: a short select list of scriptures—the canon—whose provenance was beyond dispute. Such is the usual drift of Christian apologetics in support of orthodoxy's relentless campaign against heresy.

Unfortunately, the tragic downside is almost never mentioned. It was akin to tossing out the proverbial baby with the bathwater. Even the most casual glance at the historical record shows that the Church's holy war against heresy failed to avert the bitter schisms of the third through the sixth centuries, controversies that wracked the Church top to bottom, destroying all semblance of the unity supposedly secured by the canon. This is the bitter irony that the Church, even to this day, has not acknowledged. Had the so-called heretical writings and beliefs not been quashed, those bitter internal schisms might have been attenuated or averted altogether. In a more tolerant and inclusive atmosphere of truth seeking, the wisdom contained in the Gnostic writings would have emerged to inform and illuminate, adding a greater clarity to the debates and discussions of subsequent centuries, a clarity that, judging from what we know about those debates, was in desperately short supply.

Among the weighty issues of the times, probably the most fiercely contested controversy concerned the person of Jesus—his human versus divine nature—an issue about which, as we are beginning to learn, Naassene (Gnostic) Christianity had much to say. Had the secret teachings of the Naassenes become more widely known, they might have saved Christendom from several hundred years of horrendous internal bloodletting. Indeed, Naassene mysticism might even have saved the Church from doctrinal error. But, alas, we cannot reverse the tragedies and mistakes of yesterday. We can only hope to learn from them and do better in the future.

One way to start would be to immediately address doctrinal issues in a straightforward manner. In this spirit I raise the following question: Why did the Church reject the words of the Gospel regarding reincarnation? In subsequent chapters we shall return to this and related questions. But before we do, we must learn more about the Naassenes.

3

The Sacred Jordan and the Reversal of the Flow

THE NAASSENES WERE KEENLY AWARE of the symbolism of the waters. The Sermon indicates that Jesus, like Elijah and Elisha before him, also commanded the river; but the case of Jesus is no mere repeat performance. The Sermon reads: "This, he [the Naassene] says, is the great Jordan . . . But Jesus drove it back, and made it flow upwards" (*Refutation* 5.7.41). Here, Jesus not only stops the flow of the river, but he actually reverses it! He drives the Jordan back upstream, all the way—by implication—to the source, which in this case is not the Nahr Banias, the Ain Leddan, or the Nahr Hasbani, the Jordan's three main headwater springs. The "source" here is spiritual, not physical: These are the waters of the upper firmament (Genesis 1:7–8) or, in other words, heaven.

Notably, the same idea turns up in the Testimony of Truth, one of the Gnostic gospels found at Nag Hammadi.[1] The pertinent line reads: "But the Son of Man . . . came [to the] world by the Jordan River, and immediately the Jordan [turned] back."[2] The authorship of the Testimony is not known, but scholars think it was composed in Alexandria in the second or third century C.E. Was it known to the Naassenes? Probably.

We have already discussed the evolution in meaning of the parting of the waters as evidenced first by Moses and Joshua, then by Elijah and Elisha. The Naassene Sermon indicates a further evolution: In the case of Jesus, the symbolic language becomes more obviously spiritual. Mastery over the waters no longer involves solely mastery over the physical elements. Now, the very action of mastery over the waters has become symbolic of an interior process of spiritual attainment. By making the river reverse its flow, Jesus achieves the absolute: supreme union with the Godhead—and he does it while still part of this world, which distinguishes him from Enoch, Noah, and Elijah, all all of whom represent previous cases of heavenly ascent. In the process of reaffirming the old theme of mastery over the waters, the Savior announces a new mystery that is even more profound, involving a new series of cosmic lessons on a still higher level.

It is a feat without precedent in Judaism. This is why in Gnostic Christianity all of the important events occur in association with the baptism scene at the Jordan, in which four distinct and important events are discernible: 1) spiritual initiation; 2) the descent of the dove, or Holy Spirit; 3) the reversal of the flow; and 4) the return to the source.

THE JORDAN AS METAPHOR

Let us now explore the symbolism of the Jordan in the Naassene Sermon and the Testimony of Truth. In both, the river appears as a dual metaphor: On the one hand, it represents the downward creative expression of the divine will or, in other words, the manifestation of the world. The gravity-driven Jordan symbolizes a process of materialization from subtle to gross through a series of intermediate veils, ages, or aeons. The various intermediate levels amount to a progression of increasingly dense layers, each one stepped down from a higher vibratory field above. The Gnostics believed that the world of planet Earth, the home of humanity, was located in time and physical space near the bottom rung of this overarching system—near but not at the bottom because some held that Hades, or Sheol, and, beneath Hades, the hellish realm of fiery Tartarus, were even lower and more dense. Tartarus was reserved for the lowest of the low, the damned Titans and angels cast down, dragons and demons, and other cursed entities. It was thought to be located in the infernal regions somewhere below the earth.[3]

THE REVERSAL OF THE FLOW

Whereas the downward-flowing river manifests the physical world of everyday reality, the upward-flowing Jordan refers to a latent spiritual potential, one involving a return to the divine source. We have observed that spiritual ascent was not unprecedented in Judaism; it had long been a part of tradition. We have discussed the case of Elijah as reported in II Kings. We have also mentioned the example of the patriarch Enoch (see Genesis 5:24), who was reportedly taken at an advanced age, body and soul, into heaven. Although Noah's ascent is not mentioned in the Bible, it is known from Hebrew legends and also from the Book of Enoch, which includes a long section about the Flood.[4] These cases show that while spiritual ascent had long been known in Judaism, the boon was exceedingly rare.

The Old Testament makes no mention of an upward flow or reversal. The Naassenes clearly believed this was a brand-new revelation and a major advance. Jesus had inaugurated a new age, and because of his example human fortunes had improved dramatically. For even as the downward, gravity-induced flow of the river manifests the physical world in time and space—including the incarnation of individual souls—there exists simultaneously the spiritual potential for a turning of the tide, so to speak, a reversal of the flow leading to a return to the divine source. The Naassene Sermon associates the downward-flowing river with the carnal and mortal, for in this direction "there ensues a generation of men" (*Refutation* 5.7.38–40).[5] However, "when it [the river] flows upwards . . . a generation of gods takes place" (*Refutation* 5.7.38).

Jesus demonstrates in stunning fashion the feasibility of actualizing this potential.[6] In the process of ascending (being lifted up) to the ultimate source through the many aeons, he also reestablishes the lost connection with the All—that is, the Gnostic Pleroma—or, as they say in the Hindu tradition, he becomes permanently established in God consciousness. The attainment is not the result of magic, nor is it conjured by spells or incantations. It is instead a genuine feat of mastery over the spiritual river—one to be imitated and, if possible, replicated. By reversing the flow of the waters, Jesus demonstrates that the impossible is possible. In the process of establishing a new precedent, he raises the roof beams, elevating the bar for all of humanity.

The divine nature of Jesus in no way diminishes the achievement, for in the process of incarnating into the world, Jesus, like every other human soul, is required to sip the milk of forgetfulness, relinquishing all memory of his divine nature.[7] Born a man, his humanity makes him prone, like every other human, to the weaknesses and frailties of the flesh. Yet he triumphs over the flesh. As John 16:33 tells us: "In the world you will have trouble, But be brave: I have conquered the world."

"And so can you," the words imply, which was also the understanding of the Naassenes.

JACOB'S LADDER

The Naassene scribe complements the rich metaphor of the upward-flowing river by incorporating into his Sermon another story from scripture: the Old Testament tale of Jacob's ladder (Genesis 28). The scribe adds a new twist, however, one that illustrates the transition from the Old Testament to the New (*Refutation* 5.8.19). In the original Genesis story Jacob uses a rock for a pillow and dreams a remarkable dream about a ladder strung between heaven and earth. On this ladder angels of God are continually ascending and descending. After awakening, Jacob cries out, "How awesome is this place!" He is understandably ecstatic, and he renames the spot Beth-el, meaning "house of God." He also installs the pillow stone as a memorial. Figuratively speaking, it is a foundational act. Interestingly, the symbol of the foundation stone or cornerstone turns up in the Naassene Sermon no fewer than seven times, a repetition that should alert us to its importance (*Refutation* 5.7.10, 29, 35–39).

In his dream Jacob glimpses the gate of heaven, and it is here that the Sermon breaks with tradition. In the Genesis story, humans do not have access to the famous ladder between heaven and earth. It is frequented solely by angelic beings. The Old Testament is explicit about this. Yet the Naassene Sermon hints that in the process of fulfilling tradition, the events at the Jordan also necessitate its renovation. The Sermon suggests that Jesus not only demonstrates the feasibility of reversing the flow, thereby gaining access to the gate of heaven, but he also teaches the method by which his disciples can do the same. Henceforth, human souls will have access to the ladder. The worthy will ascend like gods into the rarefied spiritual realms, ultimately to join in the heavenly company.

The Sermon actually links the Jordan with the gate of heaven, which itself is well attested to in the New Testament. In Matthew 7:13–14 Jesus says, "Enter by the narrow gate, since the road that leads to perdition is wide and spacious, and many take it; but it is a narrow road that leads to life, and only a few find it." Here, the word *life* recalls the passage from the Gnostic Gospel of Thomas (see chapter 2): "The man old in days will not hesitate to ask a small child seven days old about the place of life. For many who are first will become last, and they will become one and the same . . ." The word *life* is used in the same manner in both instances: When Jesus speaks of life in this way he is always referring to spiritual life—in other words, spiritual attainment or *gnosis*.

The narrow gate also appears in Luke 13:24, except that here it is described as a door: "Try your best to enter by the narrow door, because, I tell you, many will try to enter and will not succeed." (See also John 10:8–9.) A similar reference also occurs in the Dialogue of the Savior, one of the Gnostic gospels found at Nag Hammadi. In the Dialogue Jesus says, " . . . when I came I opened the way, I taught them the passage through which will pass the elect and the solitary ones.[8] Here the word *way* appears in place of *gate,* and it is used in almost a technical sense. According to the scholars Helmut Koester and Elaine Pagels, the Dialogue of the Savior has close affinities with the Gospel of Thomas and the Gospel of John.[9] The Naassene scribe refers to the gate no fewer than a dozen times. (See *Refutation* 5.8.18–21, 24, 31, and 44 and 5.9.22.) As we have seen, the repetition of a symbol is a sure indication of its importance.

ANOTHER CLUE IN EUSEBIUS

Another important clue related to the hidden gate occurs in the earliest written history of the Church, the *Ecclesiastical History,* produced in the fourth century by Eusebius, the court historian of Constantine. The gate turns up in Eusebius's discussion of the death of James the Just, the brother of Jesus, though the citation itself is actually the work of another ancient writer, Hegesippus, whom Eusebius quotes at length. James the Just was known for his great holiness and was the acknowledged leader of the Jerusalem community of the Nazarenes during the period after the crucifixion. In 62 C.E., however, James was brought before the Sanhedrin and was falsely accused of violating Jewish law. After a sham trial he was stoned to death on order of the high priest Ananus. Hegesippus reports that before his murder the accusers questioned James in minute detail about this same gate.[10] Evidently, word of the esoteric teachings of Jesus had been leaked and the rumors were stirring up considerable interest, not to mention controversy. While it is impossible to relate to the high priest's brutality, we can certainly appreciate his curiosity. There was nothing like this teaching in Judaism. Though the clue from Eusebius is only a small detail, it is important because it shows that the New Testament passages referring to a gate were not the result of someone's wild imagination, as the Talmudic scholar Hyam Maccoby recently insinuated, but involved genuine esoteric teachings.[11]

Given what we have discussed in this chapter, it is no wonder the

Naassenes attached such importance to the secret teachings imparted to James, which, we are told, were subsequently passed on to many others (*Refutation* 5.7.1). Judging from the Sermon, the events at the Jordan had become the focus of secret instruction, spiritual practice, and intense devotion. In chapter 12, where we investigate sacred anatomy, we will return to the hidden gate and identify the precise points shared in common with the Eastern yoga traditions that even today employ the same symbolism as the river. While in Hinduism the river is the Ganges instead of the Jordan,[12] the meaning remains the same. East or West, the subtle gate or door is the threshold between the coextensive human and divine worlds.

4

Primal Man, Son of Man, and the Messiah

THE TERM SON OF MAN IS ONE OF THE MOST mysterious expressions in the Bible. Most Christians probably pass over it without understanding its significance. The term has been intensely studied since the Protestant Reformation, yet its meaning and provenance have proved elusive. Today, biblical scholars are as far from consensus as ever. This is confirmed by a casual review of Delbert Burkett's excellent study *The Son of Man Debate*.[1] Fortunately, the Naassene Sermon affords a ready framework for the clarification of the issue; however, until the Sermon's importance is more widely recognized, the current disarray of scholarship is likely to continue.

The expression Son of Man occurs in the New Testament no fewer than forty-three times, and appears in all four Gospels. Notably, the expression turns up in one of the most important scenes in the New Testament, an episode known as Peter's Confession. The original and fullest account is Mark 8:27–33, although the scene occurs in all three synoptic Gospels. In the scene Jesus asks, "Who do you say I am?" Peter replies, "You are the Christ" (Christ = Messiah = Anointed One). In her commentary, the author Elaine Pagels suggests that by giving this answer Peter shows he is privy to the secret identity of Jesus.[2] This is the

39

standard interpretation, yet it cannot be reconciled with the evidence we examined in chapters 1 and 2: that the secret identity of Jesus concerned his soul connection with Elisha. Certainly Jesus did not have two secret identities! In fact, in the very next line, far from affirming Peter's designation, Jesus responds by instructing his disciples not to use the term: "And he gave them strict orders not to tell anyone about him." Jesus then launches into a discussion about his spiritual mission, in which he refers to himself as the Son of Man, clearly the favored name:

> And he began to teach them that the Son of Man was destined to suffer grievously, to be rejected by the elders and the chief priests and the scribes, and to be put to death, and after three days to rise again; and he said all this quite openly. Then, taking him aside, Peter started to remonstrate with him. But, turning and seeing his disciples, he rebuked Peter and said to him, "Get behind me, Satan! Because the way you think is not God's way, but man's."

When Peter hears that Jesus' destiny will involve great trials, suffering, and death, he is incredulous and begins to protest, but Jesus rebukes him sharply, using the word Satan (the devil) in a figurative sense. In this important scene Jesus tailors scripture to suit his purpose; he draws material from different Old Testament sources and refashions it to serve his unique destiny. He creates an unprecedented fusion of the Son of Man concept and the suffering servant who must be lifted up, drawn from II Isaiah 52:13 and 53:1–12. This explains Peter's shocked reaction. Being well versed in scripture, Peter knows that there was no previous relation in Judaism between the suffering servant and the Son of Man; nor was the Messiah associated with either of these ideas. The much anticipated Messiah was to be a combination of priest and king, a towering political and religious leader, a great national hero who would vanquish Israel's enemies. The very thought that the Messiah must suffer and die is offensive to Peter's ears—and his reaction in the story is probably typical of most Jews of the time. (See also John 12:34, Acts 17:3, and I Corinthians 1:23.)

But Jesus has no political ambitions, at least not in the narrow sense. True, his uncompromising message of love is an open challenge to every form of tyranny and human exploitation. To set Judaism on a new path, Jesus must go against the grain, and in this sense he is profoundly political—indeed, revolutionary.[3] Still, he is no zealot. His revolution is spiritual in nature, which is why he is not impressed with the name Messiah. On several occasions Jesus consents to be referred to as such (see John 4:25–26), but Peter's Confession shows that the Son of Man is the preferred name.

Now let us contrast the two terms, Son of Man and Messiah. The names were scripturally unrelated and had widely divergent meanings and origins. The concept of the Messiah originated within Judaism—its roots were in the prophetic books—and was recent in the sense that it reached its fullest expression only in the apocalyptic writings of the last two centuries B.C.E.[4] The term was also steeped in politics—it had to do with "man's way," not "God's way"—hence, was unacceptable from a spiritual standpoint. By contrast, as we shall see, the preferred name Son of Man was ancient and had profound spiritual meaning, as the scholar D. S. Russell has pointed out.[5] In fact, the contrast between the two names could not be greater, and Jesus' admonishment of Peter expresses this perfectly.

In the end, of course, the religious and social pressures to use the name Messiah (Christ) were too great to overcome. Even Peter, one of the pillars of the Nazarene community, seems to have abandoned the preferred name. Peter's soliloquies in Lukan Acts 3 and 4 and in the two epistles that bear his name (I Peter and II Peter) make frequent reference to "Jesus Christ" (the Messiah) yet never mention the Son of Man. (This assumes, of course, that both sources report Peter's words accurately.) The same pattern is plainly evident in the Epistles of Paul. Indeed, the absence of the Son of Man in Paul's writings has tempted some scholars to speculate that it is an inauthentic expression and that Jesus never used it.[6] But while this absence in Paul is a bona fide puzzle, it does not itself subvert the expression's authenticity. Paul's conversion, after all, occurred late, several years after the crucifixion. He never knew the living, breathing master and never heard him speak.

In fact, an abundance of evidence strongly supports the authenticity of the name Son of Man. In addition to its frequent use in the New Testament, the name turns up in no fewer than fifteen of the Gnostic gospels from the Nag Hammadi library, including the Gospel of Thomas (in Saying 86).[7] Are we to conclude that this perfect agreement between the orthodox New Testament and Gnostic scripture is mere coincidence? When orthodox scripture and so-called heretical writings concur, our confidence should soar. It is much more likely that the institutional Church, far from making up the name Son of Man, in fact abandoned its use in favor of Messiah (Christ).

While Hippolytus himself, most likely following the trend of the day, refers to Jesus as "the Christ" on several occasions (*Refutation* 5.7.1 and 21) and never once uses Son of Man, a careful review of the text of the Naassene Sermon shows that it remains true to the favored name. The Naassene scribe also refers to the master as Jesus, the blessed Jesus, and the Savior. By contrast, the name Christ (Messiah) appears only once, in a full reference to "Christ, the Son of Man" (*Refutation* 5.7.33). The Naassenes, in other words, preserved Jesus' original instruction concerning his name, and in this respect the Sermon is more spiritually accurate than the Epistles of Peter and of Paul.[8] The increasing use of the name Messiah was probably inevitable. But the marriage of the two names was never a happy one and the tension between them was never resolved. No doubt the use of both caused confusion in the first centuries C.E., just as it does today.

Now let us explore the name Son of Man in more detail. The expression appears in a number of prophetic and apocalyptic books, including the pseudoepigraphic Book of Enoch (I Enoch), parts of which are among the oldest writings in the Judeo-Christian tradition.[9] Though Enoch was either lost or suppressed—we do not know which—from a very early date, in the eighteenth century a world traveler from Scotland named James Bruce acquired several copies on a visit to Ethiopia—it had been preserved in the Ethiopian Church—and brought them home. These were the first complete editions of Enoch ever to be seen in Europe.[10] The Book of Enoch is a vast literature unto itself, and in fact is an aggregate of separate books of widely varying ages, written by different scribes. The name Son of Man appears many times in the portion of Enoch known as the Book of Parables (Similitudes), which beautifully summarizes its significance. (See I Enoch 38:2, 46:3, 48:6, 48:10, 51:3, 61:9, and 62:6 and 7.) Here he is described as a preexistent heavenly being. He looks human— his face is like a man's—yet he is in some respects angelic. He stands in a special relationship with God. He is the righteous one and the judge (compare with John 5:22) who commands the secret lore of the universe. He knows the mysteries that pertain to the beginning, the continuance, and the end of all things and he rules over what is hidden. But he is also the teacher and the revealer of secrets. From his mouth pours forth the profoundest counsel—every kind of knowledge and wisdom. Yet the Son of Man himself is the greatest secret of all. He is the chosen one who was hidden before the creation of the world. All in all, it is a most impressive spiritual legacy.

I Enoch, however, cannot be the original source. In 1947 numerous Enochian fragments turned up among the Dead Sea Scrolls, found in the caves of Qumran, a discovery that established the importance of Enoch to the Essenes. All parts of Enoch were represented in the find— except the Book of Parables. For this reason J. T. Milik, the scholar who published the Enochian fragments from Qumran along with a very able commentary, ruled out a pre-Christian date for Parables. In the course of his study he found similarities between Parables and the Sibylline Oracles, whose date of origin was already firmly established as the second century C.E. This led him ultimately to settle on a second- to fourth-century C.E. composition date for Parables.[11] And this later date rules out Enoch as the origin of the concept of the Son of Man. Whoever produced the Book of Parables borrowed his material from older sources. Nevertheless, Enoch remains an important summation.

The name Son of Man also appears in the apocalyptic Book of Daniel (7:13), composed in the second century B.C.E.[12] Like many other scholars, Pagels attributes the name to this source.[13] But it also appears numerous times in Ezekiel 2–7 and is found as well in Job 25:6 and

II Isaiah 51:12—all post-exilic books. It even turns up in Psalm 8:4 and Psalm 80:17. Yet despite this abundance of biblical occurrences, it is virtually certain that none of these is the original. While the date of Psalms is disputed, the fact that Ezekiel, Job, and II Isaiah are all post-exilic cannot be coincidence. This points to an older common source. We know that much new material from the East entered Judaism in these books and the concept of the Son of Man was a part of this legacy, as a number of prominent scholars have pointed out, beginning with W. F. Albright as early as 1940 and including D. S. Russell.[14]

THE MAN WHO EMERGED FROM THE SEA

It is of interest that the name Son of Man also turns up in a Christian apocalypse known as 2 Esdras (also called 4 Ezra). The book is not a part of the Bible and these days it is almost forgotten, yet 2 Esdras was never declared heterodox; it remains a part of orthodox Christian apocrypha. 2 Esdras 13 contains an account that is pertinent to our investigation: A man comes up out of the stormy waters of a wind-tossed sea, and everything trembles at his gaze. The image is peculiar and unforgettable. The text, however, is sufficiently garbled that the biblical scholar D. S. Russell wrote, "The obviously forced exegesis of the coming of the man from the sea in the apocalyptic writings indicates that this material had been received . . . and explained without being perfectly understood.[15] Judeo-Christianity apparently assimilated this image from older material that was not fully digested.

A link to Babylonia is certain. The man who comes out of the sea is an easily recognizable figure in surviving fragments of the writings of the Babylonian scribe Berossos, an acquaintance of Aristotle, who wrote a history of Babylonia soon after its conquest by Alexander the Great. At that time, in the fourth century B.C., there was apparently a perceived need to make available to the Greek-speaking world the lore of the newly conquered lands. In his role as chronicler, Berossos did for Mesopotamia what Manetho accomplished for Egypt. Drawing upon the temple archives of his native land (written in cuneiform), Berossos produced an account of Babylonia in the lingua franca of the day: Greek. His writings brought a basic fund of knowledge about Mesopotamian history and religion within the reach of every educated person in the Hellenized world. Unfortunately, only fragments of his work have survived. Yet several of these fragments describe how the mysterious figure of Oannes (Iannes) emerged in the earliest times from the Erythrian Sea (known now as the Persian Gulf). Upon his arrival, Oannes supposedly taught men the arts of civilization, including astronomy, medicine, agriculture.[16] In this role of teacher Oannes was the Mesopotamian counterpart of the Egyptian Osiris (see chapter 13). The Assyrians worshipped Oannes as a fish god, but they clearly inherited their knowledge of him from the Akkadians, who, in turn, surely received it long before from the Sumerians, the first settlers on the Gulf coast.

Without question, Oannes had at least some of the characteristics of the Son of Man, which raises questions about the origin of Christianity's use of the fish symbol for Christ. The facile explanation has long been that the equation Christ = ΙΧΘΥΣ (fish) pertains to the Age of Pisces, the start of which is often associated with the appearance of Jesus. But no less an authority than the famed psychologist Carl Jung ruled out the zodiac as the origin of the fish as the symbol for Christ.[17] In his fascinating book *Orpheus the Fisher*, published in 1921, the biblical scholar Robert Eisler flirted with the idea that Christian fish symbolism had originated with the fish god Oannes. Eisler even cites a line from Tertullian: "But we—the Christians—are little fishes after the type of our great ΙΧΘΥΣ (fish), Jesus Christ, [who was] born in the water.[18] In the end, however, Eisler backed away from a direct link and contented himself merely to point out the parallels. He concluded that the fish symbol originated within Judaism. By 1940, however, other Mesopotamian parallels with the Son of Man had become obvious to the scholar W. F. Albright.[19]

For all of these reasons, it is of great interest that the Assyrian fish god turns up in the Naassene Sermon: The Naassene scribe includes Oannes in his list of "First Men" from antiquity (*Refutation* 5.7.6). This can only mean that Gnostic Christians understood the parallels between Oannes and the Son of Man in the early period of Christianity.

No doubt the Naassene scribe had access to the writings of Berossos—as well as to an abundance of other material—in the famed library of Alexandria, all of which points to a Mesopotamian (or possibly Persian) origin of the concept of the Son of Man.

Although we are not ready just yet to delve more deeply into the image of the stormy sea, subsequent chapters will prepare the way for that discussion, which will be presented in chapter 13. Nevertheless, we can at least begin here to address the larger questions. The evidence we have examined thus far shows that the name Son of Man is one of the keys to the spiritual mission of Jesus on earth. The problem, however, is that there is no way to extract the term's significance from the usual Christian sources. The orthodox canon is simply too restrictive; the narrowing of scripture in the interests of combating alleged heresy has made discovery next to impossible for the average Christian. A serious investigation of the significance of the name Son of Man would draw from pertinent pseudoepigraphic, apocryphal, and Gnostic source material in addition to other ancient texts—whatever documentary evidence may present itself. Indeed, the need to widen the investigation of the name is implicit in the name itself: By favoring a name that clearly predated Judaism by thousands of years, Jesus was very consciously placing himself in a context of human history so sweeping in scope that it recedes from us into the mists of the dawn of civilization. And the Naassene scribe's insistence on preserving these links with antiquity surely reflects the Naassenes' awareness of this.

PRIMAL MAN

In her latest book, *Beyond Belief,* the scholar Elaine Pagels briefly mentions the heavenly Adam, or Anthropos, whom she identifies as the prototypic human.[20] Although Pagels does not associate this important concept with the Son of Man, the link between the two becomes evident once it is understood that the heavenly Adam was only one of many synonymous designations. The Naassene Sermon is most helpful in this regard because it documents in amazing detail just how widespread this concept of the Anthropos or heavenly Adam was in the ancient world: The Sermon mentions other equivalent names, including the Great Man from Above (*Refutation* 5.7.7), the Perfect Man (5.7.8), Adamas (5.7.6), Primal Mind (5.10.1), and, most notably, Primal Man (5.8.9). The Sermon also goes on to mention at least a dozen other "First Men" known from antiquity (*Refutation* 5.7.2–6).

Obviously the concept of Primal Man was not limited to the Naassenes. It appears to have been in general use, and this includes Gnostic Christians. Adamas, one of the designations, turns up in at least five of the Gnostic gospels from the Nag Hammadi library.[21] The Mandaeans (or Sabians) referred to the same prototypic human as the Secret Adam.[22] Initially, the Mandaeans were probably disciples of John the Baptist, and were the only Gnostic sect from the period of early Christianity to survive into the modern age, a remarkable achievement. Much later, the same prototypic figure turned up in Jewish mysticism (i.e., the Kabbalah) as Adam Kadmon.[23]

The Sermon's many references to the heavenly Adam indicate that the idea was well known in the ancient world and suggests that it, like the Son of Man, long predated Christianity. Although Primal Man is never mentioned in the New Testament, he is certainly implied in the name Son of Man. Bishop Hippolytus himself mentions Primal Man and the Son of Man in the very same line (*Refutation* 5.6.4).

So who exactly was Adamas, the Primal Man? The short answer is that he was a kind of heavenly mold or template from which humanity had been stamped—a nonmaterial perfect model that existed in the spiritual realms many aeons above the earth. The scholar Richard Reitzenstein traced the concept to Iran,[24] and the Naassene Sermon more or less affirms this origin, mentioning a Chaldean (Mesopotamian) source (*Refutation* 5.7.6). The obvious connection between Primal Man and Son of Man certainly points to a common source.

The Sermon mentions an important characteristic of Primal Man: his hermaphroditic nature (*Refutation* 5.7.14). This should not surprise us. As the blueprint for humanity, Primal Man would necessarily incorporate both male and female aspects.[25] The Sermon refers to Adamas as the rock and tells us that rock and cornerstone are equivalent (*Refutation 5.7.35*). In both mythology and alchemy the stone is considered to be hermaphroditic. In fact, the root of *hermaphrodite—herm—*means "stone," which is also the root of the name of the Greek god Hermes, the androgynous messenger of the gods. As we know from Greek mythology, Hermes shared some of the qualities of the Son of Man, so it is perhaps not surprising that the Sermon mentions him in this context (*Refutation 5.7.37*). The equivalence of rock and stone also affirms the intimate connection between Primal Man and the Son of Man: The First Epistle of Peter (I Peter 2:4–8) identifies Jesus as "the living stone" and the cornerstone. If Adamas (Primal Man) is the heavenly rock, then Jesus, as the Son of Man, must be his earthly double or representative.

The antiquity of the concepts of the Son of Man and Primal Man stands in sharp contrast to the much later Jewish concept of the Messiah, which incorporated attributes that were more worldly and nationalistic, with little in the way of spiritual depth. The Naassene Sermon is proof that at least some early Christians—ironically, the very heretics excoriated by Bishop Hippolytus for "uttering falsehoods against Christ" (*Refutation 5.7.1*)—understood the important differences between the Son of Man/Primal Man and the Messiah.

Many of the Gnostic systems describe Primal Man as an incorruptible light being.[26] The immortal souls of humans were *spinthers* (Greek for "spark") spun from this original and indestructible light source. Later, this same idea was incorporated into Jewish mysticism. Are we to conclude, on this basis, that Primal Man is equivalent to God? We can only hazard a guess: Although Primal Man is definitely a part of the heavenly company, and is therefore divine, he appears, nonetheless, to be distinguishable from the Godhead. It is as if a blueprint—Primal Man—existed in heaven, and was used to create and re-create humanity. We should also recognize, however, that the available evidence is inadequate to make a final determination about the precise relation between Primal Man/Son of Man and the Godhead. The last word on the matter remains to be written.

PART TWO

Immanence

5

The Naassene Sermon

IF THE NAASSENE SERMON IS INVALUABLE because of the glimpses it affords into early Christianity, why isn't the document better known? And why have so many Christian scholars dismissed it? There are a number of reasons. First, Christianity as we know it today bears little resemblance to what existed in the beginning, so it is not surprising that the Sermon's relevance has not yet been recognized. In addition, Naassene Christianity was Gnostic Christianity: a tradition within a tradition. It was for the few not in the sense of the elite, but in the sense of the small minority of seekers who were ready for more advanced teachings.

The Naassene Sermon also poses stubborn challenges. It has probably frustrated many more scholars than it has inspired. The document resembles a cord of interwoven strands, the result of overwriting. This layered complexity is not easily unraveled. Patient study is required to identify the various threads and their relation to one another. The Sermon does not yield up its treasure easily. Richard Reitzenstein, a prolific German scholar and one of the first to investigate the text, believed that in addition to the opinionated comments of Bishop Hippolytus, he had also identified pagan, Jewish Christian, and Gnostic Christian voices. Identifying these different voices and keeping them separate is essential to deciphering the Sermon's meaning; a reader must know at all times not only what is being said, but also who is saying it.

This multilayered complexity is not unique to the Naassene Sermon. Biblical scholars have long recognized that the Old Testament has a similar structure. According to Judaic tradition, Moses authored the first five books, but today no serious scholar holds this view. The fingerprints of successive redactors are too plainly in evidence. Far from being the work of a single individual, the first four books of the Old Testament are known to be a polyphonic composition, the work of successive scribes, at least three of whom have been identified: a Yahwist scribe, an Elohist, and a much later Priestly source.[1] The fifth book of the Old Testament is primarily the work of a writer known as the Deuteronomist, whom we have already discussed.

The Naassene Sermon is also challenging for other reasons. The text is often obscure because it includes many unfamiliar words and names from the ancient world. For this reason, to facilitate discovery, I have provided the full text of the Sermon in the appendix, as well as a glossary of known terms. Though in the introduction I already mentioned the frequent references to the Sermon in this study—for example, (*Refutation* 5.712)—I remind readers that they can follow the discussion using these citations simply by flipping to the appendix. Biblical references also appear in parenthesis, and copious endnotes cover other sources.

FIGURE? OR GROUND?

One of the earliest challenges faced by scholars in deciphering the Sermon was determining which voice in the text came first. In other words, was the Sermon essentially a pagan document, one that was later superficially reworked by Christian heretics? Or was it a thoroughly Christian document with pagan material embedded within it for some unexplained purpose? The matter of origins is vital because it bears on the nature of the Naassene community. Richard Reitzenstein believed that the document was essentially pagan, and the theosophist G. R. S. Mead apparently accepted this view.[2] Reitzenstein attempted to recover what he believed to be the older parent document by deleting from the text the running Naassene commentary, which, in his view, had been inserted later. The pagan material pertains to the various Mystery traditions, including the Phrygian Mysteries of Asia Minor, the Thracian rites of the Haemonians, the Eleusinian Mysteries of mainland Greece, the rites of Samothrace, and various Egyptian traditions. Hippolytus informs us that these last were the most ancient of all—a remark that must have fired Mead's Hermetic interests.

This multiplicity of voices and influences makes the Naassene Sermon extremely difficult to unravel. The Naassene scribe's commentary interrupts the continuity of the pagan account, and the pagan material often breaks the Christian thread. Nor is the relation between the two always clear. The question of which came first confounded early attempts to decode the text. Building on the previous contributions of Reitzenstein, Mead devised an ingenious labeling system to identify and keep separate the pagan, Jewish Christian, and Gnostic Christian voices in the text. I should mention that I dispute the shared opinion of Mead and Reitzenstein regarding the Sermon's alleged pagan origins. Indeed, we have already shown that the document contains esoteric Christian teachings. I also take issue with their distinction between a Jewish Christian voice and the voice of the Naassene scribe; I would conflate the two. Nevertheless, in order to maintain continuity with previous scholarship, in the appendix I have preserved Mead's labeling system essentially intact. It continues to be useful and should help readers to discriminate between the pagan and the Naassene elements and to recognize the voice of Hippolytus.

REFUTING REITZENSTEIN

The theory of pagan origins drew sharp fire from critics such as R. P. Casey. Eventually, because the weight of evidence within the document proved so compelling, Reitzenstein partially recanted his early views, although he never fully retracted them. Over the years scholars have continued to debate Reitzenstein's initial theory of pagan origins, but no one has succeeded in advancing the case in any substantial way.[3]

The last attempt was made in 1978 by a scholar named W. Gogolin, whose work is thoroughly reviewed and persuasively rebutted by R. Scott Birdsall in his Ph.D. dissertation.[4]

In 1970 the Italian scholar M. Simonetti made an astute observation that also effectively refuted Reitzenstein's initial theory. Simonetti pointed out that the pagan material in the Naassene Sermon often includes background information, such as the names of places, clues about the provenance of deities, and minor details about the various pagan traditions. This is significant because similar details about Judaism and Christianity are conspicuously absent from the text—as though they were taken for granted by the scribe, who fully expected that his readers would already know this information.[5] Clearly the text shows a comprehensive knowledge of scripture that no pagan would have possessed. Simonetti's observation confirms the evidence we have already examined in preceding chapters that the deep structure of the Naassene Sermon is firmly rooted in the Old Testament. Bishop Hippolytus obviously did not pursue any of the dozens of Old Testament citations in the Gnostic material that had passed into his hands, for if he had, he would have been compelled to reconsider his hasty condemnation of the sect.

The Naassene scribe's command of the Old Testament distinguishes him from other Gnostics of the day, many of whom rejected the Old Testament along with the God of Judaism. In fact, that rejection was almost standard from the time of the second-century C.E. Gnostic heretic Marcion. Obviously these Naassenes were no ordinary Gnostics.

NO ORDINARY GNOSTICS

A thoughtful comparison to other Gnostics of the time shows that the Naassenes retained the "best" features of Gnosticism while remaining free from the "worst." To clarify this, let us briefly contrast Naassene beliefs with those of other Gnostic sects.

Some of the Gnostic ideologies were justifiably viewed as divergent. Docetism, a prevalent example, was based on the idea that the Redeemer

never completely touched down both feet in this world. There were varying degrees of Docetism, but in general Docetists believed that Jesus was
a psychic entity, or a phantasm. They denied that he had a corporeal
body and insisted that he didn't require food because he subsisted on
heavenly energy or that he ate only to *appear* human. Docetists were
repelled by the thought that the body of Jesus excreted waste in the manner of animals and ordinary humans. For similar reasons they also
denied that Jesus suffered and died on the cross; being a purely spiritual
entity, the Redeemer was above pain. Docetism was a divergent strain of
Gnosticism, but there is no trace of it in the Naassene Sermon. The full
humanity of Jesus is presumed throughout.

Some Gnostic groups became notorious for certain nihilistic practices. One sect, for instance, the Carpocrations, had a dubious and probably deserved reputation for sexual libertinism. The Naassenes, however,
were untainted by this malediction. The Sermon repeatedly emphasizes
the need for sexual continence. Even Hippolytus reports that "they [the
Naassenes] enjoin [their votaries] with the utmost severity and vigilance
to abstain from sexual intercourse" (*Refutation* 5.9.11).

World-denying pessimism was another common Gnostic tendency,
and one that scholars are right to criticize. Yet there is no evidence that
the Naassenes shared this predilection. The darkly pessimistic world-
view characteristic of many Gnostics groups derived from the standard
Gnostic Creation story, in which there is dissension in heaven. For some
reason, things go dreadfully wrong in the process of materialization—
that is, during the mixing and separation of the elements. Somehow, the
lower material realm becomes estranged from the divine light. The
details of the story vary, but the outcome is usually the same: The
immortal souls of men and women become trapped in physical bodies,
cut off from their higher spiritual selves. The human souls languish in
the lower world in a state of profound alienation from God. Lacking
spiritual awareness, they become increasingly prone to worldly attachments and vulnerable to the power of evil. The Gnostic view of the
human condition is a state of acute vulnerability, angst, purposeless-
ness, utmost alienation, and even despair.

This standard Gnostic vision—or nightmare—contains an uncomfortable dose of existential truth, no less for our times than in the ancient world. But the Naassenes did not incorporate every aspect of the story—for example, concerning the Gnostic belief in the spinthers of light. Gnostics believed that the scattered shards originally spun from Primal Man still glowed like embers in the earth-bound souls of men and women. Some held that the Redeemer's earthly mission was to gather up the spinthers and return them to the original heavenly abode, thus enabling worthy human souls to escape from the lower prison. The Naassene Sermon mentions the spinthers, referring to them as seeds or pearls (*Refutation* 5.8.28, 32), but says nothing about the gathering up of the shards. There are hints that the Naassenes did not view the human body as a prison, but instead, like some mainstream Christians, honored it as a temple (*Refutation* 5.9.6,11–12). The Naassenes went much further than orthodox Christians, however, claiming to be in possession of higher teachings received from James the Just, the brother of Jesus. They alleged that an intermediary, a female teacher named Mariamne, had passed on these teachings (*Refutation* 5.7.1). Her identity remains mysterious, but their claim cannot be dismissed out of hand. We have already shown that the Naassenes did have secret teachings. Indeed, this brings us to the core message of the Naassene Sermon.

THE GREAT HIDDEN TRUTH OF THE NAASSENES

If the Naassene beliefs were rooted in Judeo-Christianity, how then do we account for the presence of so much pagan material in the text? It is an important question. In 1984 R. Scott Birdsall, a divinity student, proposed an answer in his Ph.D. dissertation, one of the most fascinating studies of the Naassene Sermon to date. He observed that the presence of pagan material in the text is beside the point because the entire corpus of the Sermon is one long series of testimonials to "the omnipresence of the primal [divine] essence in matter."[6] Another scholar, G. Sfameni Gasparro, seconded Birdsall when he wrote that the Naassenes believed that "[t]he life and order of the cosmos . . . have their foundation and source in a divine substance secretly present in matter, even in its lowest levels.[7] As we are about to discover, far from seeking to escape from the prison of the body, the Naassenes sought to cultivate gnosis within the temple.

Delve into the Naassene Sermon—indeed, open the document to almost any page—and if you are alert, you will discover a single theme throughout. Here and there Hippolytus interjects his own thoughts and shallow criticisms, yet it is obvious that much of the text was recorded verbatim from the bishop's primary source document(s). The actual compiler of these lengthy portions of the text was the Naassene scribe, whose purpose was to inform his reader of a great truth: the most sublime secret of the universe. It is a deeply hidden mystery, yet it is profound in that it is omnipresent and, hence, discoverable at every hand. Few humans find it, however, for though the secret lies in plain view, the vast majority of humans are blind to it. Even when people touch this truth they stumble over it without recognizing it for what it is. This truth, however, is the Sermon's central message, and repeats throughout the document in a variety of ways, like a mantra.

Indeed, such is the scribe's zeal that he overwhelms us with a flood of documentary material. He spares no effort, exploiting every opportunity to inform us about this most profound truth. He draws upon diverse sources. He is not averse to citing pagan material: He quotes liberally from the Greek poets Homer, Anacreon, and Pindar. He relies on Greek historians such as Plutarch. He cites Greek philosophers such as Parmenides, Heraclitus, and the legendary Empedocles. These are his witnesses, and he uses their testimony on behalf of his noble endeavor, which is to present this great truth.

One of the pagan strands in the Sermon is the hymn of the young vegetation god, the consort of the goddess who must be sacrificed annually so that the earth can be fruitful. In the ancient world this god had various names and epithets, depending on region. Attis and Adonis were the most important of these, though the Sermon cites others (*Refutation* 5.9.8). But the scribe is not concerned about the regional variations, because he is not interested in the pagan gods for their own

sake. As Birdsall points out, they are important to him only as manifestations of a more universal truth.[8] In the ancient world it was customary to impute greater authority to older traditions. In fact, the more
ancient a religious tradition was, the greater its authority. But the
Naassene scribe does not follow this convention; instead, he treats contemporary figures as equals to the renowned sages of old. In the words
of Birdsall, "He disallows all national claims to pride of place and in
fact radically devalues every individual national tradition as a mere
symbol of the hidden Gnostic truth."[9] The scribe does not favor one
pagan source or tradition over another. Indeed, he draws from them all,
enthusiastically appropriating material from a diversity of traditions,
past and present. To him all sources are cowitnesses to the secret principle of the universe. In this respect the Naassene scribe is a universal-
ist: As is done within the spiritual traditions of India, he absorbs and
incorporates—exactly the opposite of orthodox Christianity's penchant
for contraction and exclusion.

Everything is fodder, grist for his mill, raw material out of which to
fashion his Sermon and reveal this truth, which is the omnipresence of
the divine principle and the power of gnosis.

From the standpoint of the Naassene scribe, there is nothing new
about this great truth. It is as old as the Judean hills. It was present in
the beginning of the world and is still present, having neither increased
nor decreased. The problem is that we humans have failed to understand
it. We practice our religions without knowing the nature of God and
without being at all aware of his presence in the world. As Jesus says in
the Gospel of Thomas (Saying 113): "The Kingdom of the Father is
spread out upon the earth, and men do not see it." The implication is
that because men do not see it, they cannot avail themselves of it.

The Naassenes obviously believed that Jesus had come into the
world to remedy this condition of unknowing. He was the fulfillment of
Judaism, yes, but he was also the fulfillment of the ancient Mystery traditions. This probably accounts for the sect's radical syncretism. Jesus
did not come to found a new religion called Christianity. He came to
revive religion itself. He came to breathe life into the dead symbols, to

instruct humans in the true meaning of scripture, and to reveal to a worthy few the deepest mystery of all: the great and hidden truth of gnosis.

EVIDENCE OF A LOST TEACHING?

The problem, as we know, is that there is no such great truth in orthodox Christianity. How then—or from where—did the great truth of the Naassenes arise? Church doctrine affirms the old Judaic belief in a transcendent Deity, but has nothing to say about immanence. In his dissertation Scott Birdsall looks for an answer to this question in the Greek Stoic tradition: He traces certain passages and ideas in the Sermon to Plutarch, and from Plutarch to Aristotle. For example, in the Sermon the Naassene scribe uses the word *soul* in a double sense (*Refutation* 5.7.10–11). The first use refers to the soul that each human possesses. But the scribe also uses *soul* in a larger sense that resembles Ralph Waldo Emerson's concept of the Oversoul—a concept that Birdsall traces to Aristotle. As Hippolytus tells us:

> . . . soul is the cause of everything that comes to be, for all things that are nourished and grow, he [the Naassene] says, require soul. For it is not possible, he says, to obtain any nourishment or growth where soul is not present. For even the stones, he says, have souls. (*Refutation* 5.7.10)

Birdsall was not the first to detect an Aristotelian influence in the Sermon. Many years before, Reitzenstein did the same. Apparently the Stoic philosophers of Greece took up many of Aristotle's ideas and adapted them for their own needs.[10] The problem with this attribution, however, as Birdsall himself concedes, is that Aristotle applied his broader concept of soul only to living things. It was biological and did not apply to inanimate objects such as rocks and stones.[11] Yet, as we have just seen, the Naassene soul concept was all-inclusive. This suggests that we must abandon Birdsall's worthy attempt to place the origin of the great truth of the Naassenes within the Greek tradition. Aristotle, it seems, was merely another witness.

Fortunately, within the Sermon itself are clues to another possible origin. The text includes a long discussion (*Refutation* 5.8.6–12) that is illuminated by a single image: the cup. In this portion of the Sermon the scribe cites no fewer than five different Old Testament, New Testament, and pagan sources that refer to a cup, a repetition that should alert us to the importance of this symbol. We are told that "[t]his cup silently speaks the ineffable mystery" (*Refutation* 5.8.7). The cup, then, signifies the great truth. But what is this symbolic cup? From the text of the Sermon there can be no doubt: The cup in question is the famous chalice used at the Last Supper (*Refutation* 5.8.11). This cup, then, is the Grail, which, as we know, pertains to the immanence or indwelling of God. The Naassene scribe is telling us that Jesus himself is the source of the great truth!

This presents great difficulties, of course, because, as we have already observed, Christian scripture says nothing about immanence. Or does it? Can it be that we have missed something? The Naassene Sermon suggests that we have! The scribe is clearly pointing to the Last Supper as the source of the great mystery. Indeed, the Sermon appears to confirm that event's historicity. Can it be that the great truth of the Naassenes originated in the person of Jesus? And was this secret teaching an original part of early Christianity that was somehow lost? In the following chapter, we shall investigate this profound idea more deeply.

6

The Teaching That Didn't Take

There is nothing [in Christianity] to suggest the . . . view
that God is immanent in the world . . . The New Testament
knows nothing of the Stoic conception of providence. There
is a great gulf between God and the world.
RUDOLF BULTMANN, *PRIMITIVE CHRISTIANITY IN*
ITS CONTEMPORARY SETTING

As a boy I attended Catholic schools, and I remember well the catechism lessons about the Last Supper and the Holy Eucharist, in which
the nuns explained in total seriousness that Christ had transformed
ordinary bread and wine into his own body and blood. I recall no less
vividly my wonderment during the Mass—the catechism miraculously
sharpened my powers of observation—as the priest, before lifting up
the host and chalice, repeated the words, "This is my body . . . this is
my blood." It all seemed so strange! What was it all about, this mystery
known as the transubstantiation? Was it real? I remember my childish
doubts and the unsettling moment in catechism when another student—he was bolder than I—dared to express *his* doubts. "I don't
believe it!" he blurted out. I will never forget the mix of curiosity and
skepticism on the boy's face. The nun, however, quickly put an end to

our discussion: It was not for small boys to question a hallowed teaching of the Church, a teaching that had been the heart of the Mass for 1,900 years. This was something that had to be taken on faith—simple as that.

Looking back, I can't help but wonder if the stifling of that boy's healthy curiosity on the matter of the Holy Eucharist, multiplied many millions of times over the centuries, has been a contributing factor in the spiritual decline of the West. Religion dooms itself to stagnation when it fails to explore the deepest questions. Put differently, religious doctrine replaces truth seeking at the risk of irrelevance. Each succeeding generation has both the responsibility and the privilege to discover anew the truths of religion. Stifle the holy impulse to question and a generation of nihilists will soon appear to pronounce: "God is dead!" Had institutional Christianity taken a different road, had the Church actively encouraged Christians to pursue the deepest spiritual questions, perhaps a significant portion of the Christian world today would appreciate the deeper mystery of the Last Supper.

After studying the Naassene Sermon for years, I began to suspect that orthodox Christianity had suppressed one of the most important teachings of Jesus. In addition to affirming the historicity of the Last Supper, the Sermon hints that when Jesus said, "This is my body," rather than transforming the bread, he was making a much more profound statement. He was saying: "I *am* this bread. I and this bread are one. The God who dwells within me is also present in this bread, and it is imbued with the divine because matter and spirit are coextensive." Jesus could just as well have said, "The God who dwells within me also dwells within the fibers of this cotton napkin, and within this wooden table, and within these hewn stone walls that surround us, and within all of *you*." Or he might simply have pointed to an object at random and said, "I am that."

To suggest that this was a radical idea in first-century Palestine would be a colossal understatement. The deity of the Old Testament was exclusive in his transcendence. Yahweh reigned in heaven. Of course, the Hebrews of the southern kingdom (Judea) believed that

Yahweh was also present in a special way within the inner sanctum of the famous temple of Jerusalem; and no doubt the Hebrews of the northern kingdom (Israel) held similar beliefs about their own temples and high places where they too made burnt offerings and blood sacrifices. It is a curiosity of history that during the long transitional period when the great prophets of north and south were guiding Judaism over the threshold to monotheism, a coincidental convergence of priestly and secular interests was also under way. To appreciate this, we must read between the lines of scripture, with a little help from archaeology.[1] The southern scribes who wrote or compiled most of the Old Testament roundly condemned the northern Hebrews as corrupt and idolatrous, as likely some of them were. Yet their judgment seems too harsh, for idolatry and corruption were no less rampant in the south.[2] There was nothing about monotheism that required a centralized place of worship and a centralized priesthood. Yet the marriage of priestly and political interests in the southern kingdom demanded a showplace for the national God, and because no competition was acceptable, during the reign of Josiah the northern temples were razed, the high places were desecrated, and the great stones were pulled down.[3] But the dismantling of competing shrines and holy sites was not a solution, and only foreshadowed a greater cycle of destruction at the hands of the Babylonians.

In the Book of Jeremiah the matter of God's immanence is never openly addressed, but the issue runs like an undercurrent through the prophet's writings. Jeremiah chastises the southern priesthood for never asking the fundamental question "Where is Yahweh?" (Jeremiah 2:5, 8), basing his criticism on the astute observation that the priests had no direct knowledge of the Deity because they never actively sought him out. The priests, it seems, were satisfied with the mere trappings of religion, even as they pontificated against the north. The Book of Jeremiah is a ringing condemnation of the shallow priestly traditions, including blood sacrifice—and in this Jeremiah was joined by other dissenting voices, for the greatest of the prophets concurred with him and shunned the practice.[4] To be sure, the counsel of the prophets went unheeded.

The same errors were repeated during the post-exilic period, when the famous temple was reconstructed and a centralized priesthood was installed again.

Gradually, however, the once venerable priestly traditions began to lose their appeal. During the apocalyptic age this growing disenchantment resulted in breakaway communities like the Essenes, who sought a purer form of Judaism. By the last century B.C.E. the old temple tradition resembled a worn-out garment, too far gone to save (Mark 2:21).

Viewed in this light, the ministry of Jesus was the culmination of a trend that had been gathering within Judaism for centuries. As Andrew Harvey has pointed out, when Jesus drove the traders and money-changers from the temple, he was not merely striking out against the pollution of a holy place, "he was attacking the entire paraphernalia of ritual [sacrifice] and questioning its necessity in a world where direct, unaffected contact with God is always possible.[5] A much neglected clue in the account of Mark affirms this (Mark 11:15–19): Jesus "would not suffer any man to carry a vessel through the temple . . . ," a line that clearly refers to blood sacrifice. Born in a pagan cauldron, the practice had long outlived its usefulness. And so Jesus replaced it with a new and more suitable form of offering: self-sacrifice, the personal offering up to God of everything, without qualification. How fitting, too, that Jesus would underwrite his own teaching through the powerful means of a personal example.

The Naassene Sermon also suggests that Jeremiah's question "Where is Yahweh?" was finally answered at the Last Supper. Without denying the reality of a transcendent God, Jesus introduced an aspect of the Godhead never before revealed in Judaism: God's immanence. The new teaching did not conflict with the old way of describing the Deity. Rather, it was complementary; the opposite of one great truth was not the negation of the first, but, paradoxically, another great truth.

This teaching about the indwelling God was unprecedented in Judaism, but it had long been known in the East. In every Hindu tradition is told the timeless story of a truth seeker who, on meeting a renowned saint, asks with great reverence for an elucidation of the teachings. The saint responds with a dissertation of precisely three words that convey the sum total of religion: *"Tat tvam asi,"* meaning "Thou are that"—words that resonate perfectly with "This is my body" or "I am that."

Here, a clarification is in order because many Christians, including even brilliant biblical scholars like W. F. Albright, have run aground on the reef of these three simple words. Albright was a firm adherent of the orthodox belief in a transcendent God, and in his writings he complained bitterly about Hindu pantheism.[6] In fact, most Hindus are not pantheists, and neither were the Naassenes. The matter turns on a simple but crucial distinction. While it is true that Hindus believe the Godhead is present in physical matter, they do not equate God with matter because the physical world in all of its diversity of forms is itself but a veil of appearances concealing the deeper reality. In this sense matter is illusory, just as the Vedas have proclaimed for thousands of years. God dwells in matter, but matter is not God. It is more accurate to say that God and matter are coextensive. The distinction is also illustrated by another Hindu expression with the same meaning as "Thou art that": *"Neti, neti,"* meaning, "Not this, not this." In this simple phrase the disciple is encouraged to seek God through a relentless process of elimination. Penetrate matter, go deep within, overturn the world of outward appearances, move beyond duality—pursue this investigation far enough and at some point the divine light will spontaneously manifest. God is what remains when we have ruled out every "thing": the deeper unity beyond duality, the underlying matrix in a universe of shifting appearances. For this reason every detail of physical reality, down to the smallest jot, cannot help but reflect the reality of immanence, which only our mental blinders prevent us from experiencing directly. In the East this understanding is the basis for the "guru principle," the astounding capacity of a great saint to awaken the divine energy sleeping within the disciple.

The new teaching of immanence had profound implications concerning the temple, the nature of the soul, salvation, and much else, as we shall see. The link with the temple is obvious and important. Once it is understood that God dwells within, there is no further need for an external temple because the body itself is recognized as the vessel for the new sacrificial offering. The Gnostics understood this, believing that through the deeply felt offering of ourselves to God, we harvest the inner experience of the Kingdom. This idea is affirmed in Luke 10:10–12, in which Jesus tells his disciples, "The Kingdom of God is very near." Just how near is clarified in Luke 17:21, in which Jesus says, "For you must know, the Kingdom of God is within you." This interpretation finds support in the Gnostic Dialogue of the Savior, from the Nag Hammadi library, which quotes Jesus: "For I [say] to you truly, the living God [dwells] in you [and you] in him."[7] And there are plentiful references to the same idea in John's gospel (John 5:37; 6:51, 54, 59–63; 10:34; 14:11; 10:30; and 17:21–24), including the passage where Jesus prays in Gethsemane shortly after the Last Supper and just prior to his arrest. According to John, Jesus said:

> I pray not only for these,
> But for those also
> Who through their words will believe in me.
> May they all be one.
> Father, may they be one in us,
> as you are in me and I am in you.

The Gnostic interpretation of "one" is the direct experience of the Godhead within, which resonates perfectly with the teaching of immanence. Gnostic Christians believed that it was for *this* that Jesus prayed in Gethsemane, and it was for *this* that Jesus made the ultimate sacrifice: to redeem the inner experience of God for humankind. This interpretation is richly documented in the Gospel of Thomas (Saying 22), in which Jesus says: "When you make the two one, and when you make the inside like the outside and the outside like the inside, and the above like the below, and when you make the male and the female one and the same . . . then will you enter [the Kingdom]."[8]

The phrase "make the two one" is deeply mystical, and pertains to the indwelling of God. What is sainthood, after all, if not the direct realization of this great truth?

The same idea turns up in a lost scripture known as the Gospel according to the Egyptians. Hippolytus mentions it by name and even tells us that the Naassenes made use of it (*Refutation* 5.7.9). The gospel did not survive, but, fortunately, a few fragments were preserved in the writings of the early Church fathers. One of these fragments, quoted by Clement of Alexandria, a respected authority, contains the phrase "making the two one."[9]

Several passages from the Gospel of Thomas also pertain to immanence. One (Saying 77), in which Thomas quotes Jesus, is forthright: "Split a piece of wood, and I am there. Lift up the stone, and I am there." Another (Saying 106) goes even further, and quotes Jesus emphatically stating that Christians are to follow in the footsteps of the teacher: "And when you make the two one, you will become the Sons of Man, and when you say 'Mountain! Move away!' it will move away." A third passage (Saying 3) explicitly links the realization of the Kingdom with self-knowledge—a link that results in gnosis: "The Kingdom is inside of you and it is outside of you. When you come to know yourselves, then you will become known, and you will realize that it is you who are the sons of the Living Father." In other words, men and women who discover their true selves will experience their inner divinity. We know that the Naassenes were familiar with all of these passages. Hippolytus mentions the Gospel of Thomas by name—he refers to it as the Gospel according to Thomas—and he even states it was used by the sect (*Refutation* 5.7.20).[10]

It is noteworthy that the same idea turns up in I Enoch 70–71, which describes the apotheosis of the patriarch that occurs after Enoch is taken up into heaven. One passage explicitly states that Enoch was "translated"—in other words, transformed—into the Son of Man. This line causes orthodox scholars great consternation—it seems they would prefer not to take the scripture at its word—yet we know that other Jewish Christian sects had similar beliefs.[11] Hippolytus mentions one such group, the Ebionites, who taught that the disciples of Jesus were meant to share in his spiritual attainment (*Refutation* 7.33.1). Their teaching, commonly known as the belief in "many Christs," was officially condemned as heresy. The Ebionites themselves, however, probably did not refer to their own teaching by this name.[12]

The mystical language in the Gospel of Thomas and the Gospel according to the Egyptians surely explains why these scriptures were suppressed. Even today the Roman Catholic Church regards the term Sons of Man as heresy. The Gospel of John was probably retained because its mystical language is more ambiguous, hence is more easily given an orthodox spin. The usual orthodox interpretation of the "one" in the passage from John relating Jesus' words in Gethsemane does not refer to an inner experience of God, but simply refers to membership in the Roman Catholic Church. In Catholicism the role of Jesus is strictly redemptive. Church doctrine does not countenance the possibility that men and women can be saved by receiving wisdom from a teacher or guru and rejects the notion that the soul can be liberated in this lifetime. Souls receive their reward in the next life, after being saved in this life through conversion, baptism, participation in the Church by means of the sacraments, and especially through faith and obedience—a doctrine that contradicts the scriptural evidence we have examined thus far. We shall now take up the important question: How did orthodox Christianity arrive at such dismal conclusions?

LOWLY DUST:
THE CHURCH'S DOCTRINE OF THE SOUL

Beginning in the second century C.E., the Church developed its own ideas about the nature of the soul and its relationship to matter. After a long period of gestation, these evolving ideas finally coalesced in the fifth century and became the official Church doctrine of the soul. In the interest of space and brevity, the following explanation of this process encapsulates a complex evolution of thought that took place over many years.

The initial contribution was made by Tatian, a second-century theologian who was known as the Assyrian. Tatian studied in Rome under

Justin Martyr and later founded his own sect known as the Encratites, meaning "the self controlled" or "the masters of self." The Encratites were known for their strict asceticism; they were teetotalers who also practiced vegetarianism and celibacy. In fact, their practices were so strict that they were considered heterodox. Nonetheless, Tatian's rejection of the divine presence within matter and his ideas about the nature of the soul soon entered into mainstream Church thinking. His views can be found in his *Address to the Greeks,* a rambling document that denies the preexistence of the soul—in direct contradiction to the testimony of Jesus in the New Testament that seems to affirm reincarnation (see chapter 2). Linking the soul to the body by declaring that the soul perishes at death, Tatian nonetheless affirmed the possibility of the soul's resurrection on the final day of judgment.[13] His writings became grist for further developments.

The patriarch Gregory of Nyssa added another brick to the edifice of Church teaching in the fourth century when he wrote, "Neither does the soul exist before the body nor the body apart from the soul, but . . . there is only a single origin for both of them."[14] Later, Saint Jerome seconded Gregory's views when he penned a line destined to become famous: "God is daily making souls."[15] In other words, far from being immortal or even preexistent, the soul, like the body, is made from lowly dust; both are created together at conception. At a stroke Gregory and Jerome repudiated Jesus, not to mention Plato, Socrates, and many other Greek philosophers, all of whom taught the soul's immortality.[16]

From Tatian and Jerome it was but a small step to Augustine. Standing on the shoulders of the Church fathers who had preceded him, the Bishop of Hippo combined their ideas about the soul with an ultra-conservative interpretation of the story of the Fall in the Garden of Eden. The result was the doctrine of Original Sin, which has bedeviled Christians to this day. Even though Augustine conceded that his ideas found no scriptural support in the New Testament, his dark conclusions nonetheless became the official teaching of the Roman Catholic Church.[17] This explains why even today the Church teaches that small babies who die before being baptized do not qualify for immediate entry into heaven, but must first go to purgatory to be purged of their supposed stain of Original Sin.

THE ARIAN CONTROVERSY

Even as orthodoxy was taking shape in the second and third centuries, a healthy diversity of views continued to coexist within Christianity. The year 325 C.E. marked the beginning of the end of tolerance, however, for in that year the emperor Constantine convened the famous Council of Nicaea, the first large gathering of the bishops of the Church. Among the issues addressed at Nicaea, the most important was the growing Arian controversy. Between the third and sixth centuries, Christianity was rocked by numerous schisms, but among these the Arian dispute was by far the most important because its consequences were so far-reaching and long lasting.

There is no shortage of available material on the Arian controversy. We can still read the book by Gregory of Nyssa and the voluminous works of Athanasius, the chief spokesperson for the anti-Arius faction, whose writings are still looked upon as a quasi-official record. But there is no way to fully understand what happened at Nicaea without discussing immanence—the teaching that did not take.

The controversy arose when a Libyan priest named Arius identified the flaw in the Church's emerging doctrine of the soul. It was bound to happen, sooner or later; Arius just happened to be the first to follow the logic through to its troublesome conclusions. At issue was the human-versus-divine nature of Jesus. The Church taught that human souls were composed of the lowly stuff of matter, and were created along with the body at conception. Arius merely pointed out that according to this reasoning, the soul of Jesus must have been created in the same way. This conclusion precipitated a major crisis, because it implied that there was a time when the soul of Jesus did not exist. Therefore, Jesus' nature, while exalted, could not be on an equal footing with God the Father.

Athanasius, who led the orthodox contingent at Nicaea, was an outspoken firebrand. He insisted on the absolute equivalence of Father and Son, arguing that both had existed together as coequals from eternity. During the debate, which at times degenerated into shouting and name-calling, Arius was accused of blasphemy. Unfortunately, it is not possible to know Arius's views about the issues or the proceedings, at least not with certainty, because even though he was at the center of the storm, his views are preserved only in the writings of his accusers. Shortly after the council declared his ideas anathema, the writings of Arius were consigned to the flames.[18] Of course, the outcome was a foregone conclusion: The anti-Arian bishops in attendance held a majority in the council. Yet it is well documented that the vast majority of ordinary Christians and many members of the clergy who were not represented at Nicaea stood squarely behind Arius. Support for Arius was especially strong in the eastern parts of the empire.

In the end the council declared Athanasius the victor and even named a new creed in his honor. But Nicaea failed to end the Arian dispute. The heresy in its various forms proved so popular that it was not fully suppressed for another two centuries. And why was Arianism so popular? By affirming the full humanity of Jesus, Arius held out hope for ordinary people. Implicit in Arianism was the Gnostic belief that ordinary Christians could follow in the footsteps of the Savior. The views of Arius were perfectly compatible with the teaching of immanence, the indwelling of God. The real issue at the heart of the controversy, as the author Elizabeth Clare Prophet has pointed out, was not the denial of the divinity of Jesus by Arius, as the early Church asserted and the Roman Catholic Church still contends, but instead the question: "How is man [to be] saved—through emulating Jesus, or through worshiping him?"[19]

Athanasius is also credited with the doctrine of the Trinity, which, as a result of the decision at Nicaea, also entered into the mainstream of Church teaching in the fourth century.[20] The new concept of a heavenly Trinity, however, was not based on scripture, or divine revelation. It was based solely on logic: Given the equivalence of Father and Son, the Holy Spirit simply could not be left out of the equation; its inclusion became a logical necessity. The doctrine of the Trinity has no scriptural basis whatsoever, and for this reason can accurately be described as a nonmystery, a pure intellectual construct in the minds of those orthodox Christians who subscribe to it.

The personal triumph of Athanasius proved to be a hollow victory. By scapegoating Arius, the Church only magnified its original error of embracing a doctrine of the soul that repudiated the divine presence within. In hindsight it is quite possible that if the teaching of immanence had taken root in the early days of the Church, the Arian controversy and many other disputes might never have occurred.

Although the Church's initial error may have been an honest mistake, the consequences of perpetuating it were grave. By asserting the equivalence of the Father and Son, the Church was, in effect, declaring that the soul of Jesus was different in kind from the souls of ordinary people. This was fateful because it undermined the mystical element in Jesus' own teachings, and opened up an enormous gulf between God and humans. The *New Catholic Encyclopedia* clearly states the extent of this chasm: "Between Creator and creature there is the most profound distinction possible. God is not part of the world. He is not just the peak of reality. Between God and the world there is an abyss . . ."[21] This abyss was wholly artificial, the creation of the Church, yet it was also a self-serving artifice, a means for institutional Christianity to vastly increase its earthly power. Today, Roman Catholic doctrine holds that the Church is the sole bridge over the otherwise unbridgeable chasm between God and humans.

The Church's doctrine of the soul has no basis in the New Testament, as Augustine himself acknowledged. Indeed, it appears to contradict the teaching of immanence, which, as we have seen, finds strong support in the Gospels of Luke and John and in the Gnostic gospels. Moreover, there is another curious line from John (3:14) that we have not yet considered:

No one has gone up to heaven
except the one who came down from heaven,

the Son of Man who is in heaven;

and the Son of Man must be lifted up

as Moses lifted up the serpent in the desert.[22]

But if Jesus is equivalent to the Father, why does he need to be lifted up? The usual explanation is that the line refers to Jesus' crucifixion: He is to be lifted up on the wooden cross.[23] But if this is true, why, then, does John also remind us that the Son of Man must lift up the serpent like Moses did in the desert? More likely, the passage from John has no connection with the crucifixion and instead pertains to the teaching of immanence and to the realization of the inner divinity—the serpent here symbolizing spiritual energy. We shall discuss this important symbol in more detail in chapter 10 and again in chapter 12.

The Church's decision at Nicaea was not motivated primarily by theology, nor was it made in the best interests of Christians. The condemnation of Arius was a political act, one that served to consolidate the hierarchical power of the orthodox bishops. In this sense, the bishops at Nicaea merely repeated the mistake made by Jews in the postexilic period when they reestablished a centralized priesthood. The Council of Nicaea stands as a prime example of the abuse of spiritual authority. Who were its victims, in addition to the scapegoat Arius? Answer: Everyone who has professed to be a Christian.

THE END OF TOLERANCE

The emperor Constantine's official endorsement of Christianity brought about a new marriage of Church and state that reshaped the Roman Empire. The alliance was destined to continue over many centuries, with many deleterious long-term consequences for Christians. But the immediate effects were even less healthy for non-Christians and so-called heretics. Constantine was an enthusiastic patron of the Church, and he constructed many new churches and basilicas during his long reign. But he was also the first Roman emperor to approve the demolition of pagan temples and the active suppression of heresy, policies that his successors greatly expanded. Before his patronage, Christianity had coexisted with many other religions and Mystery cults, including its old rival, Judaism, but also including Mithraism, Manicheanism, Zoroastrianism, the Eleusinian Mysteries, the rites of Samothrace, the Phrygian Mysteries, and various Gnostic sects, only some of which were Christian. This coexistence ended, however, with Constantine's official sanction of Christianity. From that time the bishops of the Church had the police forces of the empire at their disposal, and they did not hesitate to use them. A law promulgated in 356 C.E. closed the pagan temples.[24] The elimination of state subsidies soon followed and pagan priests found themselves out of work. The next step was the confiscation of the vast temple estates, which were turned over to the Church. By the end of the fourth century, the bishops had banned the popular Mystery rites at Eleusis.

Throughout this period Jews were made the object of special vengeance. Not only was their proselytizing declared illegal, but they were persecuted with such ferocity that large numbers fled eastward to Mesopotamia. Present-day Iraq became the world center of Judaism for the next thousand years. Persecution of Gnostic Christians also intensified. One fifth-century account describes how the homes of known Ophites living in the province of Bithynia (present-day Turkey) were ransacked by "a furious mob" led by an orthodox bishop. It is reminiscent of an earlier, better-known episode in Alexandria incited by the patriarch Theophilus. The incident involved a Christian riot and the destruction of the pagan temple of Serapis (the Separium), including a portion of the irreplaceable library of Alexandria.[25]

The Church eventually identified no fewer than 156 different kinds of heresy. By the time of Pope Theodosius in the fifth century, more than one hundred statutes against heresy were on the books. The implementation of Church policy, which involved seizing and destroying allegedly heretical scriptures, became increasingly systematic and effective. Gnostic writings became as rare as hen's teeth. It is no wonder that the discovery of an entire Gnostic library at Nag Hammadi in 1945 generated such excitement among scholars. The Gnostic and Hermetic manuscripts from Nag Hammadi have been dated to 350–400 C.E.—the period immediately following Constantine's rule when the Christian crackdown began in earnest.

There is no reason to suppose that Gnostic Christian communities such as the Naassenes survived the Church's relentless campaign against heterodoxy. While the total number of Naassenes was probably never large, numbers do not tell the full story. No doubt the communities of Naassenes and Ebionites and other Jewish-Christian sects included gifted teachers and probably a few saints capable of elucidating for others the deeper significance of the Last Supper. The fact that the doctrine of immanence was a closely kept secret does not mitigate the subsequent tragic events. In a climate of tolerance the secret would have survived to spread widely in more propitious times. Only Christian intolerance can explain why Jesus' vital teaching regarding the indwelling of God failed to find its way into mainstream Christianity.

As it turned out, the propitious times never arrived. On the contrary, the individuals in the Gnostic Christian communities who might have made the difference became the object of one of the greatest witchhunts in human history. Swept up in a broadening net of Church repression, they disappeared into one of the anonymous eddies of history. The precious diamond introduced by Jesus fell into the memory hole of our race, and there passed out of knowing. So great was the loss that over subsequent centuries Christianity failed to advance by a single step. The passage of time has been anything but kind because the magnitude of our loss has yet to be recognized, which explains why the spiritual impoverishment of the West is ongoing. Nearly twenty centuries after Jesus first spoke the words, they lie on the page like some cuneiform text, in wait of the happy hour when Christianity will finally rediscover their meaning.

7

The Parting of the Waters (Revisited)

IN APRIL 1928 AN ARAB FARMER WAS PLOWING a field on the coast of present-day Syria, near the town of Ra's Shamra, when he broke sod over an ancient tomb. The farmer didn't know it but he had stumbled onto the necropolis of a long forgotten Canaanite city. The authorities in Beirut were promptly summoned—in this case, Charles Virolleaud, director of the French Office of Antiquities, who inspected the site and notified Paris. The following year a French archaeologist, Claude F. A. Schaeffer, arrived and began to excavate the burial field. In May 1929, after five fruitless weeks digging in the necropolis, Schaeffer gave up and started to explore the nearby Tell. Within days he unearthed hundreds of clay tablets: an entire cuneiform library that soon became known as the Ra's Shamra tablets. The peasant farmer had discovered the ancient city of Ugarit, a thriving Mediterranean seaport during the second millennium B.C.E. Excavations continued on site for twenty-nine years and demonstrated that the city had been destroyed in a single great cataclysm, a combined earthquake-fire event, after which it was never reoccupied.

In its day Ugarit had been a cosmopolitan place. In the ancient world the coast of Canaan was a vital crossroads of trade and commerce, with Assyria to the east and Hatti or Hattusaland, the empire of the Hittites, to the north. Other important coastal seaports such as Tyre, Sidon, and Byblos lay farther south, within the sphere of influence of pharaonic Egypt.

Schaeffer's hoard from Ugarit included an amazing variety of ancient texts. Most of the languages were already known: Sumerian, Akkadian, Hurrian, Hittite, hieroglyphic Hittite, Egyptian, and Cypriot.[1] One, however, baffled linguists until they realized it was a cuneiform version of a dialect of Canaanite closely related to Hebrew.[2] The importance of the Ra's Shamra tablets was obvious from the beginning, and forty years after the discovery, newly translated inscriptions were still being published. Collectively known as the Ugaritic literature, the texts have dramatically changed our understanding of the development of Hebrew culture and religion. Schaeffer described the discovery as "one of the richest archaeological troves ever found at a single site."[3] W. F. Albright called it "stunning," "sensational," and "epoch-making."[4]

From the standpoint of our discussion, their praise is justified because in 1973 Albright's star pupil, Frank Moore Cross, proposed an explanation for the biblical theme of the parting of the waters based on his analysis of the texts from Ugarit. Cross's thesis involved a comparative study of Canaanite mythology and Hebrew scripture, and was published in his 1973 book, *Canaanite Myth and Hebrew Epic*. We shall soon have a closer look at it, but first we need to review the overall implications of Ra's Shamra.

THE IMPLICATIONS OF THE RA'S SHAMRA TABLETS

The library of clay tablets uncovered at ancient Ugarit has proved to be one of the most important archaeological finds ever made. Analysis of the Ugaritic texts in light of other archaeological evidence from Palestine and Lebanon led scholars to the stunning conclusion that the language, culture, and religion of the Canaanites were homogeneous across a wide region: from Ugarit in the north to Sinai in the south. Canaanite civilization even extended into northern Egypt, where it became fused with

Egyptian religion, though this synthesis was mostly confined to the Nile delta.[5] The evidence also suggests that soon after the Hebrews settled the highlands of Palestine, they adopted many of the urban customs of their more civilized Canaanite neighbors, borrowing heavily in architecture, shipbuilding, technology, literature, and even poetry.

Beyond this, scholars made a no less remarkable determination: Both the Hebrews and Canaanites were part of a larger family of Semitic peoples. Analysis of the Ugaritic literature demonstrated that many pre-Mosaic elements of the Pentateuch (the first five books of the Old Testament) were not only held in common with the Canaanites, but had also been heavily influenced by the Assyrians, Hurrians, and especially the Babylonians.

Thanks to the texts found at Ugarit, we now know that the Hebrews adopted Canaanite religious ideas from a very early date, even from the period of seminomadic wandering. We know, for example, that the design of Yahweh's tent and tabernacle came directly from the Canaanites: It seems the home of the Canaanite god El was a tent on a mountain, virtually identical to the sacred pavilion that originally housed the Ten Commandments and the Ark of the Covenant. Further indication of this close connection can be found in the Hebrew term for the outermost curtain of the tent sanctuary—*tahas,* which translates as "the skin of the dolphin." Now, pastoral seminomads such as the Hebrews would have had little interest in the skin of a sea creature, but the Ugaritic literature abounds with references to the sea—not surprising given that many of the Canaanites were coast dwellers. In the texts, El is sometimes described as dwelling "in the midst of the sea" or at "the fountain of the double deep." The neighboring Phoenicians also used the dolphin motif in association with El.[6] These references to the sea as we are going to discover, had mythological origins rooted in antiquity.

The inscriptions from Ugarit refer to various features of Canaanite temples that formerly were thought to have been Hebrew innovations: the tabernacle, table of gold (in the sanctuary), sacred courtyard, sacred enclosure, holy of holies, ephod, and teraphim—all terms long associated with Hebrew tradition and thought to be exclusive to it. In fact, just about every detail of the famed temple of Solomon, including the pillars of Jachin (Yakin) and Bo'az, the portable lavers, and the decoration of walls and objects with figures of cherubim (winged sphinxes), lions, bulls, palmettes, and lilies, had been borrowed from the neighboring Canaanites.[7] Even the Hebrew name for the temple, *hekal*, came from the Canaanites, with ancient Sumerian origins that date back to before 2500 B.C.[8] The Ugaritic texts also mention the term *man of god,* which turns up in the Old Testament in reference to Moses, Samuel, and the prophets.[9] Further, a number of the Psalms show the influence of Canaanite prose, verse, and mythology: As the scholar H. L. Ginsberg showed, Psalm 29 was originally a Canaanite hymn that the Hebrews appropriated almost verbatim.[10] In a 1935 paper Ginsberg also shows that Exodus 15:3,6 and the Song of Deborah, one of the earliest examples of Hebrew verse, are both stylistically identical to Canaanite poetry found at Ugarit.[11] Similarly, Frank Moore Cross found archaic elements from Canaanite mythology in Psalm 24.[12]

The tablets from Ugarit indicate that the Hebrews also borrowed pagan religious practices. Inscriptions describe Canaanite religious festivals that were probably the prototypes for the Jewish Feast of the Tabernacle, Feast of Weeks, and Feast of Unleavened Bread.[13] Likewise, the Hebrews adopted many Canaanite words and names. For example, the Jebuscite city of Jerusalem, which David selected to be the seat of his monarchy, derives its name from a Canaanite god: Shalem (or Salem), one of the mythological sons of Baal. Shalem was the patron and protector of the city, and Jerusalem, or Uru-Shalem, literally means "city of Salem." King David also apparently named his son, Ab-salom, after this same god.[14] Even the name Israel, the precise meaning of which has never been determined, incorporates the name of the Canaanite god El (Isra-El). One scholar, Aharon Wiener, has translated Israel as "God's fighter,"[15] while another translates it as "he who struggled with God."[16]

From the Bible it is clear that many Hebrews did not welcome the transition from seminomadism to a settled way of life. Strict Yahwists bridled at the perceived corrupting influence of Canaanite culture and religion. Rechabites lamented with nostalgia the passing of the old ways (Jeremiah 35), and many continued to view the former pastoral lifestyle as normative. For this reason there was also strong opposition to the new monarchic institutions. In the oracle of Nathan (II Samuel 7), Yahweh, speaking through his prophet, inveighs against the construction of a centralized temple. Frank Moore Cross has argued persuasively that the passage reflects real history—in other words, that King David paid close heed to his prophet/adviser, Nathan, and retained the old time-honored traditions during the period of his rule, including a more limited kingship and a permanent tent sanctuary in lieu of a temple. According to Cross, the dismantling of the loosely organized tribal league in favor of monarchic institutions was not the work of David, but of his son and successor. Cross also argues that the prevalent belief that David planned the great temple later constructed by Solomon was no more than Solomonic propaganda. Cross attributes the stubborn persistence of this belief to Solomon's remarkable success at rewriting history to suit his political agenda. The contradictory text of II Samuel 7 shows clear evidence of subsequent editing to legitimize the temple that Yahweh himself had opposed but which Solomon needed to underwrite his new imperial institutions. The centralized kingship required the centralized authority of religion—hence, the manufactured endorsement of scripture.[17]

Today, we know that Professor Cross was on the right track but did not go quite far enough. Fifty years of archaeological surveys in Israel-Palestine have demonstrated that it was not Solomon who tampered with the Book of Samuel, but the Deuteronomist scribe(s) who lived and worked two centuries later. According to Israel Finkelstein, a leading authority, archaeology has failed to produce a scintilla of evidence for Solomon's famed temple, his grand palace, or any other of his reputed architectural achievements. The systematic archaeological surveys conducted over the last fifty years show that the great metropolis of Jerusalem described in the Bible is a fiction. Finkelstein believes the city was no more than a rustic village during the reigns of David and Solomon and that the ruins at Megiddo, Hazor, and Gezer, and at other sites long attributed to Solomon, were actually the work of Omri and Ahab, the rulers of the northern kingdom who are so excoriated in scripture. David and Solomon were historical figures—of this there is no doubt—but not on the grand scale described in the Bible. Finkelstein attributes the scriptural hyperbole to the seventh-century Yahwist revival during the reign of King Josiah. Josiah was a religious reformer under whose rule the southern scribes compiled the Pentateuch and the Deuteronomic books (Joshua, Judges, and Kings). These compilers and revisionists created the story of a united monarchy led by the southern kingdom (Judah) to reflect their own then current geopolitical aspirations. Unfortunately, we do not have space here to discuss in more detail the archaeological basis for these recent stunning conclusions. Finkelstein's book is highly recommended.[18]

THE NAME OF THE DEITY

In the years following the Ra's Shamra discovery, as more of the Ugaritic texts were translated and published, scholars sought to map out the full extent of Canaanite influence on the Hebrews and, in the process, to identify the true threshold of Hebrew monotheism. At the epicenter of scholarly interest was the role played by the Canaanite gods Baal and El. The subject is fascinating, complex, controversial, and highly relevant to our investigation.

The Ugaritic texts include a number of mythological tales about Canaanite gods in which the Old Testament names of Yahweh appear numerous times, including El Olam (Genesis 21:33, "the God of Eternity" or "Ancient of Days"); El Elyon (Genesis 14:18, "the Most High" or "the Creator"); El Shaddai (the most common use, "the Mountain One"); and El Elohim Israel (Genesis 33:20, "God of Israel"). These parallels raise fascinating and important questions about the role of Canaanite religion in the emergence of Hebrew tradition. It is remarkable how closely the Pentateuchal descriptions of Yahweh tally with Ugaritic descriptions of the principal Canaanite deities. The stereotypical image of the patriarchal judge with the long white beard who dwells in a tent on a mountain and who presides over a council of gods (or angels) is not only a metaphorical description of Yahweh; it also accurately portrays the chief Canaanite god El. The same is true of the epithets for Yahweh. For example, both of the Hebrew meanings for Elohim were used by the Canaanites: The first form denoted the plural ("the gods") and the second, the "majestic plural," denoted prestige or majesty and expressed the full range of divine manifestations and names.

We can well imagine the enormous challenge the scholars faced as they sifted through the textual jungle of linguistic puns and nuances, searching for a way to distinguish the pagan elements from true monotheism. The Canaanite storm god Baal is a case in point because Yahweh is often described in the Bible in stereotypical storm-god fashion. For example, in Deuteronomy 33:26–27 he rides the clouds: "There is none like the God of Jeshuron: he rides the heavens to your rescue, rides the clouds in his majesty." It is of interest that this is also how Baal is described in the Ugaritic legend of Baal and Anath: "I tell thee, O prince *Baal*, I declare, O rider of the clouds."[19]

Probably the classic description of Yahweh is the theophany on "the mountain of Sinai" in Exodus 19:16–19:

> Now at daybreak on the third day there were peals of thunder on the mountain and lightning flashes, a dense cloud, and a loud trumpet blast, and inside the camp all the people trembled. Then Moses led the people out of the camp to meet God. And they stood at the bottom of the mountain. The mountain of Sinai was entirely wrapped in smoke, because Yahweh had descended on it in the form of fire. Like smoke from a furnace the smoke went up, and the whole mountain shook violently. Louder and louder grew the sound of the trumpet. Moses spoke, and God answered him with peals of thunder.

Another passage, from II Samuel 22:8–16, describes Yahweh in similar language:

> Then the earth quivered and quaked,
> the foundations of the heavens trembled

(they quivered because he was angry);
from his nostrils a smoke ascended,
and from his mouth a fire that consumed
(live embers were kindled at it).
He bent the heavens and came down,
a dark cloud under his feet;
he mounted a cherub and flew,
and soared on the wings of the wind.
Darkness he made a veil to surround him,
his tent a watery darkness, dense cloud;
before him a flash enkindled
hail and fiery embers.
Yahweh thundered from heaven,
the Most High made his voice heard;
he let his arrows fly and scattered them,
launched the lightnings and routed them.
The bed of the seas was revealed,
the foundations of the world were laid bare
at Yahweh's muttered threat,
at the blast of his nostrils' breath.

The descriptions here, however, are not unique to Yahweh. In the Ugaritic literature the same language is applied to Baal. When the god speaks, his

holy voice convulses the earth [and makes] the mountains quake
and tremble.
East and west, earth's high places reel.
Baal's enemies take to the woods.[20]

Canaanite storm-god imagery is made still more complex by the fact that it was also applied to El in his "mountain god" aspect (El Shaddai). As the judge of the mountaintop, El, like Baal, commanded lightning and storm, which may explain why storm-god language persisted in Judaism even after Baalist elements had been purged.

But the parallels do not end there. Homer used similar descriptive language for Zeus, the Greek equivalent of Baal: He is the "cloud gatherer," the "earth shaker," and "hurler of thunderbolts." Indeed, this metaphorical language appears to have been universal throughout the ancient world. The various storm gods of the Near East included the Egyptian Seth, the Hittite and Hurrian Teshub, the Assyrian Assur, the Amorite Ramanu, and the Babylonian Hadad (Marduk).[21] These earth shakers were all related and may have descended from the much older Sumerian Enlil and his sons Adad and Ninurta—all storm gods. If this picture is accurate, the storm-god genealogy traces unbroken to the oldest civilizations in the Near East: Egypt and especially Sumer, which is dated at roughly 4000 B.C.E., the dawn of recorded history in the current world age.

Not all scholars have supported the view that pagan elements were incorporated into Hebrew religion. W. F. Albright was an outspoken critic of those who, in his opinion, exaggerated the influence of pagan mythology. Albright believed that the Hebrew scribes who compiled the Bible had "demythologized" it,[22] arguing that the Pentateuch, with the exception of the first twelve chapters of Genesis, was essentially free of "polytheistic elements." He contended that "[t]here is no true mythology anywhere in the Hebrew Bible. What we have consists of vestiges—what may be called the debris of a past religious culture."[23] Albright likened the many borrowed pagan elements in the Bible, including the Hebrew appropriations of El and Baal, to modern borrowings of various aspects of pagan culture. For example, while the English word *cereal* derives from the Roman grain goddess Ceres, modern breakfast cereal clearly has nothing to do with the worship of Ceres. Nor do Christians mistake Easter for a pagan festival simply because the name of the holiday derives from the Anglo-Saxon goddess Oestre. Albright similarly accounted for the Hebrew use of Dagon for "grain," Dagon being the Canaanite vegetation god.[24]

Albright's logic appears sound enough for the examples cited, but it seems weak in the case of El because the Hebrews retained not only his pagan name but also his various divine aspects. Further, this was true not only of the earliest, and arguably the least "pure," stage of Hebrew monotheism. A revival of the most archaic forms of El occurred as late as the sixth century B.C.E., as documented in the Books of Ezekiel, Job, and II Isaiah,[25] and yet again during the apocalyptic age. In fact, despite intensive linguistic analysis, Frank Moore Cross was unable to identify a clear distinction between Hebrew and Canaanite epithets for their respective deities. In the end Cross concluded that the language is simply ambiguous. The only apparent difference is that the Hebrews melded both of the Canaanite gods—Baal and El—into a single deity, which was the status of Yahweh until ninth-century B.C.E. reformers such as Elijah began to purge the Baalist elements.[26]

All of this suggests that the earliest distinguishing feature of Hebrew monotheism was not the name of the deity, but rather the introduction of a superior ethical code: the Ten Commandments. Consider, for instance, the story of Isaac in which Yahweh instructs Abraham to sacrifice his own son only to commute the sentence at the last moment. The story is peculiar—it certainly troubled the Danish writer Søren Kierkegaard—and might be inexplicable but for archaeological evidence that the Canaanites practiced child sacrifice. Apparently the practice was limited to the cult of El, the Canaanite equivalent of the Greek god Cronus, who, in Greek mythology, devoured his own children.[27] This suggests the story of Isaac was actually a morality lesson that sought to teach by recapitulating the pagan practice, then explicitly rejecting it. After the initial command, Yahweh intercedes on behalf of the sanctity of children. The moral is obvious: The Hebrews were instructed to shun the barbaric practice of their neighbors. Of course, during wartime Yahweh could still be counted on to sanction the slaughter of entire cities.

MYTHOLOGICAL ELEMENTS IN EXODUS

Frank Moore Cross continued W. F. Albright's linguistic studies of Ugaritic literature in light of Old Testament tradition, but arrived at somewhat different conclusions. Cross found compelling evidence that

Canaanite myths had actually influenced Hebrew religion, in ways both subtle and complex. As we shall now see, the mythological common ground outlined by Cross involves the ancient concept of the waters, and thus is highly relevant to our exploration of the Naassene Sermon.

In the Bible can be found a number of tellings, retellings, and references to the Hebrews' Exodus from Egypt. Whatever its historical accuracy, the story is central to Jewish tradition. By means of linguistic analysis, Cross was able to establish that one of these Exodus stories, the Song of Miriam, also known as the Song of the Sea (Exodus 15:1–18), stands apart; it cannot be reconciled with the other prose accounts. The Song of the Sea is attributed to Miriam, the sister of Moses, and is one of the most archaic fragments in the Bible. It was written in verse, which distinguishes it from the prose body of Exodus in which it is embedded. The pertinent lines read:

> Yahweh is a warrior;
> Yahweh is his name.
> The chariots and the army of Pharaoh he has hurled into the sea;
> the pick of his horsemen lie drowned in the Sea of Reeds.
> The depths have closed over them;
> they have sunk to the bottom like a stone.
> Your right hand, Yahweh, shows majestic in power,
> your right hand, Yahweh, shatters the enemy.
> So great your splendor, you crush your foes;
> you release your fury, and it devours them like stubble.
> A blast from your nostrils and the waters piled high;
> the waves stood upright like a dike;
> in the heart of the sea the deeps came together.
> "I will give chase, and overtake," the enemy said.
> "I shall share out the spoil, my soul will feast on it;
> I shall draw my sword, my hand will destroy them."
> One breath of yours you blew, and the sea closed over them;
> they sank like lead in the terrible waters.

Cross dated the song to the period of the Judges—that is, to the last centuries of the second millennium B.C.E. If this is accurate, the poem is the oldest version of the Exodus story and therefore must also be the primary source for Hebrew tradition. The early date presents a serious problem, however, because the Song of the Sea deviates from tradition in important respects. It contains no mention of the safe passage of the Israelites over a dry seabed. The destruction of the pharaoh's pursuing troops is described strictly in terms of a storm-tossed sea that capsizes and swallows the Egyptian army, who—we can assume—are following in boats. Most notably, the song contains no reference to Yahweh's parting of the sea. Cross argued that these other elements were later mythological accretions, the Song of the Sea being the original Exodus account, essentially historical and non-mythological in character.[28]

Where Velikovsky searched for a naturalistic explanation in *Worlds in Collision,* Cross found a historical solution within the Bible itself. Traces of mythology do remain in the Song of the Sea. For example, the word *majestic* is an epithet for Baal. Cross, however, judged this incidental and entirely vestigial. Of much greater importance, in his view, is the fact that the Song of the Sea reads like straightforward history. Cross argued that the subsequent additions to the Exodus account had a mythological basis, which he traced to a story in the Ugaritic literature: the legendary tale of Baal's fight with Yamm, the Canaanite sea god who is also sometimes described as a dragon (Lotan). This mythical story was unknown to scholarship before the discovery of the Ra's Shamra tablets. Yamm is the Canaanite equivalent of the Greek Typhon and the Babylonian Tiamat, the same monster who also appears in Revelation 12 and in the Old Testament as Leviathan or Rahab. Clearly, the dragon fight was a part of the cultural heritage shared by the Hebrews and all of their Semitic neighbors.[29] Although this was not confirmed until the discovery at Ra's Shamra, it is of interest that many years before, a scholar named Hermann Gunkel had made a similar case for biblical and Babylonian parallels in a famous book, *Schöpfung und Chaos in Urzeit und Endzeit* (Creation and Chaos in Primitive Time and Endtime), an amazing example of scholarly intuition.[30] In chapter 13 we shall more thoroughly investigate the cosmology of the dragon fight and its Mesopotamian origins.

Professor Cross argued that Hebrew scribes had reworked the Ugaritic story of Baal and Yamm, substituting Yahweh's name for Baal and Rahab's name for Yamm before incorporating it into scripture. Fragments of the archaic tale are clearly in evidence in Psalms 74, 77, 89, and 114. For instance, Psalm 89:9–11 reads:

> You control the pride of the ocean,
> when its waves ride high you calm them;
> You split Rahab [the dragon] in two like a carcass
> and scattered your enemies with your mighty arm.

The same idea is evident in Psalm 74:12–13:

> Yet, God, my King from the first,
> author of saving acts throughout the earth,
> by your power you split the sea in two,
> and smashed the heads of monsters on the waters.

Notice that in these examples the dragon Rahab is equivalent to the sea. Thus, splitting the dragon is tantamount to splitting (or dividing) the waters. The same archaic motif appears in Nahum 1:4; Job 7:12, 9:8, 26:12, and 38:7–11; and Isaiah 27:1, 51:9–10. Consider the last:

> Awake! Awake! Clothe yourself in strength,
> arm of Yahweh.
> Awake as in the past,
> in times of generations long ago.
> Did you not split Rahab in two
> and pierce the dragon in two?

Cross proposed that the mythological accretions to the original Exodus story had occurred during the days of oral tradition in the period of the Judges, long before Exodus was compiled and written down. During this time the Hebrews lived in close proximity to their Canaanite neighbors. Israel-Palestine is not a large region—even today, towns and villages lie in close proximity, almost within hailing distance. For this reason, in times of peace there must have been considerable sharing between the two peoples. Nevertheless, Cross thought it unlikely that the Hebrews borrowed Canaanite mythology during this period. He argued that the common mythology traced to a much older shared Semitic cultural background dating to a time long before monotheism.

He went on to propose a liturgical mechanism to account for the later additions to the Exodus story, for which he found evidence in II Isaiah 35 and 40:3–6.[31] He contended that during the period of the Judges, the Exodus Conquest was ceremonially reenacted at the annual spring festival (Passover), when the Ark of the Covenant would be borne aloft in a solemn procession from Shittim, the site of Joshua's camp east of the Jordan, across the river to Gilgal, where a covenant renewal ceremony would be consummated. Cross suggested that the Hebrews may even have temporarily dammed the Jordan for the event. In these liturgical reenactions the Jordan River substituted for the Red Sea and in this way the first Red Sea crossing was coupled with a second parting of the waters. Tradition was thus enriched.

Cross's thesis is plausible because the equating of sea and river is well attested to in both Ugaritic literature and the Bible. In the Canaanite myth of the sea dragon, Yamm the Sea is also Yamm the River Judge.[32] Thus, Yamm = sea = river *(nahr)*. Notably, the same link appears in Jonah 2:4: "And you cast me into the abyss, into the heart of the sea, and the flood surrounded me." Here, as the linguist Cyrus Gordon pointed out, the words *sea* and *flood* are equivalent to *nahr,* the word for river. All are synonymous and refer to Rahab or Yamm.[33] A similar pairing can be found in Psalm 114:

> When Israel came out of Egypt,
> the house of Jacob from a foreign nation,
> Judah became his sanctuary

and Israel his domain.
The sea fled at the sight,
the Jordan stopped flowing.
The mountains skipped like rams,
and like lambs, the hills.
Sea, what makes you run away?
Jordan, why stop flowing?

Here, sea and river are interchangeable. Cross cited yet another example, from Habakkuk 3:8:

Yahweh, is your anger blazing against the rivers,
or your fury against the sea,
that you come mounted on your horses,
on your victorious chariots.

This mythological pairing of river and sea is an extremely important feature of Near Eastern mythology. We have already touched on it in our discussion of the sacred river and the spiritual waters. (See chapters 1 and 3.) In chapter 13 we shall explore its cosmological basis.

In summary, Cross argued that the theme of the parting of the waters, so integral to both the Exodus story and Joshua's traditional crossing of the Jordan, originated and evolved through a complex process wherein annual ceremonial reenactments were influenced by ancient mythological ideas that the Hebrews held in common with the Canaanites. Real historical events preserved in memory were thus reshaped into the stories, part historical and part mythological, that only much later, when they were finally written down, became the familiar body of Hebrew tradition. If Cross's assertions are correct, W. F. Albright was not wrong when he argued that the Hebrew scribes were among the world's first competent historiographers—though it is no less true that mythological elements also found their way into scripture.

The liturgical mechanism introduced by Frank Moore Cross to explain the appearance of the theme of the parting of the waters in the

Books of Exodus and Joshua is not only fascinating and entirely plausible, but it also may well be correct. No less fascinating, though, is what Cross left out of his discussion. Conspicuous by its omission is any mention of the third and fourth instances of the parting of the waters involving Elijah and Elisha (II Kings 2:1–18), which we have discussed in chapters 1 and 2. Why did Professor Cross not consider this material, which obviously derives from the same mythological fabric? Was it because he judged that the archaic elements had become vestigial? Perhaps, for although mythological elements are certainly present in II Kings 2:1–18 and establish continuity with the ancient past, the Deuteronomist clearly has made them serve some new and as yet unexplained purpose. Let us now explore what that purpose might be.

YAHWEH DONS A NEW FACE

Like the Song of the Sea, the biblical story of Elijah has the feel of actual history. At the time I Kings and II Kings were compiled, the demythologizing process described by W. F. Albright had taken hold. The Deuteronomist appropriates the old mythological material, but now with some new use in mind. He makes a clean break with the past by explicitly rejecting the old storm-god language, in keeping with the ninth-century B.C. campaign waged by Elijah and the prophets against a resurgent Baal cult. To be sure, the history presented in I and II Kings must be treated with caution, for the books reflect the narrow geopolitical interests of the southern kingship. Yet the polytheistic revival described in the story is probably factual. Real history is in evidence and is the backdrop for the later events at the Jordan, culminating in Elijah's ascension into the whirlwind. As a result of the Canaanite revival during the lifetime of Elijah, the epithets of Baal that had long been assimilated into Hebrew religion had become an obstacle to the further maturation of monotheism and therefore had to be jettisoned.

This is played out in the account of Elijah's flight from the northern kingdom and his subsequent visitation by Yahweh (I Kings 19). In the story, Elijah has just won a dramatic victory over the priests of Baal, but that victory has triggered a political backlash. The Baalist sympathizer Ahab remains on the throne. The Yahwist reformer king Jehu has not yet appeared on the stage of history to play out his role as avenger. For the moment the scales tip back the other way and the campaign of the prophets hangs by a thread. Amid intensifying Baalist persecution, Elijah learns of a plot for his own assassination and flees for his life. The prophet makes his way into the reaches of the southern desert and finds refuge in a cave on Mount Horeb. It is no mere coincidence that this cave is the site of Moses' earlier theophany (Exodus 33:18–23). Not surprisingly, during the night Yahweh returns once again. This time, however, the Deity is described very differently. In the theophany of Moses, Yahweh appeared as the storm god, the earth shaker in the full raiment of his power and glory. On that occasion Moses was forced to avert his eyes and seek shelter in a rocky cleft lest he be destroyed by Yahweh's unbridled power. But now the Deuteronomist consciously rejects the storm-god epithets of cloud, earthquake, and fire. As in the story of Isaac, the scribe employs the device of first presenting the old pagan elements, then rejecting them. According to the account in I Kings 19, the prophet Elijah initially hides in the cave just as Moses did, before being summoned forth to witness with open eyes what is about to ensue:

> There he went into the cave and spent the night in it. Then the word of Yahweh came to him, saying "What are you doing here Elijah?" He replied, "I am filled with jealous zeal for Yahweh Sabaoth, because the sons of Israel have deserted you, broken down your altars and put your prophets to the sword. I am the only one left, and they want to kill me." He was told, "Go out and stand on the mountain before Yahweh." Then Yahweh himself went by. And there came a mighty wind, so strong it tore the mountains and shattered the rocks before Yahweh. But Yahweh was not in the wind. After the wind came an earthquake. But Yahweh was not in the earthquake. After the earthquake came a fire. But Yahweh was not in the fire. And after the fire there came the sound of a gentle breeze. And when Elijah heard this, he covered his face with his cloak.

Notice that the Deuteronomist replaces the old storm god rhetoric with a new metaphorical language: Yahweh dons a new face, now appearing in the form of Spirit. In Hebrew, Spirit is feminine *(Ruah)*, beautifully described here as a gentle breeze. The use of the cloak as a literary device is also extremely skillful. When the prophet covers himself, we know that he is undergoing an interior process: Elijah is in the throes of a sublime spiritual experience. Twenty-nine centuries later, the challenge to human understanding remains essentially unchanged.

A WORK IN PROGRESS

The subsequent account of the ascension of Elijah, which we have already discussed in chapters 1 and 2, is no less extraordinary. Its mysteries are several: the parting of the waters, the ascension itself, the role (again) of the cloak, and the descent of the Spirit upon Elisha. What does it mean to say that the prophet and his disciple part the waters by striking the river with the cloak? Cross's linguistic analysis cannot take us into this territory—a limitation that it seems he well understood.

As demonstrated by the repetitive theme of the waters, the development of Judeo-Christianity has been a dynamic process. In the hands of the Deuteronomist the waters—the dragon of old—have become the medium for a new message. Traces of the archaic elements present in Exodus and Joshua are still detectable in the Deuteronomist's account. But it is also obvious that they have become vestigial. Mythology has been reshaped for some new purpose, as evidenced by the scribe's conscious rejection of the old storm-god language. And what is that new purpose? Perhaps the Deuteronomist did not understand it himself. His inspired and unerring use of the ancient language of symbolism linking water and the Spirit suggests that mastery over the river is the key to the mystery. Even so, within the framework of Judaism, it is a work in progress and will remain unfinished for centuries, until, as we have seen, Gnostic Christianity took the final steps.

8

The Demiurge and the Wisdom Dialogue

They teach the insidious doctrine
that there is another God besides the Creator.
IRENAEUS, *AGAINST HERESIES*

For many heretics have said that the God
Of the Old Testament is one,
and the God of the New Testament is another.
AMBROSE, *ON THE HOLY SPIRIT*, 1, 4

GNOSTICS ATTRIBUTED THE WORK OF CREATION to a lesser deity or demiurge known as Ialdabaoth (also spelled Yaldabaoth or Jaldabaoth), but the notion of the demiurge was not a Gnostic invention. Nearly five hundred years before Christianity, Plato described a similar Creation scheme in his *Timaeus*. In fact, as we know from a number of pagan theogonies that have come down to us, the same formula existed throughout the ancient world.[1] The story goes something like this: In the beginning the unknowable and self-begotten first principle emerges from watery chaos and gives birth to the gods. This primal being first cleaves in two, and then consorts with itself, thus producing the next divine pair. And so it goes. Each successive generation of gods gives rise to the next until the full pantheon emerges. At some point the cosmic clock begins to tick. The various responsibilities attending Creation are delegated, after which heaven and the earth are formed along with the stars, day and night, and the elements air, fire, and earth. Very late in the game living things appear, including, almost as an afterthought, the human race.

This grand Creation scheme was, with many variations, almost universal throughout the ancient world—and this includes the Greeks, despite that remarkable flowering of speculation about man, God, and the universe known as Greek philosophy. Most of the Greek philosophers, of course, were monotheists. Yet, with some exceptions, they managed to coexist with polytheism. The great thinkers were not fooled. They understood that mythology was to be taken figuratively, not literally. The purpose of philosophy was to delve deeper—and the true foundation was obviously monotheism. The gods of Olympus were entirely derivative.

The Gnostic Ialdabaoth has been translated as "begetter of Sabaoth," which seems to have been a pejorative pun for YHWH Sabaoth, one of the names of Yahweh in the Old Testament. The demiurge is of special interest to us because the Naassene Sermon mentions Ialdabaoth (*Refutation* 5.8.30), a significant fact because the Naassenes, unlike other Gnostic sects, did not reject the Old Testament. The demiurge, of course, was wholly foreign to Judaism. Whereas the monotheistic Greek philosophers often tolerated a proliferation of lesser deities, Judaism insisted on a single entity: Yahweh. By some accounts he was attended by a council of angels, but Yahweh remained the prime mover; he alone was responsible for Creation. Even today this remains one of Judaism's distinguishing features. How, then, do we explain the presence of the demiurge Ialdabaoth in the Naassene Sermon? We have noted the Naassenes' syncretism, but syncretism alone cannot answer the question.

ORIGINS WITHIN JUDAISM

Most scholars regard the Gnostic demiurge as a rebellion against Judaism.[2] This may well be so, but it is important to realize that the demiurge was not a simple phenomenon. The rebellion involved a devaluation of the God of the Old Testament, which is partially explained by historical events—namely, the three failed Jewish revolts against Roman rule. The first and best known of these was the Jewish War of 66–73 C.E. A second uprising was put down in 115–117 C.E., during the rule of Trajan, and a third and final insurrection, the Bar Kokhba rebellion, was crushed in 135 C.E.[3] There is no doubt that these failed political revolts against Rome seriously undermined the prestige of Yahweh. And for this reason the inception of the Gnostic demiurge might date to as early as the period after 70 C.E., the year of the cataclysmic destruction of the famous temple of Herod.

But political history does not tell the full story. The devaluation of Yahweh was also rooted in a process of religious reform that had been under way within Judaism for centuries, and which only attained its full fruition in the person of Jesus. To understand this reform and how it came about, we must look to the Old Testament—in particular, to the seminal Book of Job. (Many scholars have sought answers in Genesis—which is understandable, given that the demiurge is associated with Creation—but with less satisfactory results.)

Most Christians probably assume that the God of the Hebrews in the days of Abraham was the same as the God of Moses and, furthermore, that this God was also equivalent to the Father mentioned by Jesus with such love and devotion. Any such assumptions are false, however, but not because God changed. God's nature, being absolute and eternal, never changes. What does change is human understanding. The human conception of God—the God concept—has changed many times over the course of history and will continue to evolve and mature in the future. In a famous essay called "The God of the Fathers," first published in 1929, the Old Testament scholar Albrecht Alt explored whether such a transformation had occurred at the time of Moses. Alt found clues in the Pentateuch suggesting that the Elohist scribe had amended the earliest accounts to bring the more archaic God of the early Hebrews, the God of the patriarchs, in line with the later (and more pure) monotheism of Moses.[4] His paper touched off a lively debate among biblical scholars that continues to this day.

The reform that we are about to discuss is another example of the sort of evolution observed by Alt. The need for reform of the Old Testament God concept was real enough. While some Old Testament passages describe Yahweh as merciful, loyal, forgiving, and benevolent, he is at least as often portrayed as jealous, grouchy, wrathful, irritable, proud, boastful, unforgiving, temperamental, cruel, vengeful, and even blood-thirsty, prepared to sanction cold-blooded murder or mass slaughter, including the annihilation of entire cities. Given the numerous examples of God-sanctioned mayhem in scripture, it is no wonder that discriminating readers have sometimes doubted whether this same Yahweh can inspire our confidence and trust, to say nothing of love, devotion, respect, and emulation. Oftentimes, fear and trembling seem a more likely human response. And while fear of divine retribution can be a powerful force for good and, at times, perhaps, a necessary motivator, if the goal is to uplift humanity from a moral standpoint, the example set by Yahweh in the Old Testament falls short of inspirational (to say the least).

THE BOOK OF JOB

The Old Testament Book of Job, whose author is unknown, has two main themes: the question of evil and the character of Yahweh. Many scholars rightly regard Job, along with Isaiah, Jeremiah, and Ezekiel, as representative of the high-water mark of the Old Testament.[5] The central part of the book is a series of poems that was probably composed sometime in the fifth or sixth century B.C.E. Part folktale, prophetic oracle, hymn, lamentation, didactic treatise, and epic, Job makes use of almost every genre in the Bible. The question it raises is no less pertinent today: Why does evil flourish while good people suffer? The answer the story provides broke sharply with Judaic tradition, and for this reason Job must have been highly controversial in its day. Tradition held that God would eventually reward the good man, regardless of his sufferings. Like the prophet Jeremiah, however (see Jeremiah 13:14, 24–25 and 15:6–7), the author of Job adopts a much less rosy and more sober outlook that probably reflects the bleak aftermath of the conquest and destruction of Judah by Nebuchadnezzar in the early sixth century B.C.E. Although the precise composition date of the Book of Job is not known, it is obviously from the time of exile or later.[6]

The story portrays Yahweh as openly in league with Satan. God torments the good man (Job) despite the fact that he keeps the Law and lives a morally upright life. Job's many trials are the work of Satan, Yahweh's servant (or possibly his son), who whispers false accusations in God's ear and receives permission to punish the man in order to test him and expose the wickedness allegedly concealed in his heart. Job's flocks are stripped from him, his servants are slaughtered, and his sons and daughters are killed in a mighty whirlwind. He himself is stricken with a terrible wasting disease that causes great suffering and brings him to the edge of the grave. Job's body literally becomes an open wound. To make matters worse, Job's wife and his friends turn against him: His wife urges him to curse Yahweh and to abandon all faith in God; meanwhile, his friends make superficial religious cant and castigate Job for having the temerity to maintain his innocence. One after another they admonish him, insisting that because God is punishing him, ipso facto, he must be guilty. They advise him to submit quietly to his sufferings, which obviously have been ordained by God. But Job will have none of it. Like a rock he holds fast to principle. Stubbornly he maintains his innocence and insists upon justice. At the same time, however, he remains faithful to Yahweh, refusing to condemn or even criticize the Almighty.

What is shocking about the story is the ease with which Yahweh succumbs to Satan's false witness about Job's alleged faithlessness. Being omniscient, Yahweh should be able to easily verify Job's goodness and constancy. But instead he hands over Job to Satan with a single proviso: "He is in your power. But spare his life." Though Job remains faithful throughout, before his terrible ordeal is done he curses the day of his birth. No less shocking is Yahweh's failure to acquit Job even after his innocence has been established. There is to be no moment of truth and no justice under heaven. Instead of vanquishing Satan for making false accusations, Yahweh turns on the victim. Instead of offering solace and comfort to the innocent, he badgers Job and bullies him, sneers at him with rhetorical questions, and then confronts the hapless man with a mind-boggling display of divine wrath.

In the end, poor Job is beaten down and brought to his knees. But how can it be otherwise, given Yahweh's overwhelming might? The rod of God is an awesome thing. In the end Job is reduced to a stuttering simpleton. He repents, even though he is innocent, and admits that he has been talking about things far beyond his ken. Having seen the omnipotence of Yahweh, he is prepared to eat dust. In this vein Job responds: "What reply can I give to you, I who carry no weight?" (Job 40:4; 42:2) In a final prose epilogue Yahweh shows a loving touch by restoring Job's health and property, but there is no mention of restoring his dead servants and children. The somewhat cheery conclusion feels out of step with the rest of the composition, as though a later scribe who was no less shocked than we by Yahweh's behavior added it to redeem God's tarnished image. Indeed, so subversive is the Book of Job that it is remarkable the scripture was retained in the Bible. Probably the scribal "correction" saved it from being thrown out—this and the fact that Job is a literary masterpiece. Of course, even with the modified ending, the story is far from satisfactory. Job's total submission in the face of brute force seems a lame solution to the problem of evil. Nonetheless, the book is momentous because the questions the story fails to resolve were to redound over the centuries, as we shall see, and preoccupy the final books of the Old Testament.

YAHWEH'S DEFICIENCY

So what is the root of the matter in the story of Job? Carl Jung, the founder of analytical psychology, points out in his commentary *Answer* to *Job* that for all of his infinite power, Yahweh ultimately damns himself. By humiliating Job, by making him eat dust, God unwittingly reveals his own deep character flaw—brutishness—while at the same time elevating the impotent but righteous human. Job may be powerless before the Almighty, yet he remains free to choose, and by choosing well he shows impressive moral strength. Indeed, Job's fortitude stands in marked contrast to Yahweh's rage and reproaches the Deity's ratification of evil. To be sure, Yahweh carries the day. With infinite power at his disposal, the outcome is not in doubt. Yet from a moral standpoint, Yahweh's display of heavenly fireworks and thunder fails to impress. This is the beautiful and terrible irony of the story: that Job, despite his relative impotence, comes to stand in righteous judgment over God himself. As Jung put it:

> We do not know whether Job realizes this, but we do know from the numerous commentaries on Job that all succeeding ages have overlooked the fact that a kind of Moira . . . rules over Yahweh, causing him to give himself away so blatantly. Anyone can see how unwittingly he raises Job by humiliating him in the dust. By so doing he pronounces judgment on himself and gives man the moral satisfaction whose absence we [find] so painful in the Book of Job.[7]

The word Moira here refers to fate or destiny. In Greek religion Moira was one of three personified seasons that accompanied Zeus and were often pictured hovering just above his shoulder. The point is that Zeus was governed by them even though he was the most important Greek deity. The mere thought that such a thing might also exist in monotheistic Judaism is shocking. Surely the Godhead cannot be subject to fate. Is it not God, after all, who determines the destinies of others? Nonetheless, from the story it is clear that despite his omnipotence Yahweh is lacking in something. Job apparently intuits this because in his suffering he asks: "But tell me, where does Wisdom come from? Where is understanding to be found?" (Job 28:12) In the very next verse Job answers his own question. "Wisdom?" he says. "It is fear of the Lord." Here, as Jung notes, Job shows that he is unaware of his own achievement. He does not seem to understand that in holding firm, standing on his innocence, and insisting on justice he has won a tremendous moral victory—not just for himself, but for all mankind. Job's answer may seem unsatisfactory, but it is important because during the apocalyptic age it became grist for the scribal mill, as we shall see.

Now back to the problem raised by Jung—that Yahweh is ruled by fate: Even though Yahweh as God must have access to all knowledge, for some reason in the story of Job he has neglected or forgotten, as Jung phrases it, "to consult his own omniscience." It seems that Yahweh has been split off from a part of himself, which means that he is not fully conscious—incredible! And what of his paranoid boasting? Indeed, what could possibly compel an all-powerful Being to stoop to bluster and threats in the first place? This discomfiting aspect of Yahweh's behavior, analyzed long ago by the unknown author of the Secret Book of John, one of the Gnostic gospels found at Nag Hammadi, was the key Gnostic insight: ". . . he [Yahweh] said to them, 'I am a jealous God and there is no other god beside me.' But by announcing this he indicated to the angels who attended to him that there exists another God, for if there were no other one, of whom would he be jealous?"[8]

Of whom, indeed? No scholar in the modern era has understood the theological question implicit in the Book of Job better than this Gnostic scribe of old. Nor has anyone stated it more succinctly. While the phrase "I am a jealous God" does not appear in the text of Job, it is implied—and it does occur in Exodus 20:5 and Isaiah 14:5–6. Numerous other Old Testament passages—Deuteronomy 4:35, 6:15–16, and 32:19–21; and Isaiah 4:8, 44:6, 45:5,21, and 46:4—convey a similar meaning. In fact, Yahweh's jealous tantrums are a prominent feature of the Old Testament, running through scripture like the surly residue of the old Canaanite storm god, which is precisely the point. It is of interest that the famous heretic hunter Irenaeus, writing two generations before Hippolytus, quotes the very same line about the jealous Yahweh in his lengthy treatise *Against Heresies*.[9] Was it mere coincidence that Irenaeus devoted the largest portion of his five-volume opus to an attempted refutation of the Gnostic demiurge? Or was it an accurate indication of the historical importance of Yahweh's character defect? There is no question that the controversy surrounding the demiurge was one of the major battle lines separating the Gnostics from orthodox Christianity.

Let us now investigate why Yahweh would allow Satan's experiment to be foisted on an innocent man. Jung was apparently intrigued by the same question, for he writes:

> It is indeed no edifying spectacle to see how quickly Yahweh abandons his faithful servant [Job] to the evil spirit and lets him fall without compunction or pity into the abyss of . . . suffering. From the human point of view, Yahweh's behavior is so revolting that one has to ask oneself whether there is not a deeper motive hidden behind it. Has Yahweh some secret resistance against Job? That would explain his yielding to Satan. But what does man possess that God does not have?[10]

The psychologist goes on to propose that Yahweh's behavior is driven by an ulterior concern—namely, the divine suspicion that our frail human consciousness is more keen than his own. The very idea is stunning! Consider, though, that driven by the ever-present knowledge of our own severe limitations as well as our relative impotence, we humans are required to cultivate consciousness simply to survive. We have little choice in the matter. Yahweh, on the other hand, has no such need for introspection because he is unchallenged, has no opposition, and encounters no obstacles; nothing requires him to reflect upon himself.

Stranger still is the conclusion that follows from a related question: Why would Yahweh instruct Satan to spare Job's life? Judging from God's sadistic behavior, the reason certainly can have nothing to do with compassion; Yahweh is perfectly content to wreak mayhem on Job without regret or remorse. Nor can the reason involve a former loyalty—namely, the Mosaic covenant—for the Book of Job reflects the period following the destruction of the first temple, when the old covenant must have seemed a moot article. In fact, in Job there is not the slightest pretense of a covenant. Why, then, does Yahweh spare Job's life? Is it possible that he likes having someone around to hear him boast? Does he enjoy having someone present to witness his thundering about heaven? Can it be that Yahweh actually *needs* Job? Quite probably he does, which would explain Jung's purpose in mentioning Moira, the season of destiny.

Here, an example from the Greeks may help. We know from the oldest extant account from Greek mythology, the *Hymn of Demeter,* that when Hades abducted Demeter's beautiful daughter, Persephone, and took her to his realm of the dead, Demeter, the grain goddess, became so heartsick that she refused to extend her usual bounty upon the earth.[11] Stricken by a yearlong drought and resulting crop failures, humanity faced extreme privation, even mass starvation. In this dire circumstance mighty Zeus was compelled to intervene and arrange a compromise: Zeus ordained that henceforth Persephone would spend a part of the year above ground with her mother, Demeter, and the rest below it with her new consort, Hades. Now, why would Zeus be concerned enough to intervene? Quite simply, something had to be done because a mass die-off of humanity would leave no human supplicants to perform the daily sacrifices and rituals in honor of the gods![12] Just as humankind needed the gods, so also did the Greek gods need humankind.

In the story of Job we find hints of a similar phenomenon. Yahweh makes Job suffer, yes, but he dares not exterminate him because he needs a living and breathing Job to honor and glorify his divine name. It is Yahweh's fate to require worship. Of course, the relationship between God and humans is not between equals—an enormous gulf separates Yahweh from the puny and subservient Job. Nonetheless, it is a reciprocal relationship—Yahweh needs humans as much as humans need him. The deeper conclusion to which this leads is never openly stated in the Book of Job, but it is certainly implied, which probably explains why Job was (and remains) so controversial: If Yahweh is subject to fate and if he requires worship, how can he truly be the ultimate

Godhead, the first without a second? Of course, he cannot; Yahweh as presented in Job is but a figurehead, a demiurge on a par with Zeus and the other pagan storm gods.

Job's query regarding Wisdom takes us to the heart of the matter, for wisdom is the quality Yahweh lacks. The Greek word for her is Sophia. She is the Divine Mother, the feminine companion to God, and she is well known in the East, where she is the active principle in the Godhead and has many names. In the various Hindu traditions she appears as Kali, Shakti, and Durga, among others. It is she who manifests the world, sustains it, and transforms it. East or West, she is inseparable from the Godhead. In Judaism, however, awareness of her nature and importance was a late development. That it happened at all may have been due in no small part to the anonymous scribe responsible for the Book of Job.

The problem is how to reconcile her gentle and wise nature with the gruff and irritable Yahweh. The temperamental patriarch of old stubbornly resists the intrusion of her feminine presence. The Hebrew God prefers to stand alone, imperious in his majesty, bristling with archetypal wrath. Indeed, in his raging aspect Yahweh is almost the antithesis of Wisdom. It is no wonder that many of the Old Testament descriptions of Yahweh closely resemble the Canaanite gods El and Baal—the raw material for so much of his composite character.[13] In the sixth century B.C.E. these dross elements were still very much in evidence.

The patriarchal storm god dies hard. Yet change (i.e., evolve) God must, because from the moment the author of Job exposes Yahweh's dark underside, his deficiency can no longer be ignored, neither on earth, nor in heaven. Thus, we find her—Sophia, Wisdom—described in the eighth Proverb, where we are told that her presence is as old as Creation:

> The Lord possessed me in the beginning of his way,
> before his works of old.
> I was set up from everlasting, from the beginning,
> or ever the earth was.

When there were no depths, I was brought forth;

when there were no foundations abounding with water.

When he established the heavens, I was there,

When he marked out the foundations of the earth,

then I was by him, as a master worksman,

and I was daily in his delight,

rejoicing always before him,

rejoicing in his habitable earth;

and my delights were with the sons of men.

(Proverbs 8:22–24, 27, 29–31)

Parts of the book of Proverbs are very old and may even date to the time of Solomon, but the chapters about Wisdom, including the lines cited above, were composed much later, although an exact date has never been established. Dating Proverbs has proved difficult. Jung interpreted the presence of Wisdom as evidence of Greek influence and dated the above passage to the third or fourth century B.C.[14] While this has yet to be confirmed, there is no doubt about the very late date of a similar description of Wisdom in Ecclesiasticus 24:3–30:

I came forth from the Most High,

And I covered the earth like mist.

I had my tent in the heights,

and my throne in a pillar of cloud.

Alone, I circled the vault of the sky,

and I walked on the bottom of the deeps.

Over the waves of the sea and over the whole earth,

and over every people and nation I held sway.

. . . From eternity, in the beginning, he created me,

and for eternity I shall remain.

Here she is the spirit of God who broods upon the waters in the moment of Creation. Thus, there is no doubt about her antiquity, yet Ecclesiasticus dates to no earlier than around 200 B.C.E. The description is retroactive, but the passage itself was a late addition to scripture—and is firm evidence of a process of reform of the Jewish God concept.

The same theme also repeats in the Song of Songs, in Ecclesiastes, and again in the Book of Wisdom. All of these books are part of what is today known as the Wisdom literature. All were written after the time of Job, during the apocalyptic age, and all are heavily indebted to Job—again and again taking up themes that first appear in that book. For example, the preacher of Ecclesiastes 9:16–17 states: "Wisdom is better than might, but a poor man's wisdom is never valued and his words are disregarded. The gentle words of the wise are heard above the shouts of a king of fools"; and in the Book of Wisdom 5:1–2 the scribe offers firm support for Job's right to demand justice: " . . . the virtuous man stands up boldly to face those who have oppressed him, those who thought so little of his sufferings."

In the Wisdom literature we also learn more about the nature of the great feminine companion to the Deity. As it happens, she is a marvelous boon to mankind. Wisdom 10:17 waxes eloquent about her:

> To the saints she gave the wages of their labors;
> she led them by a marvelous road;
> she herself was their shelter by day
> and their starlight through the night.

And in the Song of Songs, which pretends to be the composition of Solomon (but isn't), we find details of the wondrous union, or syzygy, of both sides of God, male and female.

THE WISDOM DIALOGUE CONTINUES

In the centuries before Jesus, the scribal dialogue about Yahweh's better half (his feminine side) was played out in the last books of the Old Testament. This was a positive and important development because it produced a deeper awareness of the sublime attributes of the Godhead. The process continued in the person of Jesus, who campaigned vigorously against every kind of superstitious nonsense, including society's morally reprehensible treatment of lepers.[15] At issue, time and again, was the old Judaic belief in a vindictive God. The ratification of Wisdom by Jesus is also evidenced by his respectful treatment of women. The text of the Naassene Sermon confirms that this new awareness of the Divine Mother was absorbed into Gnostic Christianity. The Sermon actually quotes a hymn honoring the Mother as the companion to the Father: "From thee [comes] Father and through thee [comes] Mother, two names immortal, progenitors of Aeons . . . "[16] (*Refutation 5.6.5*).

We also know from a scripture called the Gospel according to the Hebrews that Jesus made another extraordinary contribution to the Wisdom dialogue. Though this gospel was suppressed and thus did not survive, from the descriptions of early writers it seems to have closely followed the Gospel of Matthew, except that it was written in Hebrew or Aramaic instead of Greek—hence its name. The scripture was apparently so popular that it was referred to as the "fifth gospel." Most important, it included the following key passage quoting Jesus, which, fortunately, is preserved in two separate places in the writings of Origen and also in the writings of Saint Jerome: "Even now did my Mother the Holy Spirit take me by one of my hairs, and carry me away to the great Mountain of Tabor."[17] Here, the words of Jesus explicitly link the Holy Spirit with the Divine Mother, and virtually the same idea occurs in the Gospel of Thomas (Saying 101):

> [Jesus said,] Whoever does not hate his father and his mother as I do cannot become a disciple to Me. And whoever does [not] love his father and his mother as I do cannot become a [disciple] to Me. For my mother [gave me falsehood], but [my] true [Mother] gave me life.[18]

This passage is also noteworthy because of the presence of the word *life,* a word that, as we have already observed, was specifically used by Jesus in reference to spiritual life. The idea that the Spirit (spiritual life) flows from the Divine Mother was unprecedented in Judaism, and thus was a momentous development in the West. But the idea had long been understood in the East. In the Hindu traditions the same Divine Mother who brings the world into existence and sustains it also makes available a very special form of her own divine Self: a divine grace that is the Eastern equivalent of the Holy Spirit. Hindus believe that by means of this extremely subtle energy, known as the Chitti Kundalini or the Shakti Kundalini, the Divine Mother brings about the dramatic reversal of flow that leads to the heavenly source (see chapters 3 and 12). Today, the living traditions of Hinduism describe the concept of the reversal of flow in almost exactly the same language the Gnostics used in the first centuries of Christianity. The only difference is that Hindus usually describe the Gnostic Christian "descent" of Spirit as an awakening from within. From our discussion of immanence, it should be obvious that both are equivalent. Either way, it is the decisive turning point in the spiritual life of the disciple.

THE GNOSTIC RESPONSE

More than 1,900 years after the fact it is very difficult for us to comprehend the extent of the calamity that enveloped Judea during 66–73 C.E. and again in 115 and 135 C.E. From the riveting account of Josephus, the consequences must have been horrific—much worse than the damage wreaked by Nebuchadnezzar six centuries before. In the act of breaching the walls of Jerusalem and destroying the great temple, the Roman general Titus proved the prophecies of the apocalyptic age to be a colossal failure—indeed, a collective fantasy. Many Jews survived the siege, the famine, and the final battle only to be crucified. Tens of thousands of others were carried off into slavery or were thrown to the lions in the great Coliseum of Rome. Traumatized by war, many Jews in its aftermath must have questioned their faith, including the darker attributes of Yahweh. In 1927 a scholar named A. Marmorstein found evidence of this in rabbinical texts.[19] For Jews who had believed in the grand apocalyptic vision, there were only three possible options. According to the scholar Robert Grant, they could rewrite the apocalypse and postpone history; they could explain the failed prognostications by trying to show that the sacred writings had been misinterpreted; or they could simply abandon their faith.[20]

Little has been written about the war's impact on the first Christian community of the Nazarenes. One scholar who did study the matter, S. G. F. Brandon, concluded that the impact on them was no less horrendous. The war scattered Jewish Christians far and wide.[21] And if the followers of Jesus were as angry with their Jewish brothers as they were with the Romans, they had good reason: The zealots had hijacked Judaism and brought ruin upon the nation. For this reason Jewish Christians probably shared the conviction that if only more people had listened to Jesus, events might have turned out very differently. Anyone with an eye in his head, after all, could see that the zealots had been blind. The entire nation had been led off the cliff like a pack of lemmings. To think the fools had believed that Yahweh would come down out of the sky and destroy the Romans! Where was Yahweh? Was he sleeping? Or was something the matter with the national God concept?

The scattered remnants of the original Jerusalem Church found it difficult to regroup. We know that Roman pursuit continued and was intense.[22] Eventually, Jewish Christian sects did emerge, including the Ebionites and Elchasaites, and held on in places like Alexandria. But Jews would never again dominate the Jesus movement. The war and the subsequent Jewish revolts had set in motion a great reshuffling of men and ideas, and out of the rubble emerged Gentile Christianity.

So began a new phase of the Wisdom dialogue within the rich and diverse literature of Gnostic Christianity—and Alexandria was one of its primary cauldrons. Increasingly, the teachings of Jesus passed into Gentile hands. Probably for this reason, as time passed, there was less sympathy for Yahweh's noisy tantrums, less tolerance for the residue of the old pagan storm god. There may also have been a feeling that the Wisdom literature did not go far enough. To many it probably seemed that events had completely discredited the Jewish God along with his people. Thus, the God of the Jews suffered the fate history has always accorded losers. Yahweh was demoted to the lesser status of a demiurge. To be sure, the Fathers of the Church vociferously resisted this trend. Bishop Irenaeus devoted much of his leaden prose—the greatest portion of *Against Heresies*—to refuting the Gnostic "error."[23] Notwithstanding the views of men like Irenaeus, the Gnostic repudiation of Yahweh was not apostasy. Indeed, to many Christians it must have seemed like an advance. Certainly the demotion of Yahweh was not the end of God or heaven. The Godhead, after all, had not changed. What had changed was the concept of God, which simply reconstituted itself in human understanding. Indeed, the sloughing off of the less desirable elements in Yahweh's character surely helped many to clarify the nature of the Godhead, and thus was a positive development. Yahweh was rechristened Saklas, "the fool," and Samael, "the blind." Behind Yahweh, unseen by him, stood Wisdom (the Divine Mother, Sophia, Achamoth, the Ogdoad, Barbelo, and so forth), now recognized as the true boss. Yahweh was simply the hired man. Above Wisdom—indeed, over all—presided the incomprehensible Father about whom Jesus spoke in such loving terms.[24] It is interesting to note that although Wisdom was often ranked below the Father, their relationship was intimate: Wisdom was an integral part of the Godhead.

The fate of the old Yahweh was not a happy one. Some of the more extreme Gnostics dealt harshly with him. In the Hypostasis of the Archons, one of the Gnostic scriptures found at Nag Hammadi, Ialdabaoth is cast down into dark Tartarus, the hellish realm beneath Hades where the Titans had been hurled after the defeat of Cronus.[25] The Naassene Sermon, however, mentions no such dismal fate. In its milder tone we may perceive the sturdy link with the Old Testament.

Just as it is difficult for us to understand the full measure of the destruction wreaked upon Judea by the Romans, so also is it difficult for us to apprehend the Gnostic resynthesis that occurred in the war's aftermath, and why, especially from the perspective of Alexandria, that reform was so necessary.

9

Spiritual Malfeasance

There will be days when you will search for me,
and not find me . . .

GOSPEL OF THOMAS
(SAYING 38; SEE ALSO JOHN 7:34)

THE WISDOM DIALOGUE INSPIRED BY THE BOOK OF JOB reached its culmination in the teachings of Jesus—yet those same teachings never found their way into orthodox Christianity. The Church aggressively resisted the Divine Mother and succeeded in erasing every trace of her from its official doctrines.

In Christianity's earliest days, of course, things were very different. The first Christian churches were loosely organized communities in which a spirit of gender equality often prevailed. We know that women participated in discussions, taught alongside men, and sometimes even led services. Unfortunately, the early policy of openness was the first casualty of institutional Christianity. During the second century, a male hierarchy of deacons, priests, and bishops emerged. Thereafter, men dominated decision making and equality went out the window. By 200 C.E. women had been relegated to subservience. Nor did their low status improve over the many centuries.

Today, one of the justifications given for this continuing policy is the pseudo-Pauline gospel of I Timothy 2:11–12, which most scholars agree was not the work of Paul: "Let a women learn in silence with all submissiveness. I permit no women to teach or to have authority over men; she is to keep silent."

The above line exaggerates Paul's alleged bias against women. In Galatians 3:28 Paul states a more congenial view, one reminiscent of Jesus himself: " . . . in Christ . . . there is neither male nor female." Unfortunately, because Paul's views on women are also more ambiguously stated elsewhere, orthodox bishops seized on the most conservative interpretation. They also argued that because the first apostles were male, the priesthood should be as well. As a result, women were banned from leading services; Mary Magdalene's prominent role was obscured, along with the prophetic mission of the sister and the saintly daughters of the apostle Philip (Acts 21:9; Acts of Philip 108, 109, 115, 126, 142, 148). And let us not forget Mariamne, the inspired teacher mentioned in the Naassene Sermon (*Refutation* 5.7.1), who, no doubt, was dismissed as a heretic. Also suppressed was the Book of Jasher, with its glowing description of the prophetess Miriam, sister of Moses, who, curiously, also turns up in the Sermon (*Refutation* 5.8.2).[1]

Even while the Church was in full retreat regarding the role of women, some Gnostic sects preserved the original policy of gender equality. Although we have no information on this regarding the Naassenes, we know that the Valentinians, another prominent Gnostic community, actively encouraged women to participate in discussions and decision making. Women helped with teaching, baptisms, curing, and even exorcisms, functions that the institutional Church reserved for priests and bishops.[2]

But the Church's subordination of women was only the most visible sign and symptom of a deeper malady: the obfuscation of the vital role of the Holy Spirit. One of the earliest lists of orthodox scriptures appeared around the time of Irenaeus (180 C.E.). It is known today as the Muratorian Canon, named after Ludovico Antonio Muratori, the Italian archaeologist who discovered the Latin fragment in 1740.[3] Its date is disputed, but most scholars believe the list was from an earlier rather than a later period. Conspicuously absent from it is any mention of the Gospel of the Hebrews and the Gospel of Thomas, both of which, as we have seen, associate the Spirit with the Divine Mother.

The Church's official erasure of the Mother had the effect of reducing the Wisdom literature to mere scribblings from the past. The last books of the Old Testament became a quaint collection of gargoyles with no apparent connection with or relevancy to the Gospels. The Church expunged every image of the feminine from its official teachings, the sole exception being the Blessed Mary, mother of Jesus. Given the official misogyny, the question as to why Mary was retained is an interesting one. The probable answer is that there was simply no way to be rid of her. In the year 427 C.E., after the defeat of paganism, Cyril, archbishop of Alexandria, delivered a famous speech in Ephesus, Greece, in which he proclaimed Mary the "Mother of God."[4] Thereafter, statues of Mary were installed in the pagan temples in place of Artemis, Demeter, and Aphrodite. Some of the temples were even converted into Christian basilicas. No surprise that the Virgin Mary immediately acquired a quasi-divine status, a curious compensatory phenomenon that the Church fathers tolerated over the centuries even while frowning upon it.

Although the Church officially retained the Holy Spirit as an equal member of the Godhead, the Paraclete was either rendered neuter or transformed into a masculine energy imbued with the seminal virility of a pagan fertility god. We are informed in the infancy Gospels of Luke and Matthew—doubtless both late additions—that the Holy Spirit impregnated Mary, the mother of God, accounting for the virginal conception of Jesus—a contrivance that blurred and even obliterated the enormous difference between sexual insemination and the descent of grace. Another effect was to trivialize the Spirit to the point of meaninglessness. No wonder the term Holy Spirit has become a cliché! Yet we need to remember that this stands in sharp contrast with its potency in the first century C.E., when the expression generated incredible excitement.

THE GOSPEL OF HERMAS

We shall now explore how orthodox Christianity promulgated the removal of the Mother from Church teaching in the day-to-day liturgy. Although the Gospel of Hermas is no longer used and, in fact, is all but forgotten, it was one of the most important Christian scriptures in the second and possibly third centuries. Today it continues to have a recognized place among the writings of the Apostolic Fathers. The Gospel of Hermas purports to be an inspired revelation. It probably served as a teaching device and may even have been read aloud during services.

It is of great interest that it begins with a river crossing—an obvious allusion to the events at the Jordan from the Old Testament that we have already discussed: involving Joshua, Elijah, and Elisha. No doubt the reference to the Jordan served to establish the gospel's scriptural pedigree. While dreaming, a young man is shown a number of visions. In these he encounters an old woman who counsels holiness and teaches him many wondrous things and who, we are explicitly informed, is responsible for the visions.[5] In one the young man observes a crew of workmen constructing a great stone tower over a foundation of water—a remarkable image. When the man inquires about it, the old crone explains that he is witnessing the construction of God's Church.[6] Here, the tower is the Church and the workmen, it seems, are angels. The foundation of water is an extremely important mythological concept that we shall explore in more detail in chapter 13. The young man also learns that the crone is a manifestation of the Church—which, notice, means that the Church itself is responsible for the visions.[7] Although one passage dutifully informs us that the Spirit comes from above,[8] in a key section the Holy Spirit speaks through the Church: The gospel describes the Church in language that is reminiscent of the descriptions of the Divine Mother in Proverbs 8:22–24, 27, and 29–31 and in Ecclesiasticus 24:3–30 (see chapter 8): " . . . she [the Church] was created before all things . . . and for her sake the world was formed."[9]

In this way the Gospel of Hermas was used to prepare Christians for an expansion of Church authority into an area where it had no business going: The goal, it seems, was not simply to expunge the Divine Mother from Christian teaching but in fact to supplant her—that is, to establish the Church in the seat of the Divine Mother herself! Evidence for this can also be found in the writings of patriarchs like Tertullian and Cyprian, both of whom regarded the Church (rather than the human body) as the temple of the Spirit. In a denunciation of schismatics Cyprian wrote, "He cannot have God for this Father who has not the Church for his Mother."[10] A similar idea occurs in the following passage from II Clement 14:2 (whose author is unrelated to Clement of Alexandria), an apocryphal but orthodox gospel dating to around 100 C.E.: "For the scripture says 'God created man male and female.' (Gen 1:27) The male is Christ; the female is the Church. Moreover, the books and Apostles declare that the Church not only exists now, but has been in existence from the beginning." Notably, the author here never states precisely which "books and Apostles declare that the Church . . . has been in existence from the beginning"—and not without reason, for there are no such sources in canonical scripture. The line referring to the Church existing "from the beginning" again echoes the references to the Divine Mother in Proverb 8 and Ecclesiasticus 24 (see above and chapter 8). All of this surely accounts for the familiar expression Holy Mother Church.

The displacement of Sophia by the Church in the Gospel of Hermas is a shocking example of male chauvinism gone amok. There is humorless irony in the fact that the very same Church fathers who, as we have seen, installed an artificial chasm between God and humankind by repudiating immanence also sought to collapse a very real and crucial distinction between a human institution (the Church) and the prerogatives of God (the Divine Mother)—another clear example of the abuse of spiritual authority. In light of the Gospel of Hermas, the subsequent dark chapters in Church history become more understandable. A foundation of water, after all, is spiritual bedrock compared to the shaky footing of a human institution that presumes responsibility for the bestowal of visions, revelations, wisdom, and even divine grace. It could even be argued that in attempting to supplant the role of the

Divine Mother, the fathers of the Church came perilously close to the worst kind of blasphemy, for, as we have observed, the bestowal of grace—the Holy Spirit—plainly falls within the purview of the Divine Mother. It most definitely lies outside the jurisdiction of a human institution. The three synoptic accounts are unanimous and unequivocal on this: Every sin is to be forgiven except one—blasphemy against the Spirit (Matthew 12:31, Mark 3:28, and Luke 12:10). Such a judgment, frightening in its implications, may explain why it so often seems that our Christian civilization has gone to the devil.

TAMPERING WITH SCRIPTURE?

There is, however, still more soiled linen to be aired from the time of the early Church. It is highly probable that during the early second century C.E. someone in Rome or with allegiance to the Roman Church took liberties with the Gospel of Matthew. Before we examine this likelihood, however, we need to explore some pertinent background.

In a brilliant 1951 study, *The Fall of Jerusalem and the Christian Church,* the biblical scholar S. G. F. Brandon argues persuasively that the parent Church in Jerusalem (the Nazarenes) established a branch community in the neighboring city of Alexandria from an early date, certainly before the Jewish War. Alexandria was the most conspicuous omission in the apostle Paul's wide travels, and it is quite possible that Paul avoided the city simply because the Nazarenes had already established a satellite community there. Certainly the apostle had no monopoly on proselytizing; we know from the Lukan Acts that other apostles were similarly engaged. Alexandria's proximity to Palestine and its large Jewish population made it an obvious choice for missionary work and suggests that the city was one of the first places to be visited by the Nazarenes. Although it can't be proved, this early wave of preachers may have included a woman named Mariamne.[11]

Brandon contends that the Gospel of Matthew was composed in Alexandria along with the epistles of James and Barnabas. Although Matthew is fiercely anti-Pharisee in tone, it also contains passages indicating that Matthew was written for a Jewish audience, including some text that actually exalts the Pharisees. This was also the view of Irenaeus.[12] Brandon proposes an interesting explanation for this seeming contradiction: After the fall of Jerusalem, the Alexandrian Church was more successful in maintaining its Jewish character than most other Christian communities. He argues that an early draft of the Gospel of Matthew was produced there during this period of continuing Jewish influence, and he even explains how the text of the Gospel later evolved to accommodate the growing ranks of Gentile converts. In his view, the Alexandrian Church succeeded in slowing by several decades the trend toward Gentile predominance, though that change could not be forestalled indefinitely.

Overall, the Gospel of Matthew certainly does reflect a Jewish Christian point of view.[13] To be sure, Matthew condemns Jews for not following Jesus, but it also affirms their status as the favored sheep. Matthew 5:17–19 contains the most emphatic affirmation of Jewish law to be found in the New Testament:

> Do not think that I have come to abolish the Law or the prophets. I have come not to abolish but to complete them. I tell you solemnly, til heaven and earth disappear, not one jot, not one little stroke, shall disappear from the Law until its purpose is achieved.

Brandon interprets this passage as a bulwark against the perceived threat of Pauline influence. Jewish Christians were generally opposed to Paul's abandonment of the Law and his emphasis on Gentile conversion. Two other passages in Matthew also affirm the status of Jews. In one (10:5) Jesus tells his disciples to avoid preaching to pagans and Samaritans, but to "go rather to the lost sheep of the House of Israel." This same line is repeated later when Jesus encounters a Canaanite woman (Matthew 15:24–28). With the passage of time, however, the Jewish character of the Church could not be sustained, not even in the more favorable environment of Alexandria; the admittance of Gentiles gradually increased. Brandon writes in 1951:

The equilibrium constructed by Matthew was essentially artificial, for it was in reality an attempt to confine the new wine of Christianity in the old wine skins of Judaism. And as such it was doomed either to perish or to be metamorphosed, for the position of the Jewish-Christians in Alexandria could not be successfully maintained into the future, unless it were assured of a continuous stream of Jewish converts who accepted its . . . outlook . . . The failure to secure such a stream . . . meant that, with the continued influx of Gentiles, the original Jewish character of Alexandrian Christianity must be lost.[14]

Brandon found evidence of this transition in several parables in Matthew. In one, the story of the centurion's servant (Matthew 8:5–13), a Gentile shows such great faith that Jesus declares that non-Jews will find a place at the feast in the kingdom of heaven. Meanwhile, the rightful subjects who have forfeited their place (the Jews) "will be turned out into the dark, where there will be weeping and gnashing of teeth."

Another, the parable of the vineyard laborers (Matthew 20:1–16), suggests that although the admittance of Gentiles into the Church became necessary, some Jews resented it. Here, the kingdom of heaven is likened to a vineyard whose owner hires various laborers at different times of the day, then pays them all the same wage, a denarius, at day's end. The moral is that the late arrivals (the Gentiles) will receive the same measure of salvation despite the disgruntled complaints of some who arrived earlier—though the parable also casts a cloud over the Gentile character by describing the last men hired as loafers "standing idle in the marketplace." The suggestion here is that the acceptance of Gentiles, although it came to be regarded as unavoidable, was not necessarily welcomed.

The parable of the wedding feast (Matthew 22:1–14) also illustrates the acceptance of Gentiles. Here the kingdom of heaven is compared to a great feast given by a king for his son's wedding. However, when the invited guests (the Jews) fail to show up, the king sends his men to every crossroads to invite whomever they meet (the Gentiles).

Yet another example is the parable of the wicked husbandman (Matthew 21:33–44). In this story the tenants of a vineyard (the Jews) murder the son of the vineyard owner, who punishes them with a terrible retribution and then leases the land to new tenants (the Gentiles). In all of these parables the same theme is variously repeated: The original sheep (the Jews) forfeit their exclusive claim to the inheritance of the kingdom and are replaced by Gentiles.

Brandon finds additional firm evidence of anti-Pauline sentiment in the parable of the darnel (Matthew 13:24–30). In this story Jesus compares the kingdom of heaven to the field of a man who sows good seed there. Later, an enemy comes in the night and sows darnel, a weed, among the crop. When the good seed and the bad come up together, the servants ask if they should remove the weeds, but the owner responds, "No, because when you pull up the darnel, you might also pull up the wheat." The servants are advised to wait until the harvest, when bad and good can more easily be separated, at which time the bad will be burned.

Brandon explains this otherwise obscure parable as an attack on Paul: Jewish Christians understood that "the enemy" was Paul, whose abandonment of the Law would be exposed in the end, though it had to be tolerated in the meantime. Brandon's interpretation suggests that a tense standoff existed between Jewish and Gentile factions, each tolerating the other in the interests of unity. In his view, however, the continuing influx of Gentiles eventually tipped the balance in their favor, which explains the curious and otherwise inexplicable addition to Matthew's Gospel, "the parable of the darnel explained" (13:36–43): The parable was amended several decades after its initial composition to reflect the decisive shift toward Gentile predominance, which demanded the rehabilitation of Paul's reputation. The anti-Paul symbolism had become an embarrassment, so an explanatory paragraph was added explicitly identifying "the enemy" as the devil, thus removing the stigma from Paul. It is an intriguing and plausible explanation.

Brandon's assertions regarding the Gospel of Matthew find general support in the Naassene Sermon, which cites this gospel more often than the others.[15] It is worth noting, however, that the Naassenes were not the only Jewish Christians who favored Matthew. The Ebionites did as well,[16] and Jewish Christians based in Syria showed a similar preference.[17]

Though the views of S. G. F. Brandon regarding the Gospel of Matthew appear sound, his ideas about the apostle Peter are more problematic. He argues in *The Fall of Jerusalem* that Peter (Cephas) played a prominent role in the establishment of the Alexandrian Church, which in his view explains why Peter is more visible in the Gospel of Matthew than in the other gospels. According to Brandon, Matthew uses Peter as a symbol of rightful authority—another bulwark against Paul—in an episode occurring at Caesarea Philippi known as Peter's Confession, which we have already discussed (see chapter 4).[18] In a famous line (Matthew 16:18–19) not found in the other synoptic accounts, Jesus establishes the primacy of Peter: "You are Peter, and on this rock I will build my Church. And the gates of hell shall not prevail against it." The wordplay in this passage is obvious: Peter's other name, Cephas, means "rock." Brandon argues that the passage was not original but had been added to counter Pauline influence: By investing authority in Peter, one of the original pillars, Jewish Christians sought to hold the line against Paul's abandonment of the Law.

Brandon's interpretation is fascinating, yet, as we shall see, it does not tell the full story. The episode of Peter's Confession appears in all three synoptic accounts: Matthew 16:13–23, Luke 9:18–26, and Mark 8:27–33, where it is expressed most fully. In chapter 4 we found that the episode was originally a lesson about Jesus' earthly mission of suffering and sacrifice. In the lesson Jesus also shows his decided preference for the name Son of Man. In Matthew, however, all of this is obscured by the line Brandon astutely identifies as a later addition: "You are Peter, and on this rock I will build my Church. And the gates of hell shall not prevail against it." We will now turn our investigation to this problematic line.

THE BASIS FOR CHURCH AUTHORITY?

Peter's Confession is important for a reason that S. G. F. Brandon does not discuss: The famous line cited above was destined to become the main scriptural basis for the authority of the Church of Rome. Yet the metaphorical equation Peter (Cephas) = rock presents grave difficulties because the word *rock* (or *stone*) has already been appropriated elsewhere in scripture. Matthew 21:42, for example, reads: "Jesus said to them, 'have you ever read in the scriptures: It was the stone rejected by the builders that became the cornerstone?'" Here, Jesus cites Psalm 118, but he might just as well be citing Job 38:6, Isaiah 28:16, or Zechariah 10:4. The same line referring to the cornerstone appears elsewhere in the New Testament (see Mark 12:10–11, Luke 4:11–12, Ephesians 2:20, and I Peter 2:4–8).

As we have noted, the Naassene Sermon mentions the stone frequently. Crucially, it also informs us that the rock is the higher Adam, the Anthropos, the Perfect or Primal Man located in heaven (see chapter 4). In Hippolytus's words: "The word *rock,* he [the Naassene] says, he uses in reference to Adamas. This Adamas, he affirms, is 'the chief cornerstone become the head of the corner'" (*Refutation 5.7.35–36*).

Thus, *rock, stone,* and *cornerstone* are synonymous and all refer to Higher or Primal Man. We note that this affirms the intimate link between Primal Man and the Son of Man because Jesus, as the Son of Man, is heavenly Man's earthly representative or double. Amazingly, the apostle Peter himself confirms this! I Peter 2:4 describes Jesus as the "living stone." This equation, Jesus = stone, is repeated again in Peter's soliloquy to the Sadducees in the Lukan Acts (4:8–1), where Peter identifies Jesus as the stone rejected by the builders.

By now, the nature of the problem should be obvious: The identification of Peter with the rock in Peter's Confession is in conflict with the symbolic use of the stone or rock in these other passages. If Jesus himself is the rock or cornerstone from above manifested on earth, this designation is clearly unique to him as the Savior. Jesus is both rock and stone and Peter cannot share in this designation. How ironic that Peter's own words, his repeated use of the metaphor of the stone or rock for Jesus, supports this conclusion! Because we have a right to expect consistency in the use of symbolic language in the scriptures, we are on firm ground to conclude that the original author of Matthew would never have knowingly introduced this sort of ambiguity in the use of a term of such importance. I Peter 2:4 precludes Matthew 16:18.

Brandon, then, is very likely right: The famous line "You are Peter, and on this rock I will build my Church" was not a part of the original Gospel of Matthew. It is worth mentioning that the biblical scholar Rudolf Bultmann also shared this view. Bultmann was one of the most respected theologians of the twentieth century. His enormous influence was based on the many solid contributions of form criticism, a methodology he pioneered as early as the 1920s.[19] In *History of the Synoptic Tradition,* Bultmann wrote: "I freely admit that it seems to me quite impossible to take Matthew 16:18–19 ["You are Peter, and on this rock . . ."] as a genuine saying of Jesus . . . "[20] Curiously, Bultmann never stated his reasons.

THE PRIMACY OF MARK

Over the long history of Christianity, the Gospel of Matthew greatly overshadowed the Gospels of Mark, Luke, and John. Matthew was the gospel most often cited by theologians and most often used in the liturgy. It was also the preferred text for teaching. Matthew also happens to be the only gospel of the four in which the word *Church* appears—not surprisingly, in the very passage we have been investigating!

Over many centuries Christian theologians assumed that Matthew was the original source document on which the other synoptics, Mark and Luke, had been based. (Scholars agreed that the Gospel of John was based on a separate, independent source.) This surely explains why the Gospel of Matthew was accorded first place in the New Testament. It wasn't until the nineteenth century that two scholars, Karl Lachman and Christian Wilke, launched a revolution when they separately began to argue for the primacy of the Gospel of Mark. Each had made deductions parallel to the other's based on a similar analysis of scripture, and, not surprisingly, both men met fierce resistance.[21] In religious matters the weight of inertia is so powerful that genuine innovations are almost always stolidly opposed. The mainstream, if it changes at all, tends to do so very slowly. Nevertheless, truth was on the side of Lachman and Wilke, and change eventually did come. By the time of World War I, a consensus of biblical scholars had swung away from the primacy of Matthew. Today, Mark is indisputably the principal source document for the Gospels of Matthew and Luke, although a second sayings source, now lost and known as "Q," has also been identified.

It is easy to show that all three of the synoptic accounts of the New Testament are parallel to each other in structure. For example, Peter's Confession (or his Profession of Faith) also occurs in Mark 8. But the line "You are Peter, and on this rock I will build my Church" is conspicuously absent. Nor can it be found in Luke 9. Because the famous line is absent from the original source document—Mark—the obvious question arises: How did it find its way into Matthew? The Roman Catholic Church has no answer to this question. The evidence we have reviewed strongly suggests that the line in Matthew equating Peter with the foundational rock of the Church was a fabrication, the result of tampering, perhaps, by someone with a political agenda.

The oldest extant copy of the Gospel of Matthew dates to no earlier than 200 C.E.[22] If some lucky archaeological find in the future should produce an older draft—say, a copy of Matthew dating to the last years of the first century—we will probably discover that the line "You are Peter, and on this rock I will build my Church" is nowhere in evidence. The omission will be as telling as a cloven hoof print in the mud. The main scriptural foundation for the authority of the institutional Church of Rome will have been demolished, once and for all, clearing the way for the rediscovery of the Wisdom teachings of Jesus by many more Christians, leading to a spiritual renaissance in the West.

Toward this end, we shall now look more closely at the primary source document for this book, the Naassene Sermon.

PART THREE

Hridaya

10

The Primary Source Document: The Refutation of All Heresies

THE REFUTATION OF ALL HERESIES dates to the third century c.e., but the document disappeared long ago and came to light only in the mid-1900s. The story of its fortuitous recovery began in 1840, when Abel Villeman, an enterprising minister in the French government, launched a program to seek out and acquire ancient manuscripts. Villeman's effort was to bear great fruit. The minister recruited an erudite Greek scholar, Minoides Mynas, and promptly dispatched him to Greece to explore the numerous abbeys and convents of Mount Athos, long famed as a monastic center. After laboring in the region's dusty libraries for two years, Mynas returned to Paris with a sheaf of old papers and yellowing manuscripts. Though a competent scholar with an eye for antiquity, Mynas still had no idea what he had found. One of the manuscripts, titled the Philosophumena, was not much to look at. The document was not an original; it had been copied, as a later editor, F. Legge, tells us, "in a crabbed hand of the fourteenth century . . . full of erasures and interlineations, and . . . [with] several serious lacunae." Indeed, its importance might never have come to light but for an alert scholar at the Bibliothéque Royale in Paris: Benigne Emmanuel Miller. In addition to being an archaeologist, Miller was a lover of everything

Greek. While examining Mynas's collection of papers he recognized that one of them, the Philosophumena, was a treasure. In 1851 Miller arranged for it to be published at Oxford University in the original Greek with no introduction and no commentary. In 1860 the rector of a college in Rome, Abbe Cruice, arranged for a Latin translation. The first English edition followed in 1868, thanks to the efforts of Rev. J. H. MacMahon. A second English edition was published in 1921, the work of F. Legge, and a third English translation appeared as an appendage to R. Scott Birdsall's 1984 Ph.D. dissertation. In preparing this book I have drawn from all of these English translations.

THE ATTRIBUTION

Benigne Emmanuel Miller ascribed the *Philosophumena* to Origen—Origenes Adamantius—the most prolific theologian of early Christendom, who was said to have penned some six thousand manuscripts during his lifetime. His authorship was immediately disputed, however, and debate raged for a time. In the end, it was found that for reasons having to do with tone, style, and substance, the *Philosophumena* did not comport with Origen's pen; the variances were too great. In addition, it was also evident from the text that the author was a bishop of the Church, which further ruled out Origen, who had never been so appointed.

Various scholars debated the evidence supporting authorship by other writers. The number of candidates being quite limited, the search soon narrowed. Two scholars, J. L. Jacobi and L. Duncker, independently nominated Hippolytus, who, during the first half of the third century C.E., was a known bishop of Portus, Italy, Rome's seaport located at the mouth of the Tiber River. The evidence was strong. In the year 1551 a statue of Bishop Hippolytus had been unearthed in an old cemetery near Rome. His name was engraved upon the statue, along with a list of literary works, one of which is mentioned in the *Philosophumena* and claimed by its author. Other evidence also supported the match. This Hippolytus apparently had earned a reputation as a debunker of heresy; various classical sources, including the Church history of Eusebius, report that the bishop made it his business to expose and discredit divergent sects and individuals. The newfound manuscript was obviously a strongly worded polemic against many different heresies. It even included a zealous attack, for alleged corruption, on a standing pope named Callistus. Later in his life Bishop Hippolytus was banished to Sardinia by Roman decree and ultimately suffered martyrdom during the reign of Maximin the Thracian (235–239 C.E.). In sum, all of the evidence fit perfectly, and scholarship accorded Hippolytus the authorship of the *Philosophumena*. Today, the document is referred to as the *Refutation of All Heresies* (or simply the *Refutation*)[1] and has been dated to sometime after 222 C.E.

THE MATTER OF THE MISSING BOOKS

The *Refutation* was originally composed of ten books. Two of these, however, were missing at the time of discovery. The absent second and third books were apparently an account of the doctrines and mysteries of the ancient Egyptians and Mesopotamians. Book 4 (a part of which was also missing) was a denunciation of Mesopotamian astrology. Books 5 through 9, which survived, deal with various heresies of the early Church. The principal focus of our study is the first portion of Book 5, in which Hippolytus turns his rugged pen against the Naassenes. Richard Reitzenstein coined the name Naassene Sermon in reference to this part of the *Refutation*, which is made up of long verbatim quotes mingled with the bishop's comments (*Refutation* 5.7.3–5.9.8).[2] For our purposes here I employ the name Naassene Sermon in a slightly more general sense: in reference to chapters 1 through 6 of the *Refutation*.

Part of the tenth book, which included a summation of the whole, was also missing on discovery. To the theosophist G. R. S. Mead this last omission was too blatant to be accidental, because it was obvious that the absent portion of Book 10 was a summary of the material in the missing Books 2 and 3. Mead, who remains one of the most able scholars ever to comment on the *Refutation*, had some incisive thoughts on the matter:

It is a curious fact that it is precisely those books wherein this divulging of the mysteries was attempted which should be missing; not only have they disappeared, but in the Epitome at the beginning of Book 10 the summary of their contents is also omitted. This seems almost to point to a deliberate removal of just that information which would be of priceless value to us today, not only for the general history of the evolution of religious ideas, but also for filling in an important part of the background of early Christianity.

Mead himself asks:

> Why were these books removed? Were the subsequent Christian orthodox deterred by religious scruples, or were they afraid to circulate this information? Hippolytus himself seems to have had no such hesitation; he is ever delightedly boasting that he is giving away to the multitude the most sacred secrets of others. It seems to have been his special *metier* to cry aloud from the rooftops what had been whispered in their secret chambers. It was for him a delicious triumph over error to boast "I have your secret documents and I am going to publish them!"
>
> Why should those who came after him hesitate? Surely they were like-minded with Hippolytus, and would have been as delighted as he in humbling the pride of the hated Mystery institutions in the dust. Can it possibly be that they saw more clearly than he did that *other* [italics mine] conclusions might be drawn from his startling revelations?[3]

While we can be sympathetic to Mead's passionate views about the missing books, we may also be thankful that the cleric who "came after" Hippolytus failed to recognize the importance of Book 5, or it too would have been made to disappear. The loss of so much material was keenly felt by Mead, who at the time was busily gathering and editing for publication various surviving fragments of the same Mystery literature that had been the subject of the missing books—what is collectively known as the Hermetic tradition (or the Corpus Hermeticum). Mead did succeed in pulling together a number of fragments, and published them in a classic study that scholars still use, *Thrice Greatest Hermes,* which includes a commentary on the Naassene Sermon. Mead was firmly convinced that a much older spiritual tradition with roots in Egypt had long preceded and may even have paved the way for Christianity—a theme we shall revisit in chapters 13 and 14.

EMPHASIS ON PAUL, JOHN, MATTHEW, AND THOMAS

The Rev. J. H. MacMahon identified a dozen references to the Epistles of Paul in the Naassene Sermon and cited these in his generously footnoted 1868 edition of the *Refutation.* Birdsall found two more, for a grand total of fourteen. This surprising emphasis on Paul would call into question some of our conclusions in the previous chapter but for the fact that closer scrutiny of the Pauline material reveals it to be made up of verbatim Old Testament extracts that Paul cites in his epistles—and thus cannot be ascribed to Paul with certainty. In fact, the amount of confirmed Pauline influence on the Sermon is minor, and this relative paucity is exactly what we would expect of a Jewish Christian community founded not by Paul but by the Nazarenes.

The dispute between Paul and the Nazarenes on the matter of Jewish law was very real. It is documented in the Lukan Acts, though Luke tends to gloss over it, as the Talmudic scholar Hyam Maccoby has noted;[4] in the Acts the account is biased in Paul's favor and tends to downplay the conflict. That the rift between Paul and the Nazarenes was deep is attested to by Paul's own writings—Galatians, for example, which, it should be remembered, was composed long before the Lukan Acts at a time when Paul's disagreements with the Nazarenes were recent and, no doubt, still painfully fresh in memory.

It is of interest that none of the passages in the Sermon that can be confidently attributed to Paul involves the Law or issues likely to have been controversial, indicating that Naassene support for Paul may have been selective. Should we be surprised that one of these cases (*Refutation* 5.8.25) is a reference to Paul's spiritual ascent in 2 Corinthians 12:2? In Paul's own words: "[T]his same person [i.e., Paul]—whether in the body or out of the body I do not know; God knows—was caught up into paradise and heard things which must not and cannot be put into human language." Here it is the Gnostic Paul who is speaking, and the presence of this passage in the Sermon shows that the Naassenes accepted Paul's visionary experience as authentic. While we cannot know if James the Just himself was responsible for this ratification, the firm support within the Sermon for Paul as Gnostic does challenge those scholars who have debunked him as a charlatan.[5] Still, we must be cautious, for we have no historical data about the chronological development of Christianity in Alexandria and thus do not know precisely when Paul's epistles found their way into more wide use. Our discussion in the previous chapter suggests that the Sermon dates from the period after Jewish influence had already begun to wane, a conclusion further supported by the presence in the Sermon of the demiurge Ialdabaoth.

The Naassenes relied most heavily on the Gospels of Matthew and John and less on those of Mark and Luke.[6] This emphasis on John conforms with current scholarship—the oldest-known Christian manuscripts from Egypt are fragments from John's gospel. Later witnesses also attest to Gnostic Christians' heavy reliance on John.[7]

NAASSENE SCRIPTURES

The Naassene Sermon mentions only two Gnostic scriptures. One of these, the Gospel of Thomas (also known as the Gospel according to Thomas), is cited nine times in the Sermon (all of which are noted in the appendix), according to Birdsall's count. The second is the Gospel according to the Egyptians, but the sect surely used other Gnostic writings as well. In his commentary on the Latin translation of the *Refutation,* the abbe Cruice proposes several more: the Gospel of Perfection, the Gospel of Eve, the Questions of Mary (the Pistis Sophia),

Concerning the Offspring of Mary, and the Gospel of Philip. A copy of the Pistis Sophia first turned up in 1785,[8] and copies of the Gospel of Philip and the Gospel of Thomas were among the Gnostic manuscripts discovered in 1945 at Nag Hammadi. The Gospel according to the Egyptians is known only from fragments quoted in other works. Though a full copy has never been recovered, the Gospel of the Hebrews is yet another scripture that the Naassenes likely knew well, as are the Apocryphon (Secret Book) of John, the Apocryphon of James, the Dialogue of the Savior, and the Testimony of Truth, all from the Nag Hammadi library.

THE SCHOLARSHIP OF MIROSLAV MARCOVICH

One of the finest commentaries on Hippolytus ever published appeared in a recent (1986) Greek edition of the *Refutation* prepared by Miroslav Marcovich. In his English introduction the author seconds the view of G. R. S. Mead that Hippolytus had come into possession of sacred Gnostic writings and refers to them as a "golden hoard."[9] According to Marcovich, an earlier treatise by Hippolytus that did not survive, the *Syntagma*, was more general in its treatment of heterodoxy because it had been composed before the bishop came into possession of the hoard. Marcovich believes that once armed with original source material unavailable to previous heresiologists, including Irenaeus, Hippolytus determined to move against the heretics in force by turning their own writings against them. Thus, he deployed the new material in Books 5–9 of his *Refutation*. Judging from his polemic, the "golden hoard" pertained to eight different sects, including the Naassenes.

In his brilliant commentary, Marcovich deftly catches Hippolytus in the frequent act of plagiarizing Greek philosophers, even while falsely accusing the heretics of the very same practice:

[The] Gnostic exegeses quote Greek philosophers in order to reinterpret them and present them as their witnesses. In his turn Hippolytus copies the passages of the Gnostic exegeses dealing with Greek philosophers, presents them as his own discovery, and uses them as "proof" of the Gnostics plagiarizing Greek philosophy. *A plagiarist accuses a quoting writer of plagiarizing.*[10]

It is ironic that from our standpoint the importance of the *Refutation* stems largely from this penchant of Hippolytus for plagiarism. The bishop's habit of quoting entire sections has preserved a priceless lens through which we may view and bring into sharp focus the very heart of Gnostic Christianity.

From the days of Justin Martyr the Church Fathers had placed blame for the inception of all heresy on the infamous Simon Magus. Irenaeus followed this example in his treatise,[11] and Marcovich believes that Hippolytus did the same in his earlier work, the *Syntagma*. The bishop, however, altered the scheme in his *Refutation* by placing the Naassenes at the head of his list. Marcovich attributes this to the Naassene emphasis on the symbol of the serpent, which Hippolytus plainly found shocking and regarded as incontrovertible proof of paganism. Hippolytus writes that he intends to "begin with those who have presumed to celebrate a serpent, the originator of the error . . ." (*Refutation* 5.6.3). Irenaeus had previously mentioned the serpent in connection with Gnostic teachings,[12] but Hippolytus takes a much harder line, describing the alleged serpent worship as the root Naassene error from which all other heresies had sprung. The bishop likens heresy to a many-headed hydra whose heads he will lop off by refuting the original Gnostic "delusion." In so doing, he will "exterminate the monster" (*Refutation* 5.11.1).

As a symbol, the serpent is demonstrably complex, with many different religious and psychological meanings. Today, these are well known and run the gamut from positive to negative, for which reason context is crucial to identifying the meaning of a particular usage. Unfortunately, Hippolytus failed to understand the serpent symbolism as used within the context of Gnostic Christian teachings. In Naassene Christianity, the Divine Mother dispenses herself in the form of a very special grace, the Holy Spirit, which she bestows from above, bringing about the spontaneous awakening of the latent spiritual (or serpent) energy in the disciple, which the Naassenes associated with the reversal of the flow. Within the context of Naassene Christianity, then, the serpent was a symbol for this ineffable spiritual energy. (As we shall discover in more detail in chapter 12, the spiritual traditions of India employ the same symbolism even today.) The meaning is the same in the Gospel of John 3:14: "the Son of Man must be lifted up as Moses lifted up the serpent . . ." Had Hippolytus paid heed to John in light of the words of his mentor Irenaeus, he might have deciphered the connection: Although Irenaeus did not understand the symbolism either, he at least discerned the link between the serpent and the Divine Mother, stating, "For some of them assert that Sophia [the Divine Mother] herself became the serpent."[13]

A closer inspection of Book 10 of the *Refutation,* which includes the bishop's own summation of orthodox Christian doctrine, offers a clue about why Hippolytus failed to appreciate this crucial connection. Conspicuously absent from it is any mention of the Holy Spirit! This most central teaching of Jesus does not register even a passing remark, a glaring omission that is only compounded by orthodox Christian scholars when they rely on Hippolytus as an unimpeachable source on heresy.

Now that we have dealt with the text's background, it is time at last to plunge into the exciting material at the mystical heart of the Naassene Sermon.

11

The Grail

Why do you wash the outside of the cup?
Do you not realize that he who made the inside
is the same one who made the outside?

THE GOSPEL OF THOMAS (SAYING 89)

I came to make [the things below] like the things
[above, and the things] outside like those [inside.
I came to unite] them in that place.

THE GOSPEL OF PHILIP

Oh you Pharisees!
You clean the outside of cup and plate,
while inside yourselves you are filled with extortion and
wickedness. Fools! Did not he who made the outside
make the inside too?

LUKE 11:39–41

THE NAASSENE SERMON WAS NEVER INTENDED for our eyes. It was meant for an inner circle of disciples who were ready for more advanced instruction about the Wisdom teachings of Jesus. We have already identified and discussed a number of the Sermon's key elements: the concepts of Primal Man and the Son of Man, the teaching of immanence, the reversal of the flow, and the hidden gate. We shall now investigate more deeply the image of the cup or chalice, the symbol of immanence par excellence.

The cup is a prominent symbol in the Naassene Sermon, mentioned no fewer than five times (*Refutation* 5.8.6–12). Three of the citations are from the New Testament, one is from the Old Testament, and another is a fragment drawn from Anacreon, the fifth- and sixth-century B.C.E. Greek poet who produced five known books:

> Bring water, boy! Bring wine!
> Make me drunk and make me groggy.
> The cup informs me
> What kind of man I must become,
> Speaking with unspeakable silence.

Anacreon apparently nursed an over-fondness for wine and in general pursued a debauched lifestyle[1]—but the Naassene scribe is not interested in the man; he is interested in the poet's cup! In his Sermon he draws from ordinary, even profane, material and extracts from it a sacred mystery: "This cup . . . silently speaks the ineffable mystery . . . For Anacreon's cup . . . speaks to him . . . as to what sort he must become, namely, spiritual, not carnal" (*Refutation* 5.8.7).

The scribe then discusses this mystery, presenting a medley of source material whose theme is transformation (*Refutation* 5.8.7–8): The mystery of the cup is compared to the first miracle of Jesus—the changing of water into wine at the marriage feast of Cana (John 2:11). It is also likened to the kingdom of heaven within us (Luke 17:21), to a precious treasure (Matthew 13:44), and to "the hidden leavening" (Matthew 13:33). Following these citations the scribe overwhelms us with an avalanche of additional material, much of it from pagan sources, regarding transformation and the concept of Primal Man: An ordinary man is reborn and becomes "in every respect the same substance as that [Primal] Man" (*Refutation* 5.8.10). In this long section about transformation he mentions the symbol of the gate no fewer than eight times (*Refutation* 5.8.18–21), a repetition that establishes its vitally important connection with the symbol of the cup that we shall now explore and decode.

THE GRAIL: PAGAN OR CHRISTIAN?

The Sermon's fascinating juxtaposition of pagan and Christian imagery anticipated by some 1,800 years the lively debate of the late nineteenth and early twentieth centuries concerning the origins of the Grail legend. In the Grail's long history the matter of its origin had never been finally resolved. Was it pagan or Christian? One group of scholars steadfastly maintained that the Grail was quintessentially Christian, while others pointed out features of the story rooted in Celtic folklore, thereby arguing for a pre-Christian or non-Christian origin. Curiously, even as the Grail debate was raging, Richard Reitzenstein and R. P. Casey were feuding about the pagan-versus-Christian origins of the Naassene Sermon.[2]

At the epicenter of the Grail debate stood an accomplished professor of Celtic literature named Jessie Weston, author of eleven books on various aspects of Arthurian romance. In her final and most popular book, *From Ritual to Romance* (1920), Weston proposed "an elucidation of the Grail problem," in which she traced the Grail's origins to the Naassene Sermon. The study was the result of a nine-year investigation and later became the inspiration for T. S. Eliot's famous poem "The Waste Land."

In her introduction Weston agrees that various elements of the Grail story support both pagan and Christian sides of the controversy. Yet she also observes:

> [T]he theory of Christian origins breaks down when faced with the awkward fact that there is no Christian legend associated with Joseph of Arimathea or the Grail. Neither in legend, nor in art, is there any trace of the story. It has no existence outside the Grail

literature. It is the creation of romance [i.e., literature], and no genuine [religious] tradition.[3]

Weston was strongly influenced by Sir George Frazer's massive work *The Golden Bough,* which examined the nature cults of aboriginal peoples. She believed she had found similar parallels in the Naassene Sermon indicating that the Grail might well have come from a pagan vegetation ritual, which only much later was reworked with the Christian elements added. In *From Ritual to Romance* Weston states:

> . . . we can show that between these Mystery Cults and Christianity there existed at one time a close and intimate union, such a union as of itself involved the practical assimilation of the central rite, in each case "a Eucharistic feast," in which the worshipers partook of the Food of Life from the sacred vessels.[4]

This, in Weston's view, was the origin of the sacred vessel or chalice.

We have already briefly discussed the vegetation god Adonis and various pagan rites mentioned in the Sermon (see chapter 5). Weston was convinced that the Grail story had grown out of these nature cults. In the myth of Adonis, known to have originated in Asia, the youthful hero becomes the consort of the goddess of love, Aphrodite, only to be torn to pieces by a wild boar. The theme is a common one in mythology—there appears to be no shortage of mythical heroes foolish enough to allow themselves to be seduced by fickle, moon-eyed goddesses. Much later, Adonis was deified as the grain god who every year must tragically die and be resurrected in order to ensure earth's bounty. The root of Adonis is *adon,* which means "Lord" in both Syriac and Hebrew, the same root of the name Adonai, commonly used in reference to Jesus. The Adonis cult spread to Greece, although in Ionia (the west coast of present-day Turkey) the deity was known as Attis and was associated with Cybele, the Phrygian Mother goddess. Attis and Adonis probably descended from the ancient Babylonian god Tammuz (consort of Astarte or Ishtar), who, in turn, descended from the still more ancient Sumerian vegetation god Dumuzi (consort of Inanna).

Weston believed that Christianity had merely reconstituted these older pagan gods in the person of Jesus, fashioning a new myth from old fabric. She did not, however, see this as a problem for Christianity because she did not regard pagan religion as primitive. On the contrary, Weston declared that "the more closely one studies pre-Christian theology the more strongly one is impressed with the deeply, and daringly, spiritual character of its speculations." In her view the nature cults of the pagan world were a vehicle for "the most lofty teaching as to the cosmic relations existing between God and man." She even wondered out loud if the various elements of the Adonis-Attis cult were not "the *disjecta membra* of a vanished civilization."[5]

Weston's research, valid as far as it went, led her to conclusions that were certainly controversial. Yet her investigation was much too limited in scope to successfully place the Naassene Sermon in its proper religious and historical context. While pagan elements are clearly present in the Sermon, as we have already shown the scribe has appropriated them for some new purpose. In order to decode the text, therefore, it is necessary to elucidate that undisclosed intent. As we have observed, anything can be appropriated—but toward what end?

In her book Weston never investigates the various voices in the Sermon—including that of the Naassene scribe. Nor can her thesis of a pagan Eucharistic feast account for the range of source material in the Sermon, including the amazing diversity of pagan sources, such as the rites of Samothrace, mentioned along with the cup of Anacreon (*Refutation* 5.8.7–10). While we know very little about the Mysteries of Samothrace, it is plain from the Sermon that they involved much more than a Eucharistic feast. The scribe tells us:

> [T]he Samothracians hand down . . . the tradition that Adamas is the Primal Man. And there stand in the temple of the Samothracians two statues of naked men, with both hands stretched aloft towards heaven and their pudenda erect, as with the statue of Hermes on Mount Cyllene. (*Refutation* 5.8.9–10)

In Greek tradition, Mount Cyllene was the mythological home of Hermes. So, what are we to make of the god's ithyphallic pose in this passage? The image of erect sexual organs is graphic, to say the least. Yet Weston never touches on this in *From Ritual to Romance*.

In his book *Hermes: Guide of Souls*, the mythologist Karl Kerényi confirms that the famous dual ithyphallic statue of Samothrace was a double depiction of Hermes: One statue signified the god as a youth, the other as an old man.[6] Of course, we can't be certain about this because in the Hermetic tradition of Egypt there were said to be two Hermes, not one, which suggests, given the antiquity of Egyptian religion, that the double statue of Samothrace was not Greek at all, but derived from a much older Egyptian source.[7] In any event, the erect phallus is clearly the important element. The problem for Weston's theory, however, is that Hermes—known as Thoth in Egypt—was never a vegetation or fertility god: He stood at the opposite pole from Dionysus, with his orgiastic rites, and, despite the Greek legend of his several paramours, was known above all else for self-control and restraint. This was also true of the Egyptian Thoth. Indeed, Hermes was perhaps the only Olympian god capable of controlling his passions. As the psychopomp or guide of souls and the messenger of the gods, he served as the intermediary between the gods and men. Notably, in this beneficial role Hermes shared some, though not all, of the characteristics of the Son of Man, which is probably why the Naassene scribe associates him with Primal Man and appropriates him as an example of the logos principle—yet another witness (*Refutation* 5.7.29).

For all of these reasons, the ithyphallic pose can have nothing to do with sexual indulgence; instead it represents just the opposite: Here, the god's erect phallus signifies self-control or sublimation of libido. The statue's upturned arms also seem to confirm this interpretation. The Jungian scholar Erich Neumann identified this pose as "the posture of epiphany."[8] Neumann explained that the pose signifies the precious moment in which the Godhead appears. What is being represented, in other words, is a divine revelation, a theophany. Even the pagans understood that continence was necessary for spiritual insight. It is also of interest that in Greek mythology Hermes was the bearer of the famed caduceus, the heraldic staff. The implied presence of the caduceus in this context is most apt. As we shall see, it is yet another confirmatory detail. (See figs. 11.1 and 11.2 and chapter 12.) We are now ready to look more closely at the symbolism of the cup.

A SACRED BLOODLINE?

Weston's book did not resolve the debate about the Grail, but it certainly fueled it. In recent years the hunt has continued in the form of several best-selling books that have attempted to resuscitate the centuries-old idea that the Grail is not simply a mythical or spiritual entity, but the actual chalice used by Jesus at the Last Supper. These books suggest that although it was lost long ago, this chalice still survives and is squirreled away somewhere, perhaps in a Cathar castle in the Pyrenees of southern France. These authors place great emphasis on the bloodline of Jesus,[9] contending that Jesus married Mary Magdalene, and they claim to have traced the divine genealogy of this match across the centuries, even asserting that the royal blood of Jesus still flows in the descendants of the Merovingian line of kings that once occupied the throne of France. Apparently there are descendants to this day who lay claim to authority based on this divine pedigree. The treasure hunt has yet to produce the famous chalice used at the Last Supper, but due to the vessel's numinous quality, the search never fails to generate excitement.

But even if the genealogists are correct—which is possible—their emphasis on the sacred bloodline cannot be reconciled with the Naassene Sermon's explicit message that the Grail mystery is ineffable or spiritual in nature. The emphasis on the bloodline merely reconstitutes the old shibboleth of materialism, repackaging that old soporific in a new wineskin. Perhaps we should be grateful that the irresolvable dilemma faced by these champions of the sacred blood is today fast approaching a fulminant head, thanks to genetic engineering and the human genome project. Strangely enough, science may yet turn out to be the surprising handmaiden of spiritual truth. For instance, what if a

Fig. 11.1. Sixteenth-century Swiss caduceus, the symbol of modern medicine, showing the three most important nadis: ida, pingala, and the central sushumna (see chapter 12, page 164)

Fig. 11.2. This Sumerian caduceus demonstrates that the knowledge of sacred human anatomy is not a new discovery, but in fact dates to the dawn of human civilization.

microscopic flake of two-thousand-year-old dried blood should be removed from the famous Shroud of Turin (assuming for a moment its authenticity as the linen shroud in which Jesus was wrapped after the crucifixion), and sufficient recombinant material were to be recovered and successfully implanted in a female egg from which the DNA has been removed? And what if this live egg should then be implanted in a woman's uterus? Would the cloned child be the infant Jesus, a duplicate of Christ? In short, can genetic tinkering successfully gestate the Son of Man in a test tube?

It is a fascinating question and one that needs to be pondered, if only to clear the air of confusion regarding the alleged connection between the Grail and the bloodline. The answer is a resounding no. In the first place, not even state-of-the-art science can produce a genetically identical clone because the egg, even deprived of its nucleus, still contributes a tiny but significant portion of the genetic material of the resulting offspring. But even if a perfect twin were possible, the resulting child would not be Jesus or his double because the identity of the Redeemer never had anything to do with blood or genes in the first place. Rather, it had to do with the unique soul that inhabited the Savior's body, which was merely a convenient vessel. This somber conclusion may sound less glamorous and have less sales appeal, yet it is consistent with an ineffable mystery.

The materialistic emphasis on the bloodline of Jesus goes awry for another reason: It replicates the ancient Hebrew blood basis for kinship and religion, including blood sacrifice, which Jesus rendered obsolete. The emphasis on the sacred bloodline also distracts us from pursuing the deeper question: What exactly *is* the Grail? As a symbol, it has always radiated an aura of sanctity and mystery—the very qualities that account for its magnetic appeal.[10] The Sermon informs us that it represents "an ineffable mystery." Obviously this can be no ordinary chalice. Our challenge, then, is to decode its meaning in the Naassene Sermon. Toward that end we now turn to the views of Carl G. Jung.

THE CONTRIBUTIONS OF
ANALYTICAL PSYCHOLOGY

Carl G. Jung's commentary on the Naassene Sermon appeared in his book about Christianity, *Aion,* published in 1959. As the founder of analytical psychology, Jung's views on Gnosticism merit a close inspection.

It is ironic that Jung's contemporaries often regarded him as a Gnostic, among them W. F. Albright, who in his own field so skillfully melded archaeology, linguistics, and biblical scholarship. Albright himself had no patience with Gnosticism, regarding it as a dangerous flight into irrationality, and, although in his writings he was respectful of Jung, whom he recognized as a pioneering psychologist, he clearly frowned on Jung's growing influence. That the brilliant linguist regarded Jung as a Gnostic was probably due, in part, to Jung's keen interest in the Nag Hammadi library. The Jung Institute played an important role in preserving one of the codices found at Nag Hammadi: In 1952 Jung acquired one of the texts—which became known as the Jung Codex—when it became available on the world antiquities market, thereby ensuring its availability for study.

No doubt Albright's opinion was also shaped by Jung's voluminous writings on alchemy. Jung produced two volumes on the subject that were an important addition to depth psychology—and even contributed to this study—but his alchemical interests must have seemed very strange to a committed rationalist like Albright. It is noteworthy that Jung never regarded himself as a Gnostic. In his discussion of Christian symbolism, Jung made clear his unfavorable impression of gnosis, which he referred to as ". . . a psychological knowledge whose contents derive from the unconscious. It reached its insights by concentrating on the 'subjective factor,' which consists empirically in the demonstrable influence that the collective unconscious exerts on the conscious mind."[11]

Jung's phraseology might be appropriate if used to describe a dream, a hallucination, a pathological condition, a neurosis, or some other erratic feature of ordinary life. But can it accurately characterize what to the Naassene scribe was the deepest secret of the universe? That

Jung consistently used such dismissive language regarding gnosis and Gnosticism throughout his long career is confirmed by his prolific writings. In his essay "Concerning Rebirth," written in 1950, Jung shrugged off Paul's famous visionary experience on the Damascus Road as merely the irruption of material from his unconscious mind—nothing more.[12] In his writings Jung treated the Godhead as just another archetype of the human mind, though one, he conceded, that is both necessary and pervasive. He denied, however, that humans can ever finally resolve the question of God's existence. In an essay titled "The Personal and Collective Unconsciousness," first published in 1928, Jung concluded that "the existence of God is once and for all an unanswerable question."[13] We should note that the great psychologist never explained how he knew this to be true.

In his 1931 commentary on Richard Wilhelm's translation from the Chinese of a Taoist manual of yoga known as *The Secret of the Golden Flower*, Jung responded to criticism that his theories amounted to "psychologism." In his own defense Jung wrote, "It is really my purpose to push aside without mercy the metaphysical claims of all esoteric teaching [and to] bring things which have a metaphysical sound into the daylight of psychological understanding . . ." His rationale for this was that "one cannot grasp anything metaphysically, but it can be done psychologically."[14] Jung believed, in other words, that spiritual experiences lay within the realm of depth psychology and thus he sought to explain (or at least describe) them in psychological language.

While Jung's analytical psychology can be extremely useful—it has already been used in this chapter to decipher the language of symbolism in the Naassene Sermon—nonetheless, critics of his "psychologism" raise a valid point. By collapsing important distinctions, Jung occasionally fell into the trap of reductionism. The desire to explain the unknown in simpler known terms is a perfectly natural human tendency, yet we must scrupulously guard against it when attempting to account for anomalous phenomena, gnosis being a prime example. While I regard myself as a Jungian, I have never been comfortable with Jung's wholesale use of the *unconscious*. It is clear that Jung often used the word as a catchall for things he could not explain or did not understand. Certainly he deserves credit for major discoveries, among them his theories of the psyche, the archetypes, the unconscious, and, not least, the collective unconscious. But it is also true that Jung brought his preconceptions about Gnosticism to his investigation of the Naassene Sermon in *Aion*—which prevented him from seeing the world through Naassene eyes. Where the Naassene scribe found evidence of the divine presence in all things, Jung saw nothing but a flood from the unconscious. I do not pretend to know what happened to Paul on the Damascus Road, but I feel certain that Carl Jung did not know, either.

Dr. Jung was an extremely competent biblical scholar, as we have observed in our discussion of the demiurge (see chapter 8). Almost a half-century after it was published, his *Answer to Job* remains one of the finest and most courageous commentaries on the Old Testament ever written. Yet the same gifted individual who produced this splendid piece of writing also overlooked the importance of the symbol of the waters in his commentary on the Naassene Sermon. As we have observed, the reversal of the Jordan that is so prominent in the Naassene Sermon has antecedents in the Old Testament—in particular, the episode culminating in the spiritual ascent of Elijah (II Kings 2). Are we to explain the prophet Elijah's mastery over the river in terms of a spontaneous irruption of unconscious material? Recall that when the cloak falls back to earth, Elisha uses it in precisely the same manner. Are we to believe that the same flood from the unconscious overwhelms two different individuals, both saints, in succession?

In this light, the title of Jung's book *Aion* seems ironic: A spiritual ascent through numerous levels or aeons (aions) surely involves an increase in awareness—which is anything but an unconscious process. The very term *unconscious* in this context seems an oxymoron. True, mastery over the waters and spiritual ascent imply an act of surrender, but to a higher power, not a lower one. The problem is that Jung's concept of the unconscious cannot distinguish between the two. When Elisha makes his request to receive a double portion of Spirit, his teacher Elijah is appropriately humble; he does not know for certain if the wish will be granted because grace is bestowed from above. Spirit knows and Spirit has nothing to do with Elijah's unconscious. A more useful term might be the *superconscious*.

For a man who delved so deeply into the workings of the human mind, Carl Jung's religious beliefs were surprisingly conventional. His orthodox views about the Roman Catholic Church can be read between the lines of *Aion*'s final pages. Might this explain why he never drew a distinction between the Wisdom teachings of Jesus and the doctrines of the Church? The critical reserve so characteristic of Jung's other prolific work seems strangely absent from his views on institutional Christianity. To find an intellectual lacuna of this sort—comparable to the overawed attitude of a starstruck neophyte—in an otherwise gifted and mature thinker is noteworthy, at the very least. In his memoirs Jung provides a possible clue as to why:

> I always wonder about people who go to Rome as they might go, for example, to Paris or to London. Certainly Rome as well as these other cities can be enjoyed esthetically; but if you are affected to the depths of your being at every step by the spirit that dwells there, if a remnant of a wall here and a column there gaze upon you with a face instantly recognized, then it becomes another matter entirely.[15]

Jung goes on to confide that despite a lifelong wish to visit Rome, he never traveled to the Eternal City. In 1949, rather late in life, Jung prepared to board a train, seeking "to repair this omission, but was stricken with a faint while . . . buying tickets. After that, the plans for a trip to Rome were once and for all laid aside." It is interesting that Sigmund Freud shared a similar paralysis of the will with regard to Rome and, I would guess, for similar reasons. According to Ernest Jones, Freud's biographer, the father of psychoanalysis eventually over-came his deep-seated fear after struggling with it for many years.[16] But Jung never did. Was his peculiar affliction of the will related to his inability to think critically about orthodox Christianity? Rome was the symbol of Church authority no less than the seat of empire.

We can only wonder how and to what extent Jung's impairment influenced his negative attitudes about gnosis. His example is instructive: The lesson here is that we seekers after truth must never surrender our God-given powers of critical thought. And there is another: that we define the larger and more complex in terms of the smaller and simpler at the unacceptable cost of mutilating the very thing we are trying to understand. Jung's attempt to confine gnosis within the limits of depth psychology is analogous to reducing his archetypes of the psyche to the level of physiology or biochemistry—reductionism by any other name.

It is of interest that Jung's wife, Emma, reached an entirely different perspective on gnosis as a result of her thirty-year, groundbreaking investigation into the Grail legend. Though Emma's work remained unfinished at the time of her death, the project, which became the book *The Grail Legend,* was taken up and completed by another great Jungian analyst, Marie-Louise von Franz. First published in 1960, it remains the most authoritative study of the Grail ever written. After a brief historical overview of the Grail phenomenon, we shall discover what this important source has to say about the ineffable cup.

THE GRAIL LEGEND

In their introduction, Emma Jung and Marie-Louise von Franz review the vast literature on the Grail and speculate about its origins, affirming the Naassenes as a likely source but insisting that the Grail could also have originated within other religious traditions. The authors mention possible Iranian, Islamic, Cathar, Celtic, and even Vedic (Indian) sources. After this introductory discussion, they move on to address other topics and, unfortunately, never return to the question of origins. At book's end the matter remains unresolved. Jung and von Franz are undoubtedly correct that Grail analogues might have arisen in parallel fashion and quite independently in different traditions, but this should not surprise us—indeed, the universal nature of immanence almost demands this. In chapter 12 we shall examine parallels from the Hindu tradition and even identify precise points of correspondence.

Yet none of this invalidates the textual evidence within the Naassene Sermon linking the Grail with Jesus and the Last Supper, not to mention the cup symbolism in Luke 11:39–41 and in the Gnostic Gospels of Thomas and Philip cited as epigraphs at the start of this chapter. Jessie Weston was on terra firma when she traced the Grail to the Naassenes; and from there it is but a small step to the earliest period of Christianity.

Jung and von Franz concede that the appearance of the Grail legend in Europe at the close of the twelfth century fulfilled an important need: the "further [elaboration] of the central symbol of the Christian religion."[17] It requires no great leap to suppose that this "further elaboration" might in fact have been a revival of the original Gnostic Christian teaching of immanence that had been suppressed (and lost) so many centuries before. Jung and von Franz freely admit that the Grail signifies the "realization of divinity reaching right down into matter."[18] Assuming a lost teaching of this magnitude, the need for its revival would seem all the more imperative—and understandable.

The story of the Grail quest made its debut in Europe in the year 1182 C.E., the work of Chrétien de Troyes, a patron of French nobility. Although Chrétien died before completing it, his story idea caused a sensation—the Grail quest swept across Europe. Within the short space of twenty years, English, German, Welsh, and Spanish versions appeared, and these were soon followed by translations into the Scandinavian tongues. The different versions include many different elements and a multitude of characters, yet none of these concerns us here: All of them, including the aspects of Arthurian romance, are no more than accoutrements and accretions revolving around a central idea, which is the object of the quest—namely, the vision of the Holy Grail—and it is this potent symbol that interests us.

The Grail's sudden and overwhelming popularity occurred in the period immediately following the First and Second Crusades (1095–1148), when the Christian states of Europe mobilized armies to drive the Saracens out of Jerusalem and recapture the holy sites. For this reason many scholars assume that Christian soldiers acquired both symbol and legend during their occupation of the Holy Land or during the long and arduous journey to and from Jerusalem, for most of the Crusader armies marched overland through Constantinople and Asia Minor, regions rich in ancient literary and religious traditions.[19]

THE REVIVAL THAT FAILED

The Grail idea fell on fertile ground largely because the late twelfth century was a rare moment in the history of Christian Europe. Nothing like it had ever occurred before, nor has anything since. It was a time of great promise—there was general economic prosperity across the Continent— yet more important for our purpose was the remarkable spiritual flowering that also occurred at this time. Monasticism flourished;[20] the cult of the black Madonna appeared and spread as quickly as the legend of the Grail;[21] and devotional movements too numerous to count sprang up in every corner of the Continent, including the Bogomils, the Cathars (Albigensians), the Waldenses, the Poor Men of Lyons, the Brethren of the Free Spirit, Beguins, Beghards, and the Holy Ghost movement of Joachim de Fiora.[22] During this same period the foundations of the first great cathedrals were laid, and soon Gothic spires of incredible grace and beauty began to rise above the cities of Europe. Each cathedral—indeed, each spire—was a unique architectural masterpiece involving an enormous sustained investment of human and capital resources. Each was a showcase of artistic genius in painting, sculpture, stained-glass work, ironwork, masonry, and stonework, the collective effort a lasting monument to the age of faith.[23] Historians of the period generally do not associate the Grail with these developments and achievements—wrongly, according to the viewpoint of Emma Jung and Marie-Louise von Franz, who contended that the Grail was not only a literary or artistic event but a spiritual phenomenon as well.

Artistic renditions of the Grail dating to this medieval period—such as woodcuts—link the chalice with the heart of Jesus, depicting the heart and the vessel together, and often showing the heart being pierced by a lance or arrow (figs. 11.3 and 11.4). In their book, Jung and von

Franz emphasize that this wounding is not to be viewed in a negative light; on the contrary, it is a wounding of love.[24] Sometimes the heart's blood is shown flowing or dripping down into the vessel, an apt image, as we shall see in the next chapter.

Like a therapeutic dream pointing the dreamer toward the resolution of some real-life dilemma, the Grail's spontaneous appearance in Europe filled a deep spiritual need in the Christian culture of the Middle Ages, a need that the institutional Church had failed to satisfy. The Grail pointed Europe toward a spiritual renaissance and became the symbol for that awakening—but it was actually a reawakening, a remembering, of the lost teaching of God's immanence. Nothing less can account for the numinousness of the Grail and nothing less can explain the Church's swift reaction to the revival.

As we know, the promise of the Middle Ages was never realized. The spiritual awakening of the eleventh and twelfth centuries ended as one of Western civilization's most grotesque failures, aborted in the

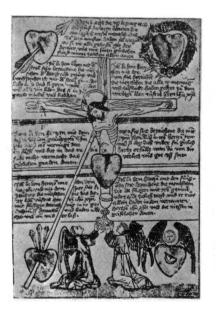

Fig. 11.3. These medieval images depict the wounding of the heart of Jesus and illustrate the link between the heart of Jesus and the Grail.

Fig. 11.4. The woman at center captures in a flask the blood of the wounded heart of Jesus, a common depiction in medieval woodcuts of the subject. This motif also appears in the image on the left in figure 11.3.

thirteenth century by the same forces of reaction that had suppressed Gnostic Christianity nine centuries before. The Church responded to this renaissance with the feared Inquisition and the so-called Albigensian Crusade, during which a million or more Cathars—deemed heretics—were slaughtered in southern France. The flowering that began with such promise ended as one of the darkest chapters in the long history of Christian intolerance, with chilling effects that—one could argue—have continued to the present day.[25]

12

The Gate of Heaven

I will give them a different heart . . .

JEREMIAH 32:39

I will give you a new heart, and put a new spirit in you . . .

EZEKIEL 36:26

THE VESSEL USED BY JESUS AT THE LAST SUPPER has long been an object of devotion, and for good reason. The chalice is the symbol of the indwelling of God. But what exactly does this mean? How does the divine reveal itself in ordinary matter? Strangely enough, an important clue can be found in medieval alchemy, which nowadays we regard as superstitious nonsense. Yet as recently as the eighteenth century, alchemy was viewed quite differently. Just about everyone is familiar with Sir Isaac Newton, the great physicist who sparked a scientific revolution with his three laws of motion. Less well known is Newton's great enthusiasm for alchemy. He was, in fact, steeped in the practice. Newton possessed one of the largest alchemical libraries in Europe and conducted alchemical experiments throughout his lifetime. Incidentally, he was also the finest biblical scholar of his generation.[1]

As practiced by men like Newton, alchemy was the forerunner of modern chemistry.[2] One of its primary objectives was transmutation: to produce gold from lead, or the proverbial silk purse from a sow's ear. Toward this end, alchemical experiments often made use of a flask or vessel in which different ingredients were combined and in which occurred a variety of transformations. So important was this container that according to a legendary writer of antiquity, Maria Prophetissa, the "whole secret [of alchemy] lies in knowing about the Hermetic vessel."[3] Theobald de Hoghelande, a sixteenth-century alchemist, wrote that "the vision" of the vessel "is more to be sought than the scriptures." According to alchemists themselves—and this is key to the Grail mystery—the vessel could at times be identical to its contents, implying a unitive or monistic level of reality above or beyond the dualistic mode of ordinary perception.[4]

Recall the words of Jesus in the Gospel of Thomas (Saying 89): "Why do you wash the outside of the cup? Do you not realize that he who made the inside is the same one who made the outside?"[5] Alchemists understood this mystical passage; they were aware—no doubt from direct experience—that the experimenter is an integral part of the experiment, an insight that did not reenter science until the twentieth century. Yet the words of Jesus as recorded by Thomas indicate that revelatory insights about non-dual reality are not the exclusive province of cutting-edge scientists or even anachronistic alchemists—on the contrary, they are available to everyone. Such fortunate experiences are usually associated with meditation, contemplation, and prayer, but they can and do occur serendipitously at any time: for example, in a fleeting instant when we succeed momentarily in suspending our beliefs about the world and about what is possible. Quite suddenly, the arbitrary distinction of "self" and "other" vanishes. Abruptly and unexpectedly, the incredible happens: Our experience shifts into a non-dual state of awareness—inside and outside are revealed to be one and the same, the body becomes an alchemical vessel holding the entire universe.

I shall never forget the day when I was first made aware of the possibility of such an expansive experience. The year was 1979; the place was the Mission of San Luis Rey on the coast of southern California;

and the occasion was the final evening of a five-day workshop called "Life, Death, and Transitions," led by the acclaimed Swiss psychiatrist Elisabeth Kübler-Ross. In 1969 Kübler-Ross had written the best-selling book *On Death and Dying*, which had become a standard part of the curriculum in medical schools and a decade later was still generating excitement. Later, Kübler-Ross expanded her path-breaking research and helped create a new field of study involving near-death experiences. That week in 1979 the workshop participants spanned the full spectrum of the helping professions: teachers, nurses, therapists, doctors, psychologists, and even a sprinkling of artists and writers such as myself. Many had come in search of personal healing—the participants included several terminally ill cancer patients who were in the process of coming to terms with their approaching death.

We were tentative during the opening session, but as Elisabeth worked her magic, the barriers came down. The participants began to share their experiences—story after story of deep personal loss and tragedy—and there was an outpouring of pain, grief, and sorrow the likes of which I had never seen. Each personal story seemed more heartbreaking than the one before. Yet as the week passed and the sharing continued, the energy level subtly shifted, and, facilitated by Elisabeth, a collective transformation occurred before our eyes. By the final evening the mood had completely changed—sixty strangers had become trusting friends and every face was beaming with newly discovered peace and joy.

On this memorable evening Elisabeth, who all week had listened dispassionately to the pain of others, shared with us a story of her own about how, one night, she had quite literally gone out of herself in a blessed experience of cosmic consciousness. The story itself is not important here—it is Elisabeth's story to tell and is recounted in her memoirs[7]—but what is relevant to our purpose is that in her attempt to describe the ineffable, Elisabeth employed as a metaphor the very same symbol of the cup that we have been seeking to decode: Her voice, raspy from smoking too many cigarettes, dropped low, and placing her hands in her lap she cupped them together and said, "We are all in the lap, cradled like small children, no matter what happens, safe and sound in the bosom of God." The room had gone completely silent, but the conviction in Elisabeth's gentle voice was like thunder. There is nothing to compare with the presence of a living saint.

THE OPHITE BOWL

Powerful evidence from archaeology confirms that Gnostic Christians had direct knowledge of higher spiritual states like the one experienced by Elisabeth Kübler-Ross. And in this respect archaeology also corroborates the textual evidence from the Naassene Sermon. Consider the artifact in figure 12.1—a unique alabaster bowl dating to the third or fourth century C.E. that ranks as one of our most important treasures from the ancient past.[8] Emma Jung and Marie-Louise von Franz include a photograph of this remarkable bowl in *The Grail Legend,* describing it as a "cult bowl from the community of the Gnostic Ophites." Hippolytus used the name Ophite (from the Greek *ophis,* for "serpent") as a generic term for Gnostic heretics of the Naassene variety; the Naassenes were a specific sect of Ophites, although they probably never referred to themselves as such.

We can see that carved figures lie in a circle within the bowl, around a central winged serpent; presumably they represent the members of the sect. Of special importance is their location entirely within the bowl. Notice the striking similarity between this alabaster vessel and the mystic rose described in the finale of Dante's *Divine Comedy* as depicted in a fifteenth-century manuscript (fig. 12.2). The parallels are unmistakable: Both are depictions of the alchemical vessel that is identical to its contents—both are expressions, in other words, of the unitive whole. The serpent in the Ophite bowl represents Spirit, with its coiled body signifying a tremendous concentration of spiritual energy. In the yoga traditions of India, kundalini or *shakti*—spiritual energy—is often represented by a tightly wound serpent. In fact, the Sanskrit word *kundalini* is derived from *kundala,* which means "coiled."[9] Until awakened, this serpent energy is said to lie dormant or sleeping at the base of the spine. The traditions of India are most explicit about the serpent's number of coils: three and a half. While we cannot, unfortunately, determine the exact number of coils in the case of the winged serpent in the Ophite bowl, interestingly, a similar sculpture of a serpent dating to the fourth century C.E., which can be found on the altar of the Church of Saint Ambrose in Milan, Italy, shows precisely three and a half coils.[10] The Milan sculpture is surely a residual trace of the Gnostic element from the early days of Christianity that survived for some unexplained reason, probably because its actual meaning was not understood.

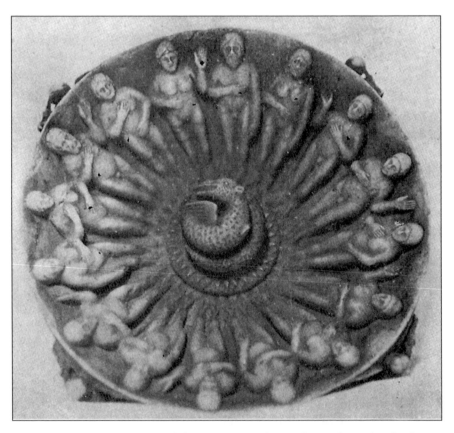

Fig. 12.1. This cult bowl of the Gnostic Ophites, dating from the third to fourth century C.E., suggests that the vision of the Holy Grail was understood from the earliest period of Christianity.

Fig. 12.2. This fifteenth-century painting of the mystic rose was based on the text of Dante's Divine Comedy *and incorporates the essential features of the Grail.*

THE SINGULARITY

We have shown that the cup symbol represents a higher order of consciousness beyond the ordinary dualistic reality of our day-to-day experience, but we have not yet established the cup's relation to the other important symbols that recur in the Naassene Sermon. The text's references to the cup and the Last Supper (*Refutation* 5.8.6–12) are immediately followed by a brief discussion about Adamas, the Primal Man. We are informed that he is manifested in the world in the form of ordinary men, who, unfortunately, have no knowledge of him and for this reason remain ignorant of their own divine nature (*Refutation* 5.8.13–17).

The Naassene scribe next enters into a lengthy discussion about the "celestial gate," which, he tells us, is the solution to the problem, for only by passing through this gate can men discover their true or spiritual identity (*Refutation* 5.8.18–21). Among the scribe's numerous references to this gate is the Old Testament story of Jacob's ladder and his vision of the "gate of heaven" (Genesis 28:7–17), which we discussed in chapter 3 (*Refutation* 5.8.19–20). He also cites passages from the New Testament—for example, John 10:9—in which Jesus says, "I am the true gate." The scribe goes on to inform us that "man . . . cannot be saved, unless he is born again by entering through this gate" (*Refutation* 5.8.20–21). We are told "that this very [man], as a consequence of the change [becomes] a god. . . . He becomes a god when, having arisen from the dead he enters into heaven through a gate of this kind" (*Refutation* 5.8.24). Here, the scribe is referring not to the orthodox Resurrection of the Dead at the end of the world, but to a casting off of earthly attachments through a process of spiritual ascent. We know this because in the very next line he tells us that the apostle Paul partially opened this same gate and ascended through it into paradise as far as the third heaven (*Refutation* 5.8.25). The Naassenes evidently took to heart the words of Jesus to the Jews: "You are as god" (John 10:34; Psalm 82:6).

Given all of this, we would still be lost concerning the specifics of how to enter the gate but for an additional clue, a reference in the Sermon to the "indivisible point." This turns up in a lengthy discussion about the Incomprehensible One: "This . . . which is nothing, and which consists of nothing, inasmuch as it is indivisible—a point—becomes through its own reflective power an incomprehensible magnitude" (*Refutation* 5.9.6). The concept of the indivisible point is well known in the Eastern yoga traditions, where it is referred to as the *bindu*, the point of maximum focus and concentration in which duality is compressed into a singularity. Although bindu has no size, no dimensionality, and no mass, it is quite real and in the East is considered the threshold between the physical world and the spiritual domains. Operationally it functions in both directions: From the standpoint of Creation, bindu is the source of spiritual light, the Logos principle, and the first sound *(nada)*, but moving in the reverse direction it is also the entry point into the spiritual world. The bindu is associated with a spiritual center, or chakra, located between the eyebrows, the *ajna* chakra,[11] but the field of bindu is said to lie above ajna, in the crown chakra *(sahasrara)* located just above the head. As one-pointed meditation deepens and the disciple penetrates bindu, the thousand-petaled sahasrara begins to unfold: The disciple begins to experience unitive states.[12]

This advanced stage of spiritual practice apparently had no counterpart in first-century Judaism,[13] although in the New Testament Jesus alludes to it in the parable of the mustard seed: "The Kingdom of Heaven is like a mustard seed, which a man took and sowed in his field. It is the smallest of all the seeds, but when it has grown it is the biggest shrub of all and becomes a tree so that the birds of the air come and shelter in its branches" (Matthew 13:31–32, Mark 4:31–32, Luke 13: 18–19). The Naassene scribe associates these two concepts—he cites the mustard seed and the indivisible point in the very same passage (*Refutation 5.9.6*)—which raises important questions. Indeed, our discovery of the indivisible point (or bindu) in the Naassene Sermon is decisive for our investigation, because it establishes an unmistakable connection with the Eastern spiritual traditions that practice kundalini yoga. Did such a tradition arise independently in the West as a result of the ministry of Jesus? Or did Jesus perhaps transmit preexisting yogic teachings from India and Tibet?

HRIT: THE MASTER CHIP

The Naassene scribe's familiarity with this Eastern concept suggests that our investigation might benefit from a closer look at Eastern scriptures, and, as we shall now see, this is indeed the case. The Vedas of India—so ancient that no one knows when they were first written down—hold the missing piece of the puzzle uniting all of the important elements and symbols in the Naassene Sermon: the cup, the gate, the river, and the reversal of the flow. The Vedas not only confirm the medieval artists' intuitive leap in associating the Grail with the heart of Jesus, but they also describe with great technical precision how the awakening of the spiritual heart center brings about the opening of the "gate of heaven." It is no coincidence that the root of the word *veda* is *vid*, which means "to know"—thus, *veda* is synonymous with *gnosis!* Although the first translations of the Vedas reached the West in the late eighteenth century, their true significance has only recently become known thanks to the 1980 book *Layayoga* by Shyam Sundar Goswami, the first English compilation of more than a hundred Vedas, Upanishads, Tantras, and Puranas. Previously, an overall assessment of these Indian scriptures was not possible in the West because only scattered or incomplete translations were available. In this regard Goswami's book was a breakthrough: the first systematic presentation in English of this vast body of scriptures.

It is of interest that the philosopher Aristotle, who was also the private tutor of Alexander the Great, taught that the seat of human consciousness lies not in the brain, but in the heart. The same idea can be found in the Upanishads (a part of the Vedas), which identify the heart chakra as the link between the cup and the spiritual channel that runs up the spine (which we shall call here the Sacred Jordan). (See fig. 12.3, page 162.) In Sanskrit the word for heart (and probably its original root) is *hrit*. This term *hrit*, however, does not refer to the fleshy organ that pumps blood through the body, but rather to a chakra located above the diaphragm, in the region of the spine. This heart center, or hrit, is extremely subtle (that is, nonmaterial) and in this respect it is like bindu—having no physical aspect, dimension, or mass, yet being quite real and, in fact, of inestimable importance. The Vedas describe hrit in its usual quiescent state as a lotus hanging in a downward position with its petals closed. When aroused, however, the lotus lifts its head and opens its petals, whence there occurs a spontaneous expansion of consciousness that is potentially limitless. (See fig. 12.4, page

163.) The Vedas say that in relation to this subtle hrit center there lies an infinitesimal void "wherein is situated the whole." The scripture's meaning is not metaphorical: "The whole" means just that—the direct experience of a non-dual, unitive state.[14] This infinitesimal void is known in the yoga traditions as *hridaya,* the heart space, where inside and outside merge and become one, but it is described by various names in other traditions: the Sacred Heart of Jesus, the great lap, the Tao, the bosom of God, and, in Gnostic parlance, the all, or Pleroma. Sometimes it is described as a fertile void because, though it is a condition of nothingness with no material substance, it contains the entire universe. This heart space is the alchemical vessel that is equivalent to its contents. Elisabeth Kübler-Ross entered into this phenomenal space during her remarkable experience of cosmic consciousness.

As far as I know, the only references to the hrit center or the heart space in Judeo-Christianity are the obscure lines from Jeremiah and Ezekiel cited as epigraphs at the beginning of this chapter as well as several passages in the Epistle of Barnabas, an orthodox apocryphal scripture that, in the view of most scholars, including S. G. F. Brandon, was written in Alexandria late in the first century. It seems to be the only source in orthodox Christianity affirming the immanence of God in conjunction with the heart center: The anonymous author of Barnabas identifies the human body as the true temple and refers to the heart center as the place where God dwells.[15] Today, perhaps not surprisingly, the Epistle of Barnabas is virtually unknown.

The hrit chakra is said to lie within the *sushumna,* the spiritual channel that starts at the base of the spine and runs up the vertebral column to the crown of the head. (Again, see fig. 12.4.) Despite its great importance, this subtle channel, which we call here the Sacred Jordan, is normally closed. Indeed, from a spiritual standpoint the challenge is to open it, and this accounts for the vital importance of the hrit chakra: According to the Vedas, the control factor that governs the opening of the sushumna lies within hrit.[16] This explains the mysterious connection between the cup and the recurring symbol of the gate in the Naassene Sermon: When hrit is aroused, the normally quiescent sushumna automatically becomes active, greatly accelerating the disciple's spiritual evolution. The frontispiece for this book (page ii) symbolizes this process. No wonder the subtle hrit center is the primary focus of meditation in all of the Eastern yoga traditions.

The scriptures of India do not always agree on the details concerning the hrit center. Although the Vedas were the basis for the most ancient spiritual teachings in India, as time passed they came to be regarded by

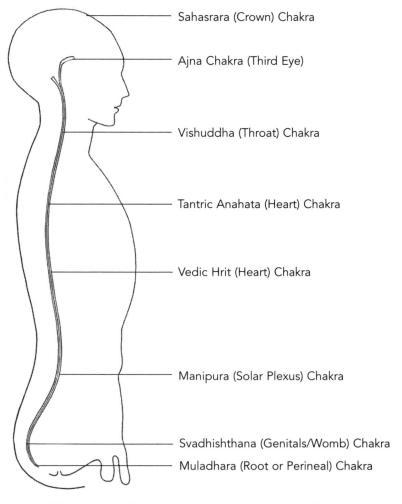

Fig. 12.3. This diagram illustrates the placement of the chakras—including the hrit—within the central channel, Sushumna or Sacred Jordan.

Fig. 12.4. This tapestry of unknown age, woven in India, currently hangs in the Siddha Yoga Ashram in Oakland, California. The image is a representation of the awakening of the spiritual heart center (the hrit).

some as too demanding. Thus, the Tantras were developed as a more accessible alternative. The Tantras simplified spiritual anatomy by collapsing the distinction between the hrit chakra (an eight-petaled lotus) and a more general designation for the spiritual heart, *anahata,* described as a twelve-petaled lotus. Some of the Tantras acknowledge hrit but regard it as a subcomponent of anahata rather than as a separate chakra.[17]

The saints and scriptures of India also occasionally disagree about the precise location of the hrit chakra;[18] however, there is unanimous agreement on its vital importance. In this respect the Indian scriptures affirm the peripatetic philosopher Aristotle's teaching that the heart is the seat of the soul. The great twentieth-century Hindu saint Sri Ramana Maharshi referred to hrit as "the center of all," and even declared that the heart center is of the same divine nature as the Godhead.[19]

THE *NADI* SYSTEM

According to the Vedas, the sushumna (or Sacred Jordan) is the principal organ of a subtle force field that provides the basis for the mind and all bodily processes. The Vedas refer to this subtle field as the *nadi* system. Although it is nonmaterial, the nadi system has a definite structure and is said to be composed of 72,000 specific motion or force lines through which *prana,* or life energy, moves. Prana, like the nadis, is extremely subtle. Of the 72,000 nadis in the body, 101 stand "in relation to hrit," meaning that they originate in the hrit center. Of these 101, fourteen are said to be most important, and of these, three are key. These three most important nadis are depicted in the caduceus, the famed heraldic staff of Hermes. Sumerian artifacts have confirmed this symbol's great antiquity; it appears to have been universally known in the ancient world. (See figs. 11.1 and 11.2, page 140.)

Two of these nadis are referred to as *ida* and *pingala*. It is said that pingala extends up the spine to the right nostril and ida to the left nostril. But the most important nadi of all is the central channel, the sushumna, which, though it lies within the vertebral column, is said to be distinct from and without direct connection to the central nervous system.[20]

Normally, the prana is said to move through the nadi system in an outward or worldly direction, sustaining the mind and all of the body's vital functions. When the hrit center is aroused, however, prana ceases to flow in the usual outward manner and instead enters the sushumna.[21] The medieval woodcuts that show the wounding of the heart of Jesus (see figs. 11.3 and 11.4, pages 149 and 150) are accurate depictions of the arousal of hrit, which is described similarly in the Vedas as the piercing or penetration of the heart center by the spiritual energy. Truly, it is a kind of wounding, as if one is being stabbed at the core of one's being, sometimes even causing a sharp but brief pain—yet followed by an ecstasy of love. This is the reversal of the flow, and from a spiritual standpoint it is by far the most important event in a disciple's life, tantamount to the biblical descent of Holy Spirit.

The sushumna is said to be composed of three sheaths, each one within the other and each of increasing subtlety. The outer sheath is the *vajra nadi;* within it is the *chitrini nadi;* and at the innermost level is the extremely fine *brahma nadi,* known as "the path of the absolute.[22] It is said that when the spiritual energy moves into the sushumna, the mind becomes calm and very stable. Of this remarkable spiritual organ Swami Vivekananda, the great disciple of Ramakrishna, wrote:

> The yogi alone has the sushumna open. When this sushumna current opens, and thought begins to rise through it, we get beyond the senses, our minds become superconscious, we get beyond even the intellect, and where reasoning cannot reach. To open that sushumna is the prime object of the yogi.[23]

Swami Vivekananda was the first Indian adept to visit the West in modern times. His incomparable teacher Ramakrishna sent him to America to attend the 1893 Chicago World Congress of Religions, at which Vivekananda delivered a stirring address that, by all accounts, caused a sensation. His appearance left a deep impression on all who were present.[24] Such is the company of a liberated soul.

Although the sushumna is subtle, at certain times it can be experienced directly. In her book *The Sacred Power: A Seeker's Guide to Kundalini,* Swami Kripananda, a monk of the Siddha Yoga lineage, describes one such experience:

> One morning while I was sitting for meditation, I suddenly felt all
> the vitality in my body withdraw itself from my limbs and gather

in the center of my body. It rose up through the central channel and exited through the crown of my head, taking my full awareness intact along with it. I felt that I was formless consciousness completely independent of my physical body, which I could observe from a few feet away. There was nothing frightening about it—I was still "me" as I knew myself, but without a body. Then, just as suddenly, I returned to my body, reentering it through the crown of the head. As the vital force descended through the *sushumna,* it shot out into all of my limbs through an infinite number of tiny channels, revitalizing them once more.[25]

The spiritual life of the disciple does not begin to unfold until the sushumna becomes active, for the sushumna is said to contain not only the various chakras, but also the *samskaras,* the residual karmic impressions generated in past lives, impressions that prevent the full awakening of kundalini or, in other words, the soul's final liberation. Before kundalini can enter the sushumna at full force, all of the outstanding issues from past lives must be dealt with and successfully resolved. Assuming this work has finally been accomplished, however, Supreme Yoga then follows naturally and spontaneously. Kundalini is aroused for the last time and the soul begins its swift and final stage of the homeward journey. The Naassene Sermon actually includes a reference to this summit of human life and religion (*Refutation* 5.9.4), one, fittingly, that we shall discuss in chapter 14, the final chapter of this book.

The sushumna, then, is "the narrow gate" in Matthew 7:13–14, Luke 13:24, and John 10:8—all passages cited in the Sermon—and the same channel mentioned in the Dialogue of the Savior, which has close affinities with the Gospel of John. The Dialogue has also been compared to the Gospel of Thomas, and was probably known to the Naassenes. In it Jesus says, " . . . when I came I opened the way, I taught them the passage through which will pass the elect and the solitary ones."[26]

Although Christian scripture never mentions the sushumna and the nadi system, their existence cannot be doubted. The Vedas and Tantras describe these spiritual organs in amazing detail, employing language so technically precise that it can only be compared to the language of science. Indeed, these Hindu scriptures are powerful evidence that the Eastern traditions advanced far beyond orthodox Christianity in the important area of mapping out and delineating the spiritual body.

Similar descriptions can also be found in Buddhism, which was born in India and developed alongside Hinduism for several centuries. As a result of this geographical association, there was considerable mixing and sharing between these two great traditions. It is no accident, for example, that in Buddhism the figure Avalokitesvara, who is associated with the heart center, is revered as the greatest of all the Bodhisattvas (highly evolved souls who incarnate on earth for the purpose of uplifting humanity).[27] Nor is it mere coincidence that Buddhists regard the experience of emptiness—in other words, the heart space—as the first important breakthrough on the spiritual path.[28] What holds for Hinduism and Buddhism is also true of Taoism, though a discussion of the relevant aspects of this tradition is beyond the scope of this book.

Christians who remain skeptical about the universality of these ideas would do well to study the drawing made by Saint John of the Cross (see fig. 12.5, page 168), a sixteenth-century Spanish contemporary of Saint Teresa of Avila. John was one of Christianity's greatest saints, and his drawing was intended as a summation of his spiritual ideas. Originally it accompanied his famous poem "The Ascent of Mount Carmel."[29] The drawing is a clear depiction of the ida and pingala nadis and the sushumna. The central channel leads to the summit of Mount Carmel, where, in John's own words, "only the honor and glory of God dwell." Saint John of the Cross lived during the height of the Inquisition, dark times indeed. During his life he endured imprisonment and even excommunication.[30] Unlike India, where saints have always been revered, the Christian West has tended to distrust and persecute its own. The Church has often viewed mystics and even great saints as psychotics, if not heretics. Nor have things changed appreciably in this regard: John's important drawing appeared in the 1973 English edition of his collected writings, yet in Christian circles it remains almost unknown.

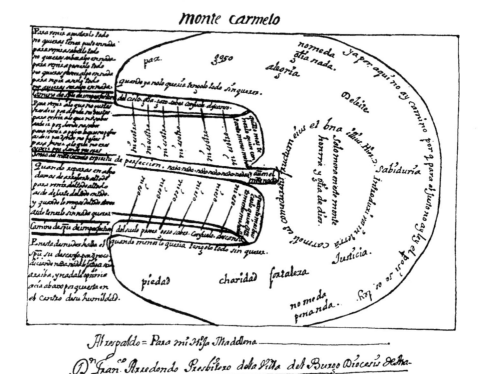

Mount Carmel

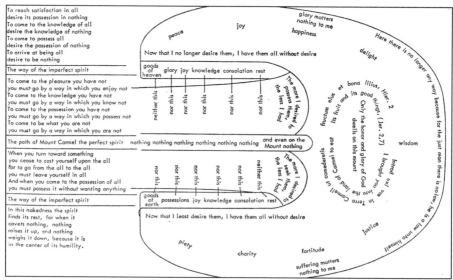

Fig. 12.5. The original drawing of Mount Carmel by Saint John of the Cross confirms the saint's direct awareness of sacred anatomy. The drawing shows the central sushumna flanked by the lesser nadis of ida and pingala.

EAST MEETS WEST

From the examples we have discussed, it is evident that sacred anatomy (i.e., the spiritual body) is a part of the collective spiritual heritage of mankind, a conclusion supported by additional powerful evidence from both East and West. When clergy and workmen, assisted by doctors and other witnesses, exhumed the corpse of Saint John of the Cross in 1859, nearly three hundred years after his death in 1591, the saint's body was found to be uncorrupted, showing no trace of decay.[31] The body was exhumed again in 1955 and was found to be in the same condition. Nor is the case of Saint John unique: Incredible as it may sound, the phenomenon of incorruptibility is extremely well documented. In fact, it is the most thoroughly documented of all miraculous phenomena, with dozens of other known cases recorded. Nor is the phenomenon limited to Christian saints: The body of Paramahansa Yogananda, who passed away in 1952, was also uncorrupted. Like Vivekananda, who preceded him, Yogananda had been selected many years before by his guru—in his case, Sri Yukteswar—to go to America and bring the yoga teachings to the West. Yogananda's spiritual attainment is a matter of record, and his famous autobiography reveals an intimate knowledge of the spiritual body. For instance, he wrote that the famous Indian saint Lahiri Mahasaya, the guru of his guru, was known as Gangadhar, which means "he who holds the Ganges," an expression referring to mastery over "the 'river' of life current in the spine," or, in other words, mastery over the Sacred Jordan.[32] Several weeks after Yogananda's death, the incorruptibility of his corpse was certified in a notarized document signed by Mr. Harry T. Rowe, mortuary director of Forest Lawn Memorial Park in Los Angeles, where the saint's body had been temporarily placed. Mr. Rowe wrote:

> The absence of any visual signs of decay in the dead body of Paramahansa Yogananda offers the most extraordinary case in our experience . . . No physical disintegration was visible in his body even twenty days after death . . . No indication of mold was visible on his

skin, and no visible desiccation (drying) took place in the bodily tissues. This state of perfect preservation of a body is, so far as we know from mortuary annals, an unparalleled one . . . At the time of receiving Yogananda's body, the Mortuary personnel expected to observe, through the glass lid of the coffin, the usual progressive signs of bodily decay. Our astonishment increased as day followed day without bringing any visible change in the body . . . No odor of decay emanated from his body at any time . . . The physical appearance of Yogananda on March 27, just before the bronze cover of the casket was put into position, was the same as it had been on March 7. He looked on March 27 as fresh and as unravaged by decay as he had on the night of his death. On March 27 there was no reason to say that his body had suffered any physical disintegration at all . . . Yogananda's body was apparently in a phenomenal state of immutability . . .[33]

Does it not seem likely that whatever phenomenon was responsible for the preservation of the body of the Christian saint John was also operative in the case of the Hindu saint Yogananda? I would argue yes, and suggest that the common factor in all such cases involves the spiritual body—in particular, the sushumna or Sacred Jordan.

ON THE UNIVERSALITY OF THE SPIRITUAL BODY AND THE DECLINE OF THE WEST

The spiritual development of the West has been seriously impeded by Christianity's failure to evolve a detailed understanding of the spiritual body. No wonder that in recent years so many Christians have gone searching elsewhere. More than a few have turned to Eastern religion, including Carl Jung, an early example of the trend, although Jung, while intrigued by kundalini yoga, approached the subject strictly from the standpoint of psychology and warned Westerners away from actually taking up the practices. In his view, ". . . the more we study [Eastern] Yoga the more we realize how far it is from us; a European can only imitate it and what he acquires by this is of no real interest."[34] Jung believed that the Westerner "who practices Yoga does not know what he is doing. It has a bad effect on him, sooner or later he gets afraid, and sometimes it even leads him over the edge of madness."[35] Jung wrote that "in the course of the centuries the West will produce its own Yoga, and it will be on the basis laid down by Christianity"[36]— words that are directly challenged by the evidence we have presented from the Naassene Sermon. Indeed, the evidence suggests that during the second century C.E.—more likely, as early as the first century—the Naassenes were practicing a fully developed system of kundalini yoga very similar to what is described in the Vedas and practiced in India today. (See chapter 14.)

If, as Christian apologists are always telling us, orthodoxy was Christianity's necessary response to the threat of rampant heresy in the first centuries, that response came at a very heavy price: Rather than developing an integral and systematic understanding of the spiritual body, Orthodox Christianity instead created an overly rigid mentality to match its institutional superstructure. Few modern Christians have escaped the long shadow cast by this disaster, including even brilliant scholars like W. F. Albright, whose hasty dismissal of the Nag Hammadi library was exceeded only by his superficial assessment of Hippolytus.[37] Albright never missed an opportunity to examine new archaeological evidence, but, strangely, he showed no interest in the Naassenes. He wrote instead of the "immense superiority of orthodox Christianity to Gnosticism, whose founders tried, like many modern theologians, to discard the rich experience of God's historical relation to His people which makes the Old Testament indispensable as a basis of Christian belief."[38] Albright's words show that he never delved into the Naassene Sermon, for if he had, he would have been compelled to concede the unassailable scriptural underpinnings to be found there. Whatever might be said of other Gnostic sects, the Sermon shows that at least one of them—the Naassenes—was deserving of a closer respectful look. But Albright's orthodoxy predisposed him to regard other traditions with condescension and contempt, including Hinduism, which he mistakenly viewed as escapist illusionism.[39] At the start of the second millennium, the choice before us in the West is not the one articulated by Albright—Western theism versus Eastern pantheism—and the simple truth is that it never was! The distinction is a false one, and reflects Albright's inability to comprehend the true nature of the spiritual revolution wrought by Jesus.[40]

The teaching about God's immanence was a radical leap in the first century C.E. and remains so in our time. Not even the pioneering psychologist Jung, who cultivated a deep interest in the East, succeeded in understanding this—perhaps because Jung, like Albright, refused to study the East on its own terms (just as he would not study the Naassenes on their own terms). Jung regarded the Eastern traditions (and likewise the Gnostic Christians) as no more than fertile ground for his psychological theorizing. Jung's commentary on the Naassene Sermon in *Aion* shows that he failed to recognize what was being presented, and in this he was no different from Bishop Hippolytus.[41]

How truly different things might have been if the patriarchs of the early Church had adopted an attitude of openness. In such a climate the ideas of the Naassene Gnostics would have survived eventually to triumph. In an open forum the essential correctness of their teachings about God's immanence and the spiritual body would have been confirmed, not by papal edicts, but through continuing study, prayer, and contemplation. And today their teachings would be mainstream Christianity.

Of course, it didn't happen. Instead of practicing openness, the Church adopted a one-size-fits-all dogmatic formula for salvation. Instead of preaching by example and persuasion, it wielded fear and repression. The Naassenes were denounced and lumped together with other heretics, some of whom, no doubt, were more deserving of the name. The dangerous Naassene scriptures were banned and consigned to the flames.

Nonetheless, it is difficult to destroy ideas, especially when they are steeped in truth. Jessie Weston pointed out this fact at the conclusion of her book *From Ritual to Romance:* "[O]f this one thing we may be sure, the Grail is a living force, it will never die; it may indeed sink out of sight, and for centuries even, disappear . . . but it will rise to the surface again, and become once more a theme of vital importance . . ."[42] As we have seen, this is exactly what happened during the eleventh and twelfth centuries. The Christian revival in medieval Europe was driven by deep spiritual hunger, and the symbol for that revival was the sacred vessel: the image of the open heart center that resurfaced on the Continent in the form of the Grail. But, once again, the Church reacted as if under siege. The radical idea of the indwelling God, so subversive to the authority of institutional religion, was violently suppressed.

Today, of course, the Catholic Church officially denies that a twelfth-century revival occurred at all. In such matters, however, the beliefs of the common folk carry more weight than do institutional disclaimers. The paintings, woodcuts, and literature of the period are evidence enough. They attest to the Grail's deep impact on Christian Europe. The twelfth-century spiritual renaissance proved the amazing resilience of the teaching of immanence, the idea so pervasive throughout the Naassene Sermon.

Had that medieval flowering, so full of promise, been allowed to reach fruition—who knows what might have happened in the West? Christianity might even have achieved a historic self-correction. The potential certainly existed for large numbers of Christians to rediscover the esoteric teachings of Jesus as they had existed in the beginning. (Should our lament be that those teachings were initially limited to so few?) In that case, Christianity might have gone on to produce something to rival the Vedas. The Grail held the potential to transform all of Christendom—and it still does. The wellsprings run eternal. But because the Church failed to open to the possible and the unlimited potentials of the Spirit, instead of an open blossom we got the dungeon and the rack, yes, and the plethora of ills that are the sure signs of the continuing spiritual decline of the West.

13

The Primordial Waters

That day Yahweh will punish . . .
Leviathan, the fleeing serpent,
Leviathan the twisting serpent;
He will kill the sea dragon.

ISAIAH 27:1

To God belong earth and all it holds,
the world and all who live on it;
he himself founded it on the ocean,
based it firmly on the nether sea.

PSALM 24

IN CHAPTER 7 WE DISCUSSED the Canaanite story of Baal's fight with Yamm, the sea dragon. References to this cosmological battle can be found in the Bible in Isaiah 27:1 (quoted in this chapter's epigraph; see also Job 7:12, 9:8, 26:12, 38:7–11; Psalms 89, 77, 74, and 114; and Revelation 12 and 20). The common element in all of these accounts of this archaic battle is water—a sea or a river—mythologically represented as a dragon. Though it may seem strange to us, this equivalence

174

had a universal currency in the ancient world that was old and familiar even in the time of Jesus.

The second verse of Genesis tells us that in the beginning "[t]he world was empty and chaotic; darkness covered the waters." Here, Genesis is referring to a time before Creation when chaos, conceptualized as a great dark roiling sea, ruled all that was. This primeval ocean existed before time itself. It was formless, without shape or dimension, and stretched forever in every direction. Yet the primordial sea was said to be composed of two parts: the upper firmament (or upper waters)—Tehom in Hebrew, Tiamat in Akkadian, both meaning "deep"; and the lower firmament (or lower waters)—Apsu or Absu in Sumerian, meaning "abyss," a loanword whose meaning has not changed in six thousand years.

In the Babylonian creation story, which was the basis for the Canaanite and Hittite accounts, the first act is the spontaneous sexual coupling of the upper and lower waters. Tiamat (or the biblical Leviathan or Rahab) is the female half of this pair, and Apsu (or the biblical Behemoth) the male. There is also, however, the suggestion that this first pair was itself spawned from the original undivided waters of chaos through self-division. In any event, the copulation of the watery parents sets in motion the familiar theogony: The various gods are born and subsequently they take over the continuing process of Creation. The Babylonian account was probably based on a much older Sumerian version that was already ancient when it was passed on to the Babylonians, and Genesis is a part of this mythological tree. In Genesis, however, an attempt has been made to demythologize the story and cleanse it of its polytheistic elements. There is no theogony in Genesis and no great chain of being that produces heaven and earth. Instead, it is Yahweh, the Most High, who alone attends to Creation. The fact that Yahweh "soars above the waters," however, is a glaring inconsistency, given that the waters have no surface. This shows the story's mythological basis—such logical flaws are common in mythology.

THE DRAGON FIGHT

Primeval chaos does not willingly accede to Creation. Chaos is by its very nature antithetical to order and tends to beget more of the same. Therefore, order must be introduced before Creation can proceed; the powers of chaos must be tamed or at least temporary restrained. This struggle to introduce order is the essence of the dragon fight— a universal motif in the Creation myths of the ancient world. We have already discussed the Canaanite version, Baal's fight with Yamm the sea dragon, which we know thanks to the Ra's Shamra tablets. In this case, however, the details are sketchy because the inscriptions from Ugarit are fragmentary. More can be gleaned from the Babylonian version of the story, of which a complete copy exists in the longer Creation epic known as the *Enuma Elish*.[1] It is a tale of order versus chaos and change versus inertia, themes that appear later in the Bible in Yahweh's archaic battle with Leviathan (Rahab).

In the *Enuma Elish,* Tiamat and Apsu, the primordial pair representing the upper and lower waters, respectively, give birth to the gods only to discover that their progeny have become a nuisance. The precise word used in the Babylonian text is *noisome.* The implicit analogy is to parents whose unruly children prevent them from sleeping, also suggesting an attitude of primeval inertia that is challenged by activity, change, and progress. Every mythological hero must overcome one expression or another of this same elemental inertia. Initially, Tiamat shows the natural sympathy and loyalty of the indulgent mother: She knows her brood are a problem, but she is reluctant to act. The gods, after all, are her own flesh and blood. She urges her mate, Apsu, to be more patient. However, Mummu, who is Apsu's attendant, succeeds in egging him on to violent rebellion. Word of Apsu's revolt soon reaches the ears of the gods and causes panic in heaven. For a time the divine council is helpless; the gods rush about in a state of confusion. Only the wise and cunning god Enki (Ea) remains calm. Rising to the occasion, he casts a spell over Apsu, which puts Apsu to sleep, enabling Enki to destroy him easily.

After the victory Enki constructs a dwelling place upon the body of Apsu—in other words, he builds a house directly over the waters of the abyss. It is a peculiar image, yet it resonates perfectly with the young man's vision in the Shepherd of Hermas (see chapter 9). Recall that in the Christian story the young man witnesses the construction of the tower (i.e., the Church) upon a foundation of water. This idea of a house or temple built upon water is a universal religious concept—it turns up even in Tibetan Buddhism in an old legend about a vast subterranean lake under the chief temple of the famous Potala Palace of Lhasa.[2]

Angered by the death of her mate Apsu, Tiamat creates a horde of monsters, every one of which is a different manifestation of herself. With this new army she marches against heaven and attacks the gods. Tiamat is, as it turns out, a much more formidable opponent than Apsu, and this time even Enki is cowed. The forces of chaos set heaven in pandemonium—but fortunately in this moment of supreme crisis a champion emerges: Enki's son Marduk, a storm god. Marduk engages Tiamat in deadly hand-to-hand combat, and after a desperate battle he succeeds in casting a net over her and her brood of monsters. Then, when the mother of chaos opens her ferocious jaws, Marduk blows into her mouth. The winds at his command fill Tiamat's belly like a balloon, at which point he lets fly an arrow that splits her heart. The precise word used in the Babylonian text is *splits,* the same word that appears in the later biblical references to the fight (Psalms 89:9–11, 74:12–13; Nahum 1:4; Job 7:12, 9:8, and 26:12; and Isaiah 27:1 and 51: 9–10; see also chapter 7).[3] This is the mythological origin of the theme of the parting of the waters. Moreover, it repeats again, for Marduk next "splits" (again the exact word used) the carcass of Tiamat "like a shellfish, into two parts," out of which he constructs the world parents, earth and sky.

Now that primeval chaos has been defeated, Creation can proceed in an orderly fashion. But chaos has not been entirely vanquished: The monsters created by Tiamat, though still trapped in Marduk's net, have not been destroyed. In the story the monsters survive, and with them the potential for future trouble. The possibility remains that one day they might escape and again wreak havoc. This idea turns up in the Book of Revelation 20:1–3 and 7–10, despite some minor differences: In John's account an angel replaces Marduk; the forces of chaos, now collectively known as Satan, are masculine rather than feminine; and they are constrained by a chain instead of a net:

> Then I saw an angel [Marduk] come down with the key of the abyss in his hand and an enormous chain. He overpowered the dragon [Tiamat], that primeval serpent which is the devil and Satan, and chained him up for a thousand years. He threw him into the abyss and shut the entrance and sealed it over him to make sure he would not deceive the nations again until the thousand years had passed. At the end of that time, he must be released, but only for a short while.

We notice that here the author of Revelation adds a new twist, a moral theme, thus transforming a process that is neither good nor bad into an ongoing struggle against evil. This illustrates the enormous difference between ancient and modern viewpoints and probably explains why so many Christians regard natural disasters and even death itself as the work of the devil. By adding a moral interpretation, Christianity obscured the original mythology, which in this instance reflects a surprisingly sober and clear-eyed understanding of the world. The ancients were aware of the need for order, but they also observed that chaos, destruction, and death are elemental forces of nature that can never be defeated and are, at best, held in abeyance.

The omphalos stones discovered at Delos, Delphi, and Khorsabad, the sites of the ancient oracles, confirm this, and suggest that while the ancients sought to influence nature, they did not share our modern penchant for dominating her.[4] The egg-shaped stones centrally placed in these oracular shrines sometimes had carved upon them a woven or net-like pattern with dragons or serpents (representing chaos) caught in the net. (See fig. 13.1.) Each oracle was regarded as the navel of the earth—

Fig. 13.1. An omphalos stone discovered at Delphi, site of the ancient oracle. The surfaces of such stones are often covered with carvings reflecting ancient cosmology—for example, Marduk's battle to subdue the dragon (i.e., the primordial waters, or chaos).

the word *omphalos* means "navel." These, then, were the listening posts where "sensitives"—that is, psychically gifted individuals— sought to commune with elemental energies. Judging from the carvings on the stones, the priests' role was not limited to divination. Their bigger challenge was to propitiate heaven, or, in other words, to mitigate as much as possible the uncontrollable forces of nature and, thus, to achieve a temporary reprieve from the next inevitable catastrophe, whether flood, drought, fire, or earthquake.

THE ROLE OF NATURAL CATACLYSMS IN THE EVOLUTION OF RELIGION

What else but some great natural disaster can account for the biblical Flood? The fact that the story is a universal feature of cultural myth around the world is the surest indication that some catastrophe did occur, perhaps repeatedly and on a monumental scale—large enough to leave a deep and lasting impression on human consciousness. Such was Plato's view.[5]

Among the possibilities, the most likely is the earth impact of a comet, the fragment of a comet, or an asteroid. There is no doubt that such objects do periodically strike the earth, perhaps as often as once every five to ten thousand years. Most of these impacts have likely occurred in water—oceans cover 70 percent of the earth's surface—generating tsunamis hundreds or even thousands of feet in height. One of these rolling mountains of seawater would easily wreak devastation beyond anything we have experienced in recorded history. Even one such event would be sufficient to exert a profound influence on the development of religious ideas, which could easily explain the Bible's account of the Flood and the ubiquitous nature of similar stories in other cultures and religions. Truly, a display of such mind-boggling power would from a human standpoint be taken as self-evident proof of the existence of the gods or God. It would also inspire terror, awe, and dread and invite speculation about the cosmos: altogether the stuff of mythology. God's (or the gods') wrath or vengeance would be perceived as second in importance only to the fertility of nature and the wonder of procreation.

Blood sacrifice and other burnt offerings to the gods (or God) probably soon followed, intended as a means of appeasement. We know that the Semitic neighbors of the Hebrews, including the Canaanites, practiced human and child sacrifice (as we have already seen in relation to the story of Isaac). The scriptural evidence for such practices among the Moabites and Aramaeans can be found in II Kings 3:26 and in Amos 2:1. The former relates how Mesha, king of Moab (located in Transjordan), sacrificed his firstborn son and heir on the city wall in full view of the Israelites, who had besieged him. His further exploits were recorded on a famous stele known as the Moabite or Mesha Stone. In the stone's inscription the king brags about how he slaughtered the entire population of Nebo, a city of some seven thousand inhabitants, as a ritual offering to the Moabite god Ashtar-Chemosh.[6]

King Mesha practiced human sacrifice, but he was a mere dabbler compared to the Aztecs of Mexico. In their book *The Feathered Serpent and the Cross,* authors Joyce Milton, Robert A. Orsi, and Norman Harrison report that the Aztec king Ahuitzotl "celebrated the dedication of the temple of Huitzilopochtli in Tenochitlán by marshaling four lines of prisoners past teams of priests who worked four days to dispatch them. On this one occasion as many as 80,000 were slain during a single ceremonial rite."[7] Most of the victims were prisoners of war taken by the Aztecs in their military campaigns against rival tribes. Based on their research, the authors estimated that by the start of the sixteenth century, shortly before the conquest of Mexico by Cortés, the Aztecs were sacrificing some 250,000 human victims annually.[8] The reason for the slaughter on such a vast scale was not blood lust. Nor was its purpose couched in some great religious mystery. According to the Aztecs themselves, the slaughter had one goal: to delay the end of the world. The Aztecs apparently believed that only by sacrificing human lives in sufficient numbers could they stave off, at least for a time, the dreaded power of heaven, some new expression of divine wrath or, in other words, watery chaos. Their fear surely hints at an old but indelible memory handed down over time: the recollection of a terrible cataclysm in the distant past that almost rubbed out the human race.

Early in the twentieth century, William Niven, a mineralogist-turned-archaeologist, discovered evidence in the highlands of central Mexico suggesting that just such a catastrophe, or a series of them, had occurred there. He was exploring ancient ruins in the province of Guerrero, near Acapulco, when the local Indians brought him strange artifacts that he traced to a site between the villages of Texcoco and Haluepantia, just north of Mexico City. There he found numerous excavations, for the area was a rich source of clay, sand, and tepetate used by builders in the nearby expanding metropolis. Niven, in exploring the pits, extended their depth, which led to one of the most startling discoveries in the history of archaeology: He found an ancient city buried under thirty feet of deposits and debris.[9] It had been interred initially by several feet of volcanic ash, over which lay three distinct layers of sand, gravel, and clay of varying depths, each separated from the one above by hardpan. The evidence suggested to Niven that major floods had repeatedly inundated the great valley of central Mexico, which seems almost incredible given that the region lies at an altitude of seven thousand feet, though whether the region's great volcanoes may have played a role has apparently never been investigated.

The field of archaeology responded to Niven's discovery by dismissing it out of hand; the evidence was too anomalous to be taken seriously. Niven's estimate that the ruins at the lowest level dated to 50,000 years ago implied an origin and history of human civilization in Central America wildly beyond our current understanding. Yet Niven's discovery of periodic natural catastrophes in that part of Mexico would account for the Aztecs' collective sense of fear and dread, which must have been based on memories linked to some distant but no less real event(s).[10]

THE DOUBLE DEEP AND THE RING OF OCEAN

But chaos comprises only one level of meaning of the waters. We shall now explore another: Once chaos has been subdued and Creation is under way, the upper and lower waters serve as a kind of foundation for the universe itself. There is abundant evidence for this idea in ancient Near Eastern religion. For example, in Genesis 7–8 we are told that "God made the firmament, dividing the waters that were below the firmament from those that were above it." The idea also turns up in Ugaritic literature (see chapter 7), in which El's abode is on the mountaintop, also described as the source of the waters:

> Toward El at the sources of the rivers,
> in the midst of the fountains of the double deep.[11]

Here the "double deep" refers to the division of the waters into upper and lower. The lower waters comprise the abyss and include the seas of the earth, freshwater springs, lakes, canals, and rivers. It is perhaps no surprise that the Canaanites' chief god was thought to dwell at the head of these waters—on a mountaintop—which also placed him in a special relation to the upper waters, which lie above the firmament (that is, above the sky).

The upper waters were thought to form an ethereal sea or river that encircles all of Creation. This idea is actually expressed on an early Babylonian map showing the known world with Babylon at its center, surrounded by the *naru marra-tum,* the bitter river—that is, the upper waters.[12] The same idea later found its way into Homer's *Iliad* in the famous battle shield of Achilles made by Hephaestus, the divine craftsman. On the shield the upper waters were displayed around the outermost margin.[13] The lesser-known shield of Heracles was fashioned in a similar manner.[14] The Greek name for the upper waters, "Ocean, the parent of the gods," is mentioned with great deference by Homer[15]— the upper waters held a central place in Greek religion, as in Judaism. Though Ocean is nominally one of the Titans, he never makes an appearance on the stage of Greek mythology, remaining instead in the background. Unlike the other gods, Ocean has no personality; he is an elemental condition, the backdrop for the ongoing mythological drama of gods and men.

Like the Babylonians, the Greeks gave expression to the upper waters (Ocean) in the maps of the day. These old maps have no modern counterparts because they included representations of metaphysical ideas, which obviously have no place in modern cartography. It seems, however, that some of the ancients shared our modern view, for the historian Herodotus wrote: "I cannot help laughing at the absurdity of the mapmakers—there are plenty of them—who show Ocean running around a perfectly circular earth . . ."[16]

THALES

Given the prominence of the symbol of the waters in the Naassene Sermon, it is hardly surprising that the Naassene scribe mentions the first Greek philosopher, Thales, who lived in the seventh century B.C.E.

(*Refutation* 5.9.13).[17] He was the first of the seven sages and was justly famous as the teacher of the great philosopher Anaximander, but he is probably best known for his belief that water is the foundation of everything. According to Thales, the universe is a hemisphere resting on an endless watery expanse and the earth is but a flat disk floating on the interior of this hemisphere. Yet Thales was not the first to entertain such ideas; as we've seen, the primordial waters (Ocean) are found in Homer, who preceded Thales by some two centuries. Whether Thales got the idea from the blind bard we do not know. More likely, Egypt was his source. Hippolytus tells us that the Greek philosophers learned their mystical ideas from the Egyptians, the oldest race of men except for the Phrygians (*Refutation* 5.7.22,28). We know that in his earlier years Thales studied at the feet of Egyptian priests, so he likely learned from them about the waters.

EGYPTIAN ORIGINS

Ancient Egypt had no standard Creation myth. According to the Egyptologist R. T. Rundle Clark, " . . . a canonical or official cosmology never existed in ancient Egypt; there seems to have been a feeling that the creation of the universe was too mysterious and complex to be explained always in the same terms."[18]

This surely helps to account for the bewildering complexity of Egyptian religion, which seems to have far surpassed that of the Babylonians and Sumerians in the subtlety and multiplicity of its expression. Nevertheless, in general, Egyptian ideas about Creation paralleled those of Mesopotamia. The fundamental landscape of the primordial waters was the same. One of the oldest Egyptian Creation accounts, recorded in the Pyramid Texts, tells how the god Atum—the "self-created" one who gave rise to the other gods—emerged from the primordial sea.[19] This first divine being was visualized as a mound or island rising up out of the ocean and containing within himself the seed for duality and for all of subsequent creation. In the god Atum we find the monotheistic basis for Egyptian religion that is so easy to miss because of the wild proliferation of lesser Egyptian deities. This multiplicity of Egyptian gods obscures the underlying monotheism, which can be confirmed by probing the descriptions of the various high gods, including Tem, Atum, Nu, Ptah, Re (Ra), and Amon. Closer inspection shows that the names are but masks for the underlying deity, who in all cases is the same. Was this deity God?

THE WATERS AS FOUNDATION

In our discussion of the Shepherd of Hermas in chapter 9, we encountered the image of the tower (Church) constructed upon a foundation of water and we observed that a similar idea survives in Tibetan Buddhism. This belief that water is the true foundation of every temple was a common theme in the ancient world, as evidenced by scripture, mythology, and even architecture. We have already observed that in the *Enuma Elish* the god Enki constructs his dwelling directly over the abyss, and Marduk replicates this pattern after his resounding victory over Tiamat (chaos):

> They raised the summit of Esagila [Marduk's temple]
> (over and) opposite Apsu (the abyss),
> and built the upper (counterpart
> to the) ziggurat of the Apsu.
> For [the gods] Anu, Enlil, Enki (Ea), and him,
> they established seats.[20]

While extant copies of the *Enuma Elish* date to the first half of the first millennium B.C.E., according to the Mesopotamian scholar Thorkild Jacobsen, the "language in which [the copies] were written . . . seems somewhat older than the Akkadian of that date, and suggests that the epic was composed earlier, say, sometime during the . . . latter half of the second millennium B.C."[21] Yet we know that the provenance of the story is even more ancient because the gods (such as Enki) and places (such as Eridu) mentioned in the *Enuma Elish* are actually

Sumerian names that long predated Babylon. Enki, the deity who established the earliest-known precedent for temple construction above the abyss, was the patron god of Eridu, the oldest of the Sumerian city-states, dating to 3800 B.C.E., which indicates that the concept of the foundational waters traces to the dawn of recorded history.[22]

THE BIVALENT WATERS

Long after Enki's famed temple at Eridu had fallen into ruin, the waters of the abyss resurfaced in the Hebrew Bible. In one of his famous visions the prophet Ezekiel saw multiple rivers of water flowing from the base of the temple of Jerusalem (Ezekiel 47:1–12). The rivers traveled in all directions and expanded into a flood so deep and wide that there was no way to cross over. In the vision Yahweh asks Ezekiel: "Do you see, son of man?" The question is clearly intended to awaken Ezekiel to the fact that these waters represent the hand of God. A similar idea occurs in the final apocalyptic chapter of Zechariah (14:8–9), which describes the end time when "Yahweh takes the field": "When that day comes, running waters will issue from Jerusalem, half of them to the eastern sea, half of them to the western sea; they will flow summer and winter; and Yahweh will be king of the whole world."

The message in this passage from Zechariah is that the waters will flow on the Day of Judgment, yet the image also recalls the Ugaritic description of the home of El on the mountaintop, the source of rivers. The tone of Zechariah's vision is apocalyptic, but that of Ezekiel's is very different. In Ezekiel the waters are not destructive but instead are wholesome and life supporting: "Wherever the river flows, all living creatures teeming in it will live. Fish will be very plentiful, for wherever the water goes it brings health, and life teems wherever the river flows."

Both of these passages are a part of the scriptural basis for John's baptism of redemption, and they may also have given rise to the rabbinic idea that the sons of Israel were fishes swimming in the waters of the Torah.[23]

We see, then, that the idea of the primordial waters was multifaceted.

In a region such as the Near East, where drought-induced famine was common, the fructifying waters had a special resonance. Water in the form of rainfall for crops and runoff for irrigation was a precious resource. It represented the slender margin between starvation and abundance—or, at least, sufficiency—which probably explains why the waters of the abyss were most often viewed as beneficial and life supporting.

The potential for storms, floods, and other natural catastrophes existed, but even when the waters were destructive, the Hebrews preferred to believe that a purposeful hand was in evidence. This is plainly seen in an old Jewish legend involving King David: While digging the foundations of the great temple, King David encounters a shard of stone at a depth of fifteen hundred cubits. Just as he is about to lift it, the shard begins to speak, saying, "Thou must not do it." When David asks why not, the stone replies, "Because I rest upon the abyss." But the king is not in the habit of taking orders and he pays no heed to the warning. He removes the stone, whence the waters of the abyss suddenly rise up and threaten to flood the earth. Luckily, David's counselor, Ahithophel, who is standing nearby, has the presence of mind to inscribe the name of God upon the shard before tossing it back into the abyss, whereupon the waters immediately subside and disappear into the earth. Indeed, the waters retreat to such a depth that the king grows concerned that the earth might lose its moisture. So David, renowned as a musician, sings the "Song of Ascents" to bring the waters back up to their proper level.[24]

This relationship between the stone and the waters, however, did not originate with the Hebrews. The same stone can be found in earlier Babylonian accounts, where it appears as "the bolt, the bar of the sea,"[25] but it is actually older still, and traces back to ancient Sumer."[26] The Hebrews called it the *eben shethiya* and every year they commemorated it at the Feast of Tabernacles, when a special libation of water was poured over it for the purpose of maintaining water's balance—neither too much nor too little—upon the earth.[27]

Nowhere did this dual nature of the lower waters find more resonance than in Egypt. The country was primarily agricultural, even though 95 percent of its land was (and is) unproductive desert. Egyptian civilization clung to the fertile but restricted Nile valley and life depended on the great river's annual flood. The narrow habitable strip along the banks of the Nile represented the realm of order. By contrast—and this is reflected in Egyptian mythology—the surrounding desert was the ferocious land of chaos and death. True, in abnormally wet years the swollen Nile could be destructive, flooding towns and drowning live-stock and villagers. But the prospect of drought-induced famine was even more serious, and so, not surprisingly, the yearly flood associated with Osiris was viewed as primarily beneficial and fructifying.

Thus, the Egyptian case shows that the theme of the waters was expansive enough to encompass creation, destruction, fertility, and regeneration—even, as we shall see, the ascent of the soul, which brings us to a remarkable ancient temple whose megalithic architecture hints at the role of Spirit.

STRABO'S WELL

Near Abydos, Egypt, there exists one of the most extraordinary archae-ological sites ever discovered: a half-ruined temple known as the Osireion. Of its origins we know nothing, but we do know that it was associated with the cult of the Egyptian god Osiris, who dates to the earliest period of Egyptian civilization. The Osiris cult of ancient Egypt was national in scope with two centers, one in the northern delta, at Busiris, and another at Abydos, on the west side of the Nile about three hundred miles south of present-day Cairo. Though the center at Abydos emerged later, because of its central location it drew pilgrims from a much larger region and thus came to far surpass Busiris in importance.

According to Egyptian tradition, Osiris—like Jesus—was both human and divine. The divine genealogy ranks Osiris among the fourth generation of gods, placing him at the dawn of Egyptian culture and religion known as Zep Tepi (the first time). The role of Osiris was pro-found: In Egyptian religion he and his vizier Thoth (Hermes) are cred-ited with teaching mankind the arts of civilization.[28] According to

Plutarch, author of the only surviving account of the legend, Osiris was later slain by his brother, Seth, and was subsequently avenged by his son, Horus. In time, the legend of Osiris and his son became the Egyptian model for kingly rule and royal succession.[29] Each pharaoh was regarded as a reincarnation of Horus and in death became identified with Osiris. The Egyptians apparently believed that Osiris returned again and again to mediate the ascent of the soul of the recently deceased king.

The Greek geographer Strabo was the first to describe the Osireion after touring Egypt in the first century B.C.E., at a time when Egyptian civilization was already in steep decline.[30] Sometime during the next few centuries, the Osireion disappeared from history. It was not rediscovered until the modern age, in the winter of 1901–1902, by the great archaeologist Flinders Petrie while he was investigating the vast temple complex of Pharaoh Seti I at Abydos. During his exploration, Petrie stumbled onto ruins some forty-one feet below the level of Seti's temple. The structure was entirely buried by sand, which probably accounts for its remarkable state of preservation; part of the roof was even intact. Petrie noted that the ruins were very different in style and design from the other nearby temples; the construction comprised cyclopean-sized blocks of red sandstone and granite, some estimated at one hundred tons or more in weight. The enormous blocks used in the roof entablature were a mind-boggling thirty-three feet in length and another large stone bordering the nave was twenty-five feet long. The walls of the inner atrium were bare of the hieroglyphic writing that can be found in most Egyptian temples, including the adjoining complex of Seti I. Petrie and his colleague Margaret Murray realized immediately that the Osireion was of great antiquity.[31] Cyclopean stone architecture is almost unknown in Egypt. In fact, it is found at only one other site: Giza, with its funerary temples and pyramids.

But the archaeologist Henri Frankfort, who led the excavations at Abydos between 1925 and 1930, took issue with Petrie and Murray regarding the age of the structure. He favored a much more recent date, proposing that the temple had been constructed at about the same time

as the nearby temple of Seti I (that is, in the middle of the second millennium B.C.E.) He also insisted that the structure was the cenotaph of
the god Osiris.[32]

Frankfort's views became part of the canon of archaeology, and
over the years have seldom been disputed. Recently, however, a maverick writer, Graham Hancock, did challenge them, suggesting that Petrie
and Murray's earlier hunch was the correct one.[33] If this is the case, the
Osireion is among the oldest structures on the planet.

No less remarkable than the megalithic scale of the Osireion was its
design, especially its placement more than forty feet below the desert.
There was a clear purpose for this: namely, to situate the structure in
relation to the water table, which even today lies just beneath the temple's stone floor. The dimensions of the Osireion are about one hundred
feet by sixty feet, enclosing a large central chamber described by
Margaret Murray as a hypogeum.[34] The remains of massive outer walls
that once surrounded and enclosed this inner chamber are some twenty
feet thick, and are constructed of gigantic blocks of red sandstone fit-
ted together in jigsaw fashion with incredible precision.

Over the course of two full work seasons (1913–1914), hired workers laboriously removed thousands of tons of desert sand from the
Osireion. When the stone pavement of the inner court was finally laid
bare, two pools and a moat were revealed. The pools were found to be
shallow, but this was not the case with the seven-foot-wide moat, which
encircled the stone floor of the central atrium, effectively making it an
island. In the process of clearing away the sand, steps emerged that had
been cut into the stone foundation leading down into the moat. As
more sand was removed, there occurred a rapid infiltration of water
from below until, despite thousands of years of total neglect, the pools
and moat were completely filled—no doubt just as the original builders
had intended.[35] All of this seemed to confirm Strabo's description of "a
remarkable structure built of solid stone . . . [containing] a spring which
lies at a great depth, so that one descends to it down vaulted galleries
made of monoliths of surpassing size and workmanship."[36] Soon after
the discovery of the moat, Margaret Murray wrote that the ruin

"appears to Dr. Petrie to be the place that Strabo mentions, usually called Strabo's well."[37] Interestingly, geological work done on site by H. F. Ferrar in 1914 established that the pools and moat were, in fact, not fed by a spring as Strabo believed, but by a desert aquifer that was (and is) continually recharged by the nearby river. The aquifer fans out from the Nile in the manner of a broad sheet—a slow-moving river of water beneath the desert.[38]

But perhaps the most amazing feature of the Osireion's moat was its great depth, which was not easily determined, even after it was cleared of sand and rubble. In his memoir Henri Frankfort recounts the unsuccessful attempts to probe the depths with a fifteen-foot pole. Only after a mechanical pump was brought in and used to draw down the water by some thirteen feet did he finally discover the bottom twenty-five and a half feet below the level of the court.[39] The moat followed the stone foundation all the way down to solid bedrock, indicating just how integral it was to the design of the temple.

The Osireion's massive stone foundations were essential to support its enormous weight. Deep retaining walls were also uncovered some distance away from the temple, paralleling its outer walls; their placement was apparently a check against subsidence and prevented the sands from shifting around the foundation. In the process of clearing the moat, workers also discovered enormous stone thrust beams connecting the outer walls of the temple with the central atrium. They had been installed to add support and crossed the moat some thirteen feet below the level of the court. Professor Edouard Naville, who led the excavations at Abydos during 1913 and 1914, concluded that the temple was "a large reservoir where water was stored during the high Nile."[40]

No one has yet explained how the builders of the Osireion overcame the Herculean problems associated with constructing such an imposing megalithic structure atop a live aquifer. Nor has archaeology determined the temple's purpose. Naville, who, like Petrie and Murray, was convinced of the Osireion's great antiquity, believed that the structure was "neither a temple nor a tomb, but a gigantic pool, a water-work . . ."[41]

Frankfort's theory that it was a cenotaph of the god Osiris barely scratches the surface. If form follows function, then the very design of the structure offers an important clue to its purpose. The fact that the moat transformed the Osireion's central court into an island is significant given the ancient Egyptian belief that every temple embodied the religious concept of the primeval hill or mound that supposedly had emerged from the primordial waters at Creation. This very idea was plainly engineered into the Osireion. It is also significant that the moat was designed with steps to afford easy access to the aquifer. Did the religious life of the Osireion involve purificatory immersions in the lower waters of the abyss? The stone steps into the moat recall the tanks of Khirbet Qumran, which many scholars believe was the site of the Essene community that produced the Dead Sea Scrolls. Some of the tanks at Qumran were almost certainly used for baptismal immersions—lustrations had long been a part of Jewish tradition. Yet it must be conceded that the rock pools of Qumran are primitive compared to the awe-inspiring, monolithic interior of the Osireion. Nor is the Osireion the only evidence attesting to the ancient practice of purificatory bathing. In a series of articles beginning in 1920, W. F. Albright documented the existence of a "cult of water" in Mesopotamia, which he traced to the upper Euphrates valley around 2800 B.C.E. and which apparently survived to as late as the third century C.E. Based on his research, Albright believed that the practice of ceremonial bathing had originated not with the Hebrews, but with their Semitic ancestors in Mesopotamia. Whether Albright knew of the pools and moat of the Osireion is doubtful; his published books make no mention of Abydos.[42]

OSIRIS = UPPER WATERS

To the ancient Egyptians, the Nile had cosmological significance above and beyond its practical importance: The river's waxing and waning beautifully expressed the unending process of creation, death, and renewal—levels of meaning that may have been reenacted during the annual eight-day Osiris festival at Abydos. While we know very little about the festival, its events may have included dramatizations, perhaps even a passion play about the god's death and resurrection. We do know that Osiris, passive in death, represented the ebbing of life that occurs in Egypt during the seasonal drought. At this time of year the desert heat lies upon the land of Egypt like death itself and every living thing wilts, even in the fertile valley of the Nile. But the dead god also contained within himself the latent regenerative force of nature, and in this respect Osiris resembled other vegetation gods such as Adonis, Attis, Tammuz, and Dumuzi.

The multifaceted Osiris, however, was much more than just a vegetation god; he fired the emotions of the people like no other Egyptian deity—he seems to have inspired true devotion.[43] In Plutarch's account of Osiris, the only surviving record of the tragic story, the dead god calls out for help. His plea is answered by his son, Horus, who descends into the underworld to perform over the corpse of his father the ceremonies that the Egyptians believed were absolutely essential for the soul of Osiris to ascend to the stars. We know that astronomy was integral to the legend. The Egyptians linked Osiris with the constellation Orion and Isis, his wife-sister, with Sirius, the Dog Star. These star connections were incredibly precise, yet their actual significance remains shrouded in mystery.[44]

The funerary rites that were viewed as essential to ensure the ascent of the dead pharaoh's soul (equated with Osiris) were not public events, and thus were not a part of the Abydos festival. They coincided with the annual rising of the Nile and, though we cannot be certain, were presumably conducted by priests within the temples at Giza and Abydos. Thus, the flooding of the river was linked with the agricultural stirring of the dead land, the return (or reawakening?) of Osiris, and the ascent of the dead king's soul. In Utterance 670 of the Pyramid Texts, which date to the time of the Old Kingdom and are the most ancient religious scriptures ever found in Egypt, we read: "O Osiris the King, you have gone, but you will return, you have slept, [but you will awaken], you have died, but you will live."[45]

From the standpoint of our investigation, the Pyramid Texts are extremely important because they clarify the relationship between Osiris and the waters. We have explored the belief, universal in the ancient world, that the lower waters of the abyss formed the foundation of every temple. We have also shown in our discussion of the Osireion that this idea was not simply an abstraction but was architecturally expressed in grand fashion. Given this incorporation of the lower waters, it is of great interest that a passage in the Pyramid Texts explicitly identifies Osiris himself with the upper waters. Utterance 366 states that Osiris is:

> The Great Circle, in your name of "Great Surround,"
> an enveloping ring, in the "Ring that encircles the Outermost lands,"
> a Great Circle in the Great Round of the Surrounding Ocean.[46]

What is striking here is the similarity of these words to those of Lord Krishna as recounted in chapter 10 of an extremely ancient Hindu scripture known as the Bhagavad Gita:

> I am the eternal serpent, the joined ends of which are a symbol of
> the beginningless and endless ring of eternity. Among the creatures
> of the deep, I am the God of the Ocean. I am the judge of the Day
> of Judgment. I am spirit.

The two passages are nearly identical, and clearly have the same meaning. This raises important questions: May we conclude on this basis that Lord Krishna and Osiris were parallel figures? Did they occupy a similar historical and religious niche? If so, what about Jesus, whom many contemporary Hindus regard as a reincarnation of Krishna? Scholarship, of course, cannot provide a final answer to these questions, at least not without additional evidence, but the questions are no less intriguing.

In his classic study *Myth and Symbol in Ancient Egypt*, the respected Egyptologist R. T. Rundle Clark mentions Utterance 366, but almost as an afterthought, as if he does not quite know what to make of it. He certainly does not stress its importance. This is noteworthy because if the waters were not of paramount importance, then why did the Egyptians go to such lengths to incorporate the idea into the design of the Osireion? The temple's remarkable construction required a supreme commitment of resources and labor and a level of engineering acumen so dazzling that thousands of years later it has yet to be explained.

There is no reason to doubt the equation Osiris = Ocean (the upper waters). Plutarch repeats the formula without equivocation.[47] So does the Naassene scribe in his Sermon (*Refutation* 5.7.23), which likely was not based on Plutarch's account; he was, after all, an outsider to Egyptian tradition. Surely the scribe, writing in Alexandria, had access to native source material. In any event, the formula equating Osiris and the upper waters can be independently verified from the inscriptions and artistic carvings discovered by Petrie and Murray at Abydos.[48]

We can draw a number of conclusions from all of this: The upper waters clearly represented a higher plane of existence beyond ordinary human ken—the realm of the gods, tantamount to the world of the Spirit. The waters here are nothing less than the upper firmament mentioned in Genesis—also synonymous with the "living waters" mentioned in the New Testament (John 4:14). The diverse Gnostic sects who differed with one another and with orthodox Christians on so many issues appear to have been in agreement on this. Hippolytus quotes at length from one of these Gnostics (*Refutation* 5.27.1–3) whose name was Justinus: "There is a distinction between water and water," the heretic writes. He goes on to describe the upper waters as "the living waters" and says that to drink of them is to be baptized in the Spirit. Justinus refuses to elaborate further, however: "I swear by him who is above all things . . . to preserve these mysteries and to declare them to no one . . . ." But why such secrecy? Justinus tells us in the very next line: because drinking of the upper waters involves seeing "what eye has not seen and ear has not heard and has not occurred to the human mind." Here the heretic Justinus sounds exactly like the Gnostic Paul! (See 2 Corinthians 12:1–6.) He has no such reticence, however, when it comes to discussing the lower waters. He describes them with the alienated repugnance of the world so typical of Gnostics in general.

Yet we know that the upper and lower waters were connected. Homer tells us that the lower waters somehow flowed from the upper. The *Iliad* mentions "the great strength of deep-flowing Ocean [the upper waters], from whom flow all the rivers, every sea, and all the springs and the deep wells."[49] Homer restates here the general principle of the downward-flowing river that manifests the physical world, a theme repeated in the Naassene Sermon. But why were the ancient temples said to be founded upon the lower waters? Did the Egyptians, for instance, associate the annual rise in the water level of the Osireion's moat and pools with a resurgence of the Spirit? Did they believe that the annual flood—the return of the god Osiris (the upper waters)—purified and resacralized the space within the temple? Is it coincidence that in ancient Egypt the annual Nile flood was said to flow from the thigh of Osiris?[50] We will return to this question shortly.

According to Strabo, a boat canal once linked the Osireion with the Nile, some eight miles distant.[51] The location of this canal has yet to be discovered, but we know for certain that a canal system did exist at Giza and Thebes and that at least one other ancient text refers to canals at Abydos.[52] Indeed, similar waterways probably linked many of the great temples to the Nile and hence to one another. The river and its canal system, which was still intact in Roman times, was the super-highway of ancient Egypt; it was essential for commerce but was also used during the funerary processions of the dead pharaohs, who were carried in royal barques to their elaborately prepared tombs at Abydos, the Valley of the Kings, and elsewhere. The timing of the funereal rites with the inundation ensured that they would be performed at the most propitious moment of the year, coincident with the return of Osiris (Spirit), thereby ensuring that the dead pharaoh's soul would ascend to the stars.

THE EGYPTIAN DRAGON FIGHT

The Canaanite and Babylonian accounts of the dragon fight already discussed in this chapter have their Egyptian counterpart in the legendary duel between Seth (Set) and Horus, the son of Osiris. The Egyptologist E. A. Wallis Budge, former keeper of antiquities at the British Museum, believed that this duel was the prototype for all subsequent dragon fights.[53] Yet Budge's comparison is somewhat misleading, because it fails to account for an important feature of the Osiris myth.

In its earliest form the mythical fight between Horus and primeval chaos paralleled the Mesopotamian account,[54] but the earliest versions did not involve Seth, the murderer of Osiris. Apparently there were a number of different recensions,[55] one of which describes a time after Creation when the forces of chaos survive in the form of a monstrous serpent named Aapep. Each day before dawn the fight to maintain order must be rejoined by Horus lest Aapep succeed in preventing the sun from sailing across the sky. Each day the monster must be defeated anew and bound in chains, just as Tiamat's progeny were bound in Marduk's net and just as Satan was bound and cast into the pit in the Book of Revelation.[56] While in later times the villain Seth came to be identified with this early monster, originally he represented the principle of limitation and human mortality. This explains why the dead pharaoh's body was embalmed; it had to be protected at all costs from Seth, who governed the natural process of death and the forces of putrefaction. The king's soul could ascend only in the propitious season, and so his body had to be preserved in the meantime.

Who, then, was Osiris and what was his role? Although Osiris and the monster Aapep (the Egyptian Tiamat) were both associated with the upper waters, the two could not be more different. The distinction between them illustrates the multivalent nature of the waters theme. Osiris (symbolizing Spirit) stands in relation to Aapep (representing chaos) as the Naassene Redeemer (Jesus) stands in relation to the Old Testament monster Leviathan (Rahab) and the Canaanite Yamm. In his commentary on the Osiris legend, the former Massachusetts Institute of Technology historian William Irwin Thompson argued that in its spiritual heyday the Osiris cult, far from being a primitive religion, was a full-fledged initiatory tradition comparable to the yoga traditions of present-day India.[57] If this is true, then Egyptian religion sprang up around Osiris in a remote age in the same manner that Hinduism coalesced around Lord Krishna and Christianity around Jesus—in which case Osiris and Krishna also deserve the title Son of Man.

Are there clues in Egypt's strange funeral rites supporting this idea? We know that the funerary processions of the dead pharaohs began at Giza during the summer flooding of the Nile, which during the pyramid age was heralded by the heliacal rising of Sirius, the brightest star in the heavens. According to the Pyramid Texts, the funeral barques proceeded upstream, against the flow of the river:

> Wake up for Horus, stand up against Seth; raise yourself, O Osiris, first born son of Geb [the earth god], at whom the Two Enneads tremble. The herdsman waits on you, the festival of the new moon is celebrated for you, so that you may appear at the monthly festival. Fare southward [upstream] to the lake, cross over the sea, for you are he who stands untiring in the midst of Abydos; be a spirit in the horizon, be long-enduring in Mendes.[58]

Another passage reads:

> Betake yourself to the waterway, fare upstream to the Thinnite nome, travel about Abydos in this spirit-form of yours which the gods commanded to belong to you; may a stairway to the Duat be set up for you to the place where Orion is, may the Bull of the sky take your hand, may you eat of the food of the gods.[59]

The word Ennead refers to the familiar theogony, the generation of the gods. A *nome* was apparently a political subdivision, similar to a state or province. *Duat* is a mysterious word that possibly refers to the world of Spirit, though its precise meaning has never been determined. "Orion" refers to the constellation of the same name, and the "Bull of the Sky" may be another. While the text remains obscure, its references to upstream movement are unmistakable. Many centuries later, a similar idea resurfaced in Greek mythology in Hesiod's description of the river Styx:

> There dwells a goddess loathed by the gods,
> dreadful Styx, eldest daughter of Ocean whose stream
> flows back on itself; she dwells apart from the gods
> in a stately palace roofed by lofty rocks and ringed
> by silver pillars that tower into the sky.[60]

According to Greek myth, the Styx, which was both river and goddess, was the most important branch of Ocean, the Greek equivalent of the upper waters of Genesis.[61] According to the Roman writer Virgil, the Styx ran nine times around Hades, the Greek nether realm or land of the dead.[62] Its cold dark waters were said to be the stuff by which the gods swore great oaths. Indeed, so potent were its waters that if a god swore falsely, he or she would be damned to lie in a coma for a period of time, then face a further punishment: ostracism by the rest of the gods. It is of interest that the length of this sentence increased from the early period of Greek civilization to classical times. In Hesiod's day (eighth century B.C.E.) the period of ostracism was nine years; by the time of Empedocles (fifth century B.C.E.), the sentence had increased to 30,000 years.[63]

Why were these waters that flowed backward into the nether realm so sacred that not even a god could violate them with impunity? The answer is that despite their conspicuous polytheism, the Greeks understood—at least, in their sober moments—that the gods of Olympus were not the final authority. There was a higher power, a more inclusive law, an ultimate truth or All to which even the gods served obeisance. In this regard the Greeks were no different from their tutors, the Egyptians. The later Greeks referred to the primal entity as Phanes or Protogonos, the first-begotten one. The Egyptians had many names, but perhaps the most important, as we have noted, was Atum, the self-created.

THE BAPTIST AND THE NEW RESTORATION

The ministries of John the Baptist and Jesus take on new meaning in light of our exploratory plunge into the primordial waters. According to the biblical scholar Robert Eisler, John's ministry derived primarily from two Old Testament sources: the Flood of Genesis and the vision of Ezekiel (Ezekiel 47). To this we might also add the apocalypse of Zechariah 14. In his brilliant study *Orpheus the Fisher,* Eisler claimed that the Baptist, as the son of a priest, was fully versed in the legend of the *eben shethiya,* the bolt or foundation stone beneath the temple, the stone that modulated the lower waters.[64]

Eisler also made note of the waters of the Torah, which, according to rabbinic tradition, Yahweh revealed to Moses as he wandered in the desert. Even when destructive, the lower waters served heaven's purpose, which was purification. John may have viewed his ministry of repentance in precisely these terms. Perhaps he foresaw the coming storm that in just a few years would overwhelm the nation. Judaism had long prescribed ritual immersions for Gentile converts, but John believed that the children of Israel had abandoned "God the fountain of living water" (Jeremiah 2:13), and for this reason he exhorted them to renew their birthright through a symbolic drowning of their old sinful selves in the purifying waters. Those who repented or "turned back" (Zechariah 1:5, Jeremiah 25:5) would become the survivors of the approaching cataclysm, just as Noah and his kin had survived the Flood. Indeed, the meaning of Noah, "God is appeased," suggests this interpretation.[65] The baptized few would swim in the waters of the Torah just as the fishes swam in the waters that flowed from beneath the temple into the Jordan (Ezekiel 47). The purified few would survive to participate in the new restoration (Tikkun). Eisler's plausible interpretation is perfectly consistent with the Naassene Sermon.

IMPLICATION OF THE BODY AS TEMPLE

But John's ministry of repentance involving the lower waters was only the prelude to the main event. The deeper mystery involved the descent of Spirit (the upper waters) upon Jesus at the Jordan. We are informed that the miracle occurs in the very moment when Jesus comes up out of the river (Mark 1:10, Matthew 3:16). Scripture here reaffirms the ancient language of the "double deep." Given the new teaching that the human body is the true temple of the Spirit, the implications—including the direct knowledge of sacred anatomy, which was surely the most closely guarded secret of Gnosticism—are astounding. If the body is the true temple, then the watery foundations must stand in relation to the body, which recalls the ancient Egyptian belief that the waters flowed from the thigh of Osiris. Did the lower waters refer in some mysterious way to the sacral-pelvis? The joined bones of the sacrum and pelvis together literally mean "sacred basin." The very name suggests a half-forgotten knowledge of sacred anatomy.[66] Might the lower waters of the Torah be said to lie in this basin? Yes, though it is not enough simply to swim in the lower waters. The lower realm must be resacralized, by mingling its waters with the upper "living water" (John 4:14, Jeremiah 17:13). The Naassene scribe informs us that the Redeemer Jesus accomplished this by reversing the flow of the river, or, in the old mythological language, by turning the river back upon itself (*Refutation* 5.7.41).

This Naassene interpretation accords perfectly with all that we have said about the symbols of the Grail and the stone, which, as it happens, are nearly equivalent. In *Parsival,* for example, the German version of the Grail legend, a stone actually replaces the chalice. Both stone and Grail refer to God's immanence.[67] He who knows the mystery of Adamas, the bolt from the deep, the *eben shethiyah,* has already gained access to heaven's gate.

14

The Incomprehensible One

No man can see me, and live . . .

EXODUS 33:20

But the Advocate, the Holy Spirit,
whom the Father will send in my name,
will teach you everything . . .

JOHN 14:26

You will see heaven laid open, and above the Son of
Man, the angels of God ascending and descending . . .

JOHN 1:51

IN JUDAISM IT WAS AXIOMATIC: Man cannot know God. The face of the Almighty was too awesome to behold; no man could survive the experience. The purpose of the famous curtain that hung in the temple of Jerusalem was to shield the priests from the power, the glory, and the wrath that would destroy them if they gazed upon the holy of holies.[1]

Jesus, however, rendered the curtain obsolete, along with the old temple traditions. Indeed, it was his firsthand knowledge of the God who dwells within the human heart—the true holy of holies—that illuminated his opposition to every form of superstitious nonsense, especially the Old Testament belief in a vindictive God. By insisting that the Father is a God of love, not of wrath and vengeance, Jesus broke sharply with the past and even turned tradition on its head.

But there was more: Jesus left his disciples with the solemn promise that the Spirit would be made available for the purpose of teaching them all things (John 14:26, 16:13). Henceforth, by means of the Spirit, a man or a woman could know the Father through the Son (John 14:6–7). Ordinary people could duplicate Jesus' achievement, and in large numbers become the Sons of Man. Thus, direct knowledge of the Godhead was made available to the many. It was a revolution in the art of the possible. But no sooner did Jesus set all of this in motion than the institutional Church turned its back on and even suppressed the Wisdom teachings, thus aborting the incipient spiritual revolution. This explains why in orthodox Christianity there is only one meager firsthand account of gnosis: Paul's testimony regarding the third heaven (II Corinthians 12). No wonder that over the centuries so many Christians despaired of Jesus' promise.

The Naassene Sermon takes up the issue of knowing the Father (gnosis) precisely where Paul leaves off. The Sermon identifies the Father by a family of names, which recur throughout the text and include the Preexistent One, the Unportrayable One, and the Incomprehensible One—significantly, names that also appear in several gospels of the Nag Hammadi library.[2]

But the Naassene scribe is not satisfied merely to identify the various names; in his Sermon he goes on to describe an elevated spiritual state that is nothing less than the face of the Almighty itself. Employing the language of symbolism, he affords his reader an existential and phenomenological glimpse of the absolute pinnacle of religion—an achievement for which there was no precedent in first-century Judaism. Not only is there nothing like it in the Old Testament, but there also appears to be nothing similar in all of the vast literature of Christianity. The Naassene account stands alone, a precious jewel.

The discussion of the Father begins with a cryptic passage, involving the obscure term Amigdalus (*Refutation* 5.9.1), meaning "almond." In our time the word is used in medical anatomy, and refers to a part of the human brain. The Sermon informs us that Amigdalus is the Father of the universe, ". . . having in himself the perfect fruit, as it were, throbbing and moving in his depth . . ." The text, minus the interpolated comments of Hippolytus, continues:

> The Spirit . . . is there where . . . the father is named, and the Son is there born from this Father. This . . . is the many-named thousand-eyed Incomprehensible One, of whom every nature—each, differently—is desirous. This . . . is the word of God, which is a word of revelation of the Great Power. Wherefore it will be sealed, and hid, and concealed, lying in the habitation where lies the basis for the root of the Universe: aeons, powers, intelligences, gods, angels, delegated spirits, entities, nonentities, generables, ingenerables, incomprehensibles, years, months, days, hours, [and the] indivisible point from which what is least begins to increase gradually. That which is . . . nothing and which consists of nothing, inasmuch as it is indivisible—a point—will become through its own reflective power an incomprehensible magnitude. This . . . is the kingdom of heaven, the grain of mustard seed, the point which is indivisible within the body. And . . . nobody knows this point save the spiritual only. (*Refutation* 5.9.4–6)

Here we have a description of gnosis. Notice, the text mentions the "indivisible point," which we have already identified as bindu. The text also mentions the mustard seed (Mark 4:31–32, Matthew 13:31–32, Luke 13:18–19), though in a context that pushes the concept far beyond anything in the New Testament. Suddenly we are on ground uncharted by orthodox Christianity.

Yet what is perhaps most startling about the above passage is its perfect congruence with a portion of another ancient manuscript, known today as the Egyptian Book of the Dead, whose name likely bears no relation to the manuscript's original religious purpose. Apparently there were a number of different recensions in use in Egypt in the pharaonic age. The one that Sir Wallis Budge drew from in preparing the first English translation is known as the Papyrus of Ani. The Book of the Dead was already ancient when the Naassene Sermon was composed in the early period of Christianity, yet it includes a description of the Egyptian God Re (or Ra) that bears a striking resemblance to the passage from the Sermon quoted above:

> This holy God, the lord of all the gods . . . the holy Soul who came into being in the beginning, the great God who lives upon truth, the first God of primeval time, the Being through whom every other god has existence . . . the Being whose birth is hidden, whose evolutions are manifold, whose growth is incomprehensible . . . traverser of eternity, the aged One who renews his youth, who possesses myriads of pairs of eyes, and innumerable pairs of ears . . .[3]

This image of the Divine Being drawn from ancient Egyptian religion is almost identical with that described in the Naassene Sermon. Obviously, the Egyptians had a much more advanced God concept than most of us moderns have been willing to concede. Skeptics, of course, will object here in the strongest of terms. They will dispute the textual evidence, very predictably asserting that this strange concurrence means absolutely nothing, because—they will argue—the Naassene Sermon itself is nothing but an ersatz fabrication, entirely derivative from some ancient pagan text. They will argue: Were not the Naassenes based in Alexandria? Yes, indeed, and for this reason they surely had access to many original pagan manuscripts (as I have already noted). Therefore, you see, it is all so obvious: The text has nothing to do with the Father mentioned by Jesus. The Naassene scribe merely copied the heathen language from some ancient Egyptian original—end of story.

This objection is predictable and may even sound persuasive on its face. It cannot stand, however, because the very same description of the Father can also be found in Hindu accounts, both ancient and contemporary. For example, it can be found in *Play of Consciousness,* the spiritual autobiography of Swami Muktananda, a Hindu saint whose life and attainments are extremely well documented. Swami Muktananda was the third Indian yogi (after Vivekananda and Yogananda) to visit the West in modern times, first coming to America in 1969. Muktananda's book includes one of the most detailed accounts of kundalini yoga ever published. In it the saint describes his many years of spiritual wandering across India in search of his guru; his spiritual initiation by the God-man Nityananda; his subsequent meditation/yoga practices, including the awakening and movement of spiritual energy through his body, the spontaneous yogic breathing *(pranayama),* and the many spontaneous cleansing movements *(kriyas* and *mudras)* that he experienced; and much more.

One of the experiences he describes is an obvious parallel to Ezekiel 12:22–27. Indeed, the resemblance is so astonishing that Muktananda's description might have been drawn verbatim from the Old Testament. In the Book of Ezekiel the prophet tells how the Spirit entered him during one of his famous visions: He is commanded by Yahweh to shut himself inside his house. There, presumably while sitting in meditation, "bonds" are laid upon his flesh. His tongue is made to stick to the roof of his mouth, which renders him "dumb." Now, compare this physical description with a portion of Muktananda's account relating his own experience:

> I got up every morning to sit for meditation, and as soon as I sat down I was seized by a powerful force . . . I . . . experienced a number of *mudras* . . . There was the *nabho mudra,* in which my tongue was stuck against my palate, and my breath retained.[4]

This phenomenon of the tongue spontaneously pressing up against the palate is well known in the yoga systems, and is said to lead to the even more advanced *kechari mudra,* involving the total reversion of the tongue associated with the opening of the higher spiritual centers in the head.

The Naassene description of Amigdalus "throbbing and moving in his depth . . ." finds resonance in Muktananda's spiritual tradition of Kashmir Shaivism. In Shaivism the first act of Creation is described as a throb or pulse *(spanda)*, motion out of motionless Shiva (Brahman), which then manifests the universe. According to Hinduism, this first spark of Creation did not happen once upon a time; it is an ongoing process, a dance without beginning and without end. It is said that the Lord of the universe has shrunk himself into an infinitesimal jot, which lies hidden within the body of the spiritual seeker—the very same idea expressed in the Naassene Sermon, and remarkably similar to the Gnostic idea of the spinther.

In the Eastern traditions the rediscovery of this indivisible point or seed is regarded as the goal of all spiritual practice because it leads to the experience of the divine Self (God realization). Indian scriptures metaphorically describe the jot, or bindu, as a sesame seed, which accords perfectly with the mustard seed mentioned in the Naassene Sermon and described in Matthew 13:31. (See also Mark 4:31–32 and Luke 13:18–19.) In the parable, the mustard seed "is the smallest of all the seeds, but when it has grown it is the biggest shrub of all and becomes a tree so that the birds of the air come and shelter in its branches." In Kashmir Shaivism this jot or seed, also known as the blue pearl, is said to spring forth spontaneously from the eyes of the yogi and dance before him as he sits in deep meditation. Swami Muktananda writes: "It is a tiny blue light. Its effulgence is enchanting. Who can describe its beauty?"[5] Eventually, this seed assumes a human shape, a "blue person," an exceedingly rare vision that Hindus regard as the ultimate realization of God as form. Muktananda recounts his sublime experience:

> The wonderfully radiant blue pearl, with its countless different rays shining from within, came closer to me and began to grow. It assumed the shape of an egg and continued to grow into a human shape . . . Suddenly a divine radiance burst forth from it . . . What a beautiful form he had . . . He wore on his head a crown set with

nine jewels. These were not inert material creations of this earth, but were composed of pure consciousness . . . He came toward me, making a soft humming sound, and made some kind of gesture . . . He walked right around me and stood still. Then, looking at me, he made a sign with his eyes. Then he said, "I see everything from everywhere. I see with my eyes. I see with my nose. I have eyes everywhere." He lifted up his foot and said, "I see with this foot, too. I can see everywhere. I have tongues everywhere. I speak not just with my tongue, but also with my hand, and with my foot. I have ears everywhere."[6]

There can be no mistake: It is the same Incomprehensible One described in the Egyptian Book of the Dead and in the Naassene Sermon. Muktananda goes on to explain that later he found a similar description of this blue person in the Bhagavad Gita (13:13–14): "He has hands and feet everywhere. He has eyes, heads, and faces, on all sides. He has ears everywhere. He knows all and exists pervading all."

Although no similar description from Babylon or ancient Sumer has yet come to light, it is quite possible that a Mesopotamian counterpart will eventually be discovered among the hundreds of thousands of cuneiform tablets from Ra's Shamra, Mari, Nineveh, Nippur, and other sites that gather dust in the museums of the world for want of enough trained scholars to decipher them. Although we should expect a Mesopotamian counterpart to be crafted in the distinctive language of the Babylonians or Sumerians, the unmistakable image of the many-eyed Incomprehensible One will nonetheless be immediately recognizable.

GOD WITHOUT FORM

The vision of the blue person, the Incomprehensible One, was not quite the end of Muktananda's spiritual journey. He goes on to describe his final dissolution into absolute consciousness: the experience of God without Form. When this occurred to Muktananda, the blue dot that for months had poised shimmering before him in his meditations suddenly expanded to encompass the entire universe, taking his essence along with it. This was the final breakthrough and the end of Muktananda's puny ego. His description in *Play of Consciousness* is eerily similar to the Naassene Sermon's account of the "infinitesimal point" that becomes "through its own reflective power an incomprehensible magnitude" (*Refutation 5.9.5*). Nor can there be any doubt that the Naassene text is describing here an actual experience, rather than a process of Creation, for in the very next line the scribe informs us: "No one knows this point except the spiritual only."

Clearly the Father is more than capable of revealing himself to worthy individuals of whatever faith and whatever period in human history, and has likely done so innumerable times. Are those who would dispute this so arrogant as to think they know the mind of God? This is precisely the attitude of parsimonious Christians who insist upon their own exclusivity.

LAST THOUGHTS

We who live in the present age are continually dogged by the past because of our deep need to come to terms with the human predicament. Today our noble endeavor to understand ourselves has never been more urgent. We live, after all, in a time of quickening, information overload, and rapid technological advance. As the future rushes upon us, mere knowledge avails us very little because each new answer, each new technological "fix," only confounds us with a dozen new questions and myriad confusing possibilities. The achievements of science cannot explain—in fact, do not even begin to explain—the deeper mystery of our existence. Even in the midst of scientific discovery we find ourselves traversing dim regions. The more we amass empirical knowledge, the more we seem to grasp at phantoms. The farther we advance, the more a final answer—truth—eludes us. Nearly two centuries ago Thomas Chalmers clearly described our predicament when he wrote in his critique of science: "[T]he greater the circle of light the greater the circumference of darkness . . ." Yes, and the only power capable of dispersing that darkness is gnosis. Eighteen hundred years ago the Gnostic Christian Naassenes understood this more clearly than do we sophisticated moderns.

In the ancient world the mythological symbol of the waters had a universal currency. Jesus clearly built upon this foundation and used it to introduce the teaching of God's immanence, unprecedented in Judaism, involving the direct experience of our own divinity and a comprehensive awareness of sacred anatomy. The association of a new idea with a known quantity is a familiar teaching device. Yet within three centuries of the crucifixion the mystical teachings of Jesus had been all but extinguished in the West. Fortunately, as we have learned, those same teachings survive today in the flourishing yoga traditions of India. Rudyard Kipling was miles wide of the mark when he wrote that "East is East and West is West, and never the twain shall meet." The truth is that they have already met, for East or West, gnosis remains the same. The Absolute never changes—good news for Christians in search of their own roots.

APPENDIX 1

The Refutation of All Heresies Book 5

MANY YEARS AGO the scholar Richard Reitzenstein coined the name Naassene Sermon in reference to the first chapters of Book 5 of the *Refutation of All Heresies,* the text of which appears on the following pages. Readers should understand that this is my own compilation of the Sermon based on the three available translations from the original Greek. I have relied most heavily on Birdsall's translation, which was a part of his doctoral dissertation ("The Naassene Sermon and the Allegorical Tradition," Ph.D. dissertation, Claremont Graduate University, 1984). Birdsall is often preferable because of his superior rendering of those passages pertaining to immanence. I have also drawn from Rev. J. H. MacMahon's translation (*The Refutation of All Heresies,* Edinburgh: T. and T. Clark, 1868) and F. Legge's edition (*The Philosophumena,* London: Society for Promoting Christian Knowledge, 1921). My goal has been to make the Sermon as accessible as possible to modern readers.

The endnotes to this appendix represent the best of MacMahon, Legge, and Birdsall, as well as those of G. R. S. Mead, but also include a few of my own. In addition, I've provided a glossary (see appendix 2) to aid in the understanding of unfamiliar words or concepts. In those few cases where the text of the *Refutation* remains unclear, I have followed

Birdsall's practice of retaining the original Greek. I have also preserved Greek nomenclature throughout (e.g., Hermes instead of Mercury, Cronus instead of Saturn, Zeus instead of Jupiter).

It is noteworthy that in his 1921 translation F. Legge inserted the name Joshua for Jesus in the crucial line referring to the scene at the Jordan (*Refutation* 5.7.41), indicating that he believed the text refers in this case to the Book of Joshua. This error is understandable because the names Jesus and Joshua are nearly identical; both derive from Yeshua, and Birdsall's translation ("Jesus/Joshua") reflects this. Still, the context of the Sermon excludes Joshua: According to tradition, Joshua halted the Jordan by means of the Ark of the Covenant, but he did not reverse the river's direction. Legge's mistranslation of this key passage indicates that he failed to recognize this distinction and thus missed the central Naassene idea of the reversal of the flow. Rev. MacMahon deserves credit for getting it right in his 1868 translation.

I have employed F. Legge's numbering system for books, chapters, and verses (e.g., *Refutation* 5.7.15) because it is the standard in use among scholars. I have also preserved Rev. MacMahon's chapter headings. Please note that each of the bracketed interpolations appearing throughout the text is the work of one of the three translators.

Although Hippolytus mentions several other heretical sects in the opening paragraphs of Book 5 (the Peratae, the Sethians, and Justinus), I have omitted the subsequent chapters concerning these sects. With a very few exceptions, their beliefs are not pertinent to our study of the Gnostic Christian Naassenes.

G. R. S. MEAD'S KEY

Mead employed the letter *H* to designate the voice of Bishop Hippolytus; *C* to designate the voice of the Christian scribe; and *J* to designate the voice of the Jewish Christian who, in his view, preceded the Christian scribe and overwrote the original pagan voice, designated as *S*. I have retained this system (bolding these single-letter designations throughout the text) with some slight modifications. As I've already made clear, I don't agree that the pagan voice is the original source; I believe that the Naassene scribe simply appropriated older pagan material. In addition, I hold that the distinction between Christian and Jewish Christian voices is unnecessary; I would equate *J* and *C*.

BOOK 5: THE NAASSENE SERMON

5.1.1 H The following are the contents of the fifth book of the Refutation of All Heresies:

5.2.1 The assertions of the Naassenes, who style themselves Gnostics, and who advance opinions previously propounded by the Greek Philosophers, and by those [pagans] who have handed down mystic [rites]. The Naassenes have constructed their heresies from [both of] these sources.

5.3.1 The tenets of the Peratae, whose system was based on astrology—not on Holy scripture.

5.4.1 The doctrine of the Sethians, who patched together their system by plagiarizing the Greeks, including the following wise men: Musaeus, and Linus and Orpheus.

5.5.1 The tenets of Justinus, based on material furnished by the historian Herodotus—not on Holy scripture.

Chapter 1

5.6.1 H I think that in the four preceding books I have very elaborately explained the opinions propounded by all the speculators among both Greeks and Barbarians, respecting the Divine Nature and the creation of the world. Nor have I omitted the consideration of their systems of magic. Making this information available to my readers has required an extraordinary amount of toil. I have been driven by my anxious desire that many will advance in learning, and in steadfast knowledge of the truth. (2) Therefore, let us hasten on to the refutation of the here-sies, and build on the foundation of the preceding chapters. For from the philosophers the heresiarchs have derived their starting-points, [and], like cobblers, patching together the blunders of the ancients, each according to his particular interpretation, and have advanced them as novelties to those who are susceptible to deception, as we shall prove in the following books. (3) In the remainder [of our work], the opportunity invites us to approach the treatment of our proposed subjects, and to begin with those who have presumed to celebrate a serpent, the origina-tor of the error [in question], through certain expressions devised by the energy of his own [ingenuity]. The priests, then, and first champions of the system [of the serpent], have been called Naassenes, so named from the Hebrew, in which the serpent is called *naas*.[1] (4) And they also call themselves Gnostics, alleging that they alone have sounded the depths of knowledge. Now, from the system of these [speculators], many others, leaving out various parts, have constructed other heresies, which, though each is somewhat different, are essentially one. For one can find the same [tenets], though conveyed under the guise of different opinions, as the following discussion will prove.

These [Naassenes], then, according to the system advanced by them, magnify, [as the originating cause] of all things else: a Man [Anthropos] and a Son of Man. (5) And this Man is a hermaphrodite, and is denomi-nated among them: Adamas. And many and various hymns are made to him. The hymns, however—to be brief—they couch in form as follows: J "From thee [comes] Father, and through thee [comes] Mother, two names immortal, progenitors of Aeons, O denizen of heaven, thou illustrious Man." (6) H But they divide him as Geryon into three parts. For, say they, of this man one part is rational, another psychical, another earthly. And they suppose that the knowledge of him is the originating principle of the capacity for knowledge of God, expressing themselves thus: J "The orig-inating principle of perfection is the knowledge of Man, while the knowl-edge of God is absolute perfection." (7) However, [H the Naassene] says J all these qualities—rational, psychical, and earthly—have derived and descended into one man simultaneously. This is Jesus, who was born of

Mary. And these three men [H the Naassene] says, J are in the habit of speaking [through Jesus] at the same time, all together, each from their own proper substances to those peculiarly their own. For, H according to them, J there are three kinds of things existent—angelic, psychical, earthly. And so there are also three churches—angelic, psychical, and earthly. And their names are: Chosen, Called, and Captive.

Chapter 2

5.7.1 H These are the heads of very numerous discourses that [the Naassene] asserts James the brother of the Lord handed down to Mariamne.[2] In order, then, that these impious [heretics] may no longer speak falsely of Mariamne, James, or the Savior Himself, let us come to the mystic rites [whence comes their fable], both the Barbarian and Greek. And let us see how these [heretics], collecting together the secret and ineffable mysteries of all the Gentiles, are uttering falsehoods against Christ,[3] and making dupes of those who are not acquainted with the Gentiles' secret rites. (2) For their foundational doctrine is the Man, Adamas, and according to them it is written, concerning him, "Who shall declare his generation?,[4] learn how they fictitiously apply this to Christ, partly deriving from the Gentiles the undiscoverable and distinguished generation of man [the biblical Adam].

(3) S "Now earth," say the Greeks, "gave forth a man, first bearing a goodly gift, wishing to become mother not of plants devoid of sense, nor beasts without reason, but of a gentle and highly favored creature." (4) "It, however, is difficult," [H the Naassene says], S "to ascertain whether Alalcomeneus, first of men, rose upon the Boeotians over Lake Cephisis; or whether it were the Idaean Curetes, a divine race; or the Phrygian Corybantes, whom the sun first beheld springing up after the manner of the growth of trees; or whether Arcadia brought forth Pelasgus, of greater antiquity than the moon; or Eleusis [produced] Diaulus, an inhabitant of Raria; or Lemnos begot Cabirus, fair child of secret orgies; or Pallene [brought forth] the Phlegraean Alcyoneus, oldest of the giants.[5] (5) But the Libyans affirm that Iarbas [Garamas] is first born, and on emerging from arid plains commenced eating the

sweet acorn of Zeus. But the Nile of the Egyptians," he says, "up to this day fertilizing mud, [and therefore] generating animals, renders up living bodies, which acquire flesh from moist vapor."[6]

(6) And the Assyrians say that fish-eating Oannes [Iannes] was [the first man] produced in their country. J The Chaldeans, however, claim that Adam [the biblical Adam] was the first, and that he lay inanimate, unmoved, [and] still as a statue, being an image of him who is above, H celebrated [in the hymns] as Adamas [Primal Man], having been begotten by many powers, concerning whom the account is detailed and extensive.

(7) J In order, therefore, that the Great Man [Adamas] from above may be overcome completely, C "from whom," as they say, "the whole family named on earth and in the heavens"[7] J came into being. To him was given also a soul, so that through the soul the enslaved image of the Great and most Glorious and Perfect Man above might suffer and be punished. (8) Then, again, they ask: what is the soul? And whence did it come? And what is its nature, that, coming to the man and moving him, it should enslave and punish the image of the Perfect Man? They do not, however, [on this point] institute an inquiry from the scriptures, but derive this [question] from the mystic [rites]. S And they affirm that the soul is very difficult to discover, and hard to understand; for it does not remain in the same shape or the same form, or in one passive condition, so that one might speak of its character, or comprehend its essence.

(9) H They have these manifold changes [of the soul] set down in the gospel inscribed "according to the Egyptians." J They are, then, in doubt, as all the rest of men among the Gentiles, whether [the soul] is from the Preexistent One [Adamas], or from the Self-begotten [one], or simply from Chaos. And first they fly for refuge to the mysteries of the Assyrians, who believe in the threefold division of man. For the Assyrians were the first to advance the theory that the soul has three parts, yet [is essentially] one. (10) S For every nature, [H he says], S, each in its own way, yearns for soul.[8] For soul is the cause of everything that comes to be, for all things that are nourished and grow, [H the

Naassene says], S require soul. For it is not possible, H he says, S to obtain any nourishment or growth where soul is not present. For even the stones, H he affirms, S have souls, for they have the capacity for growth. But growth cannot take place without nourishment, for it is by addition that things grow, and the addition is the nourishment of things that are being nourished. (11) Every nature, then, of celestial, [H the Naassene says], S and of earthly and subterranean things, desires a soul. The Assyrians call this entity Adonis, or Endymion. And when it is called Adonis, Aphrodite, [H he says], S loves and desires the soul with this name. H According to them, Aphrodite is [associated with] birth. (12) S But when Persephone, also known as Kore, becomes enamored with this same Adonis, there is born, H he says, S a certain mortal soul separated from Aphrodite.[9] But should the Moon [Selene] lust for Endymion, and fall into love of his beauty, the nature, H he says, S of the higher beings also requires a soul. (13) But if, H he says, S the Mother of the gods castrates Attis, even while retaining him as an object of affection, the blessed nature, H he says, S of the super-cosmic and everlasting [beings] alone recalls to itself the masculine power of the soul.

(14) H For [according to the Naassene], S Man's nature is hermaphroditic. H According to this account of theirs, J the intercourse of woman with man is demonstrated, in conformity with such teaching, to be an exceedingly wicked and filthy [practice]. (15) For, [H says the Naassene], J Attis has been cut off, namely, from the earthly parts of creation which came from below, and went over to the everlasting substance above, C where, H he says, C is neither female or male,[10] but a new creature,[11] a new man, which is hermaphroditic. H As to what they mean by the expression "above," I shall explain it when I come to the proper place [for treating this subject].

(16) And they assert that not only Rhea attests to their account, but all of creation. And they declare that this is also what is meant by the saying: C "For the invisible aspects of Him, such as His eternal power and glory, are discernible through the things He has made, perceivable from the creation of the world. And for this reason there is no excuse

for men, who, though they ought to have known God, glorified Him not, nor gave Him thanks; but their foolish heart was rendered vain. (17) For, professing themselves to be wise, they became fools, and changed the glory of the incorruptible God into images of the likeness of corruptible man, and of birds, and four-footed beasts, and creeping things. And so God handed them over to vile passions. For even their women transformed what is natural into that which is perverse," (18) H what they believe as natural we will declare later. C "And likewise also their men, leaving the natural use of woman, burned in their lust for one another, men doing what is unseemly with other men." H Now, these [Naassenes] believe that what is unseemly is the first and blessed and unformed substance, the cause of all things that are molded into forms. C "Thus they receive the inevitable and due consequences of their error."[12]

(19) H For they say that the words that Paul spoke contain their entire hidden and unspeakable mystery of blessed pleasure [i.e., spiritual bliss]. For, according to them, the promise of washing [baptism] is none other than the unfading pleasure that results from being washed in life-giving water, and anointed by silent [chrism = oil].

(20) Moreover, they assert that not only do the mysteries of the Assyrians support their doctrine, but so also do those of the Phrygians, concerning the Blessed Nature—concealed, and yet at the same time disclosed—of all things that have been and are coming into existence, and moreover will be, C [a Blessed Nature] which, [H the Naassene says], C is the Kingdom of Heaven to be sought for within man.[13] H And concerning this [Blessed Nature] they hand down an explicit passage from the gospel according to Thomas, as follows: C "He who seeks me will find me in children from seven years old; for there concealed shall I be made manifest in the fourteenth age."[14] (21) H But this is not [the teaching] of Christ,[15] but of Hippocrates, who uses these words: "A child of seven years is half a father." And so it is that these [heretics], placing the originative nature of the universe in causative seed, [and] having ascertained the [aphorism] of Hippocrates, that a child of seven years old[16] is half of a father, say that in fourteen years,

according to Thomas, he is manifested. (22) This, with them, is the ineffable and mystical λόγόσ (logos).[17] They assert, then, that S the
Egyptians, who after the Phrygians are of greater antiquity than all
mankind,[18] and who admittedly were the first to proclaim to all the rest
of men the rites and celebrations of all of the gods at once, as well as
their forms and activities, possess the sacred and reverend mysteries of
Isis, which are not to be revealed to the uninitiated. (23) These, however, are nothing else than what was sought and snatched away by her
of the seven robes, the black-clad one: the mysteries concerning the
pudendum of Osiris. H For they say that S Osiris is water.[19] But the
seven-robed nature, encircled and arrayed with seven ethereal robes—
H for so they call the planets, speaking allegorically, and calling them
ethereal—S is shown to be the changeable generation, creation transformed by the ineffable and unportrayable, inconceivable and formless
One. (24) J And this, [H the Naassene says], J is the Scriptural saying,
"The just man will fall seven times, and rise again."[20] For these falls, H
he says, J are the changing positions of the planets [stars?], moved by
Him who sets all things in motion.

(25) H They affirm, then, S concerning the essence of the seed
which is the cause of all existent things, that while it is [itself] none of
these created things, yet, it produces and forms everything that comes
into being, speaking as follows: "I become what I wish, and I am what
I am."[21] For this reason he says that the mover of all things is itself
unmoved.[22] For the maker of everything remains what he already is,
and does not become any of the things that he makes. (26) H [The
Naassene] says that He alone is good, C and concerning Him the Savior
spoke these words:[23] "Why do you say that am good? One alone is
good, my Father who is in the heavens, who causes the sun to shine
upon the just and unjust alike, and who sends rain upon saints and sinners."[24] H But as to whom the saintly ones are, and the sinners, to both
of whom He sends the rain, this we shall discuss later, after the rest.
(27) S This is the great and secret unknown mystery of the universe,
concealed and revealed among the Egyptians. [H For the Naassene
says], S there is no temple [in Egypt] in which the hidden things have

not been placed, naked, looking up from below and crowned with all of its fruits of things that come into being. (28) And [H he affirms] S that this thing stands not only in the holiest temples in front of the statues, but also, for everyone to know about, C like a light, not under a bushel, but set upon a lampstand,[25] as it were, proclaiming its message from the housetops,[26] S in all byways, and all streets, and near the actual dwellings, placed in front as a certain appointed limit and boundary of the dwelling; and this is the good of which everyone speaks. For they call this "bringer of good," H not knowing what they are saying. S And the Greeks, who received this mystical [custom] from the Egyptians, preserve it even until now. (29) S For we behold, [H says the Naassene], S that the herms [i.e., stones] are honored among them. And the Cyllenians especially honor the λόγοσ (logos). For Hermes is the λόγοσ (logos), who being interpreter and author of what has come into being, what is now coming into being, and what in the future will come into being, stands honored among them, fashioned into this form, which is the phallus of a man, pointed upward from below. (30) And because the [deity] of this description, that is, Hermes, [H the Naassene says], S is the conjurer of the dead, and the guide of souls, and the source of souls, he did not escape the notice of the poet, who expresses himself thus:

> *Cyllenian Hermes called forth*
> *the souls of gentleman suitors.*
>
> HOMER, ODYSSEY, 24.1

Not Penelope's suitors, H says he, S O wretches! but the [souls] awakened and brought to recollection of themselves,

> *From honor so great, and from bliss so long.*
>
> EMPEDOCLES

J That is, from the Blessed Man above, or the Primal Man, or Adamas, H as they believe, J souls that have been conveyed down here into the realm of clay, that they may serve the Demiurge of this creation,

Ialdabaoth,[27] a fiery God, fourth in number. (31) H For so they call the father of the particular world: the Demiurge.

> S *And in hand he held a lovely*
> *wand of gold that enchants human eyes,*
> *whosoever he wishes, while others who slumber he rouses.*
>
> HOMER, ODYSSEY, 24.3

(32) This, H he says, S is the one who alone has the power of life and death. J Concerning this, he says, it is written, "You will rule them with a rod [wand] of iron."[28] The poet, however, H he says, J since he wanted to embellish the incomprehensible [potency] of the blessed nature of the λόγόσ (logos), invested him not with an iron, but a golden wand. S And he enchants the eyes of the dead, H as he says, S and raises up again those that are slumbering, those who have awakened and become suitors. (33) C Concerning these, H he says, C the scripture says: "Awaken you who sleep, and arise, and Christ will give you light."[29] This is the Christ, H he says, C the Son of Man who takes form in everything that has been made, who is portrayed from the unportrayable λόγόσ (logos). (34) S This, H he says, S is the great and unspeakable mystery of the Eleusinian rites, *Hye! Cye!* [Rain! Conceive!] H And he affirms that J "all things are subject to him,"[30] and this is that which has been spoken, "Their sound is gone forth unto all the earth,"[31] just as it agrees with the expression

> S *Hermes leads by waving his wand,*
> *and the twittering souls follow.*
>
> HOMER, ODYSSEY, 24.5–7

The disembodied spirits follow continuously in such a way as the poet by his imagery delineates, using these words:

> *And as when bats in a wondrous cave*
> *fly about humming when one drops*
> *from the ridge of rock, and stay close to one other.*
>
> HOMER, ODYSSEY, 24.6

(35) J The word "rock," H he says, J he uses in reference to Adamas. This Adamas, H he affirms, J is "The chief cornerstone become the head of the corner."[32] For in the head is the form-giving brain, out of which the entire family is fashioned.[33] "Which Adamas [rock]," H he says, J "I place in the foundations of Zion." He mentions, H he says, J the form of the man by speaking allegorically. (36) The rock is interposed [within] the teeth, as Homer says, "enclosure of teeth,"[34] that is, a wall and fortress, in which exists the inner man, who thither has fallen from Adamas, the Primal Man above, who is [the rock], who has been "severed without hands to effect the division,"[35] and so has been borne down into the image of oblivion, being earthly and clayish. (37) H And he asserts that S the twittering souls follow him, the λόγόσ (logos):[36]

Thus, twittering, they went together, for Hermes ruled them—
[That is, he guided them]
along harmless paths dark and dank.

HOMER, ODYSSEY, 24.9

In other words, [he guided them], H he says, S into the eternal places free from all wickedness. For where, he says, did they go?

Over Ocean's streams they came, and Leuca's cliff
[the white rock],
And by the portals of the sun and land of dreams.

(38) This is Ocean, H he says, S "origin of gods and origin of men"[37] constantly turning in its ebb and flow, sometimes upwards, sometimes downwards. J But when, H he says, J Ocean flows downwards there ensues a generation of men; but when it flows upwards to the wall and fortress and the cliff of Luecas [white rock], a generation of gods takes place. (39) This, H he asserts, J is what is written: "I said, Ye are gods,[38] and all children of the highest;" "If ye hasten to fly out of Egypt, and repair beyond the Red Sea into the wilderness," that is, from earthly intercourse to the Jerusalem above, which is the Mother of the living.[39]

"If, moreover, again you return into Egypt," that is, into earthly intercourse, "... You shall die."[40] (40) For mortal existence, H he says, C is
the generation below, born of water only, but the immortal is that
which is above,[41] born of spirit. And what [is born] below is carnal, that
is, H he says, C what is written: "That which is born of the flesh is flesh,
and that which is born of the spirit is spirit."[42] H This, according to
them, is the spiritual generation. (41) C This, H he says, C is the great
Jordan[43] which, flowing on below, and preventing the children of Israel
from departing out of Egypt, in other words, keeping them in terrestrial
intercourse, H for Egypt is with them the body. C But Jesus drove it [the
Jordan] back, and made it flow upwards.[44]

Chapter 3

5.8.1 H Adopting these and similar [opinions], these most marvelous
Gnostics, inventors of a novel grammatical art, magnify Homer as their
prophet—as one, [according to them], who, after the manner described
in the mysteries, announces these truths. And they mock the uninitiated
[the innocent] by reconciling the Holy scriptures with such notions.
And they make the following assertion: "He who says that all things
come into being from a single source are in error; but he who says that
they arose from three is in possession of the truth, and will account for
everything." (2) [H The Naassene says], J for one is the nature of the
Blessed Man who is above, [namely] Adamas. And one is the mortal
nature, which is below. And one is the kingless generation, begotten
above, where, H he says, J is Miriam the one who was much sought
after,[45] and Jothor [Jethro = Iothor] the mighty sage, and Sephora
[Zipporah] the gazing one, and Moses whose generation is not in
Egypt, for children were born unto him in Midian. (3) S And this, H he
says, has not escaped the notice of the poets.

Threefold was our partition;
and each obtained his share of honor.

HOMER, *ILIAD*, 15.169

C For, [H the Naassene says], C the magnitudes must be declared, but declared by everyone, everywhere, in such a way "that hearing they do not hear, and seeing they do not see."[46] J For unless, H he says, J the magnitudes are spoken, the world could not exist. (4) These are the three ponderous words [of these heretics], CAULACAU, SAULASAU, and ZEESAR.[47] CAULACAU is Adam, who is farthest above; SAULASAU is the mortal one, below; and ZEESAR, that is, the Jordan, is between, and flows upwards. S This, H he says, S is the hermaphroditic man [present] in all. But those who are ignorant of him call him Geryon with the three-fold body—Geryon, i.e., as if [in the sense of] flowing from earth—while the Greeks commonly refer to him as the "celestial horn of the moon," because he mixed and blended all things in all. (5) C "For everything," H he says, C "came into being through him, and not even one thing was made without him. What came into being in him is life."[48] This life, H he says, C is the ineffable generation of perfect men, which was unknown to preceding generations. But the passage, "nothing was made without him," refers to this particular world, which was brought into being by the third and fourth [of the quaternion named above]. (6) J For this, H he says, J is the cup [Condy] "the goblet out of which the king draws his omens, while he drinks." This, H he says, was found hidden among Benjamin's "fair seeds."[49] S And the Greeks likewise, H he says, S speak of this in the following terms:

> *Bring water, boy! Bring wine!*
> *Make me drunk and make me groggy.*
> *The cup informs me*
> *What kind of man I must become,*
> *Speaking with unspeakable silence.*
>
> ANACREON, 26.25,26

(7) C This cup of Anacreon, H he says, C silently speaks the ineffable mystery that alone is sufficient when understood by men. J For Anacreon's cup, H he says, J is speechless; and [yet] Anacreon affirms that it speaks to him, though in language mute, as to what sort he must

become, C namely, spiritual, not carnal, J if he shall listen in silence to the concealed mystery. C And this is the water in that good wedding, which Jesus made into wine by transforming it. This, H he says, C is the mighty and true beginning of miracles[50] which Jesus performed in Cana of Galilee, and [thus] manifested the Kingdom of Heaven. (8) This, H says he, C is the Kingdom of Heaven that lies within us as a treasure,[51] as leaven hid in the three measures of meal.[52]

(9) S This, H he says, is the great and ineffable mystery of the Samothracians, which only those who are initiated, H he says, S are permitted to know. J For the Samothracians expressly hand down, in the mysteries that are celebrated among them, the tradition that Adamas is the Primal Man. (10) S And there stand in the temple of the Samothracians two statues of naked men, with both hands stretched aloft towards heaven, and their pudenda erect, as with the statue of Hermes on Mount Cyllene. J The aforesaid statues are images of the Primal Man, C and of that spiritual one that is born again, in every respect the same substance as that Man. (11) This, H he says, C is the passage spoken by the Savior: "If ye do not drink my blood, and eat my flesh, ye will not enter into the kingdom of heaven."[53] But even, H he says, C "if you drink of the cup which I drink,[54] whither I go, ye cannot enter there."[55] (12) For he was aware, H he says, C of what sort of nature each of his disciples had, and therefore what each of them needed in order to attain, each according to his own peculiar nature. For, H he says, C he chose twelve disciples from the twelve tribes, and spoke through them to each tribe. On this account, [H he says], C not everyone has heard the preaching of all twelve of the disciples. For what is not according to their nature is beyond their nature.

(13) S The Thracians who live around Mt. Haemus, H he says, and the Phrygians also, call him Corybas, because, taking the beginning of his descent from the 'crown of the head' (χόρυφής) J and from the unportrayed brain, S and passing through the dominions of things below; [yet] we do not perceive how and in what manner he descends. (14) J This, H he says, J is what is meant by the expression: "Though we have heard his voice, we have not seen his shape."[56] For the voice of

him that is set apart and portrayed is heard; but [his] shape, which descends from above from the Unportrayed One—what sort it is, nobody knows. Though it resides in an earthly mold, yet no one recognizes it. (15) This, he says, is "the god that inhabits the flood," according to the Psalter, "and who speaks and cries from many waters."[57] The "many waters," **H** he says, **J** is the manifold race of mortal men, from which [generation] he cries and vociferates to the Unportrayed Man, saying, "Preserve my only-begotten daughter from the lions."[58] (16) In reply to him, **H** he says, **J** it has been spoken, "thou art my son, O Israel,[59] fear not, even though thou pass through rivers,[60] they will not drown you; even though you pass through fire, it will not scorch you."[61] By rivers, **H** he says, **J** he means the fluid substance of generation, and by fire the impulsive principle and desire for generation. "Thou art mine; fear not."[62] (17) And again, **H** he says, **J** "if a mother forget her children, so as not to have pity on them and give them food, I also will forget you."[63] Adamas, **H** he says, **J** speaks to his own men: "But even though a woman forget these things, yet I will not forget you. I have painted you on my hands."[64] (18) In regard, however, of his ascension, **C** that is, his rebirth, that he may become a spiritual, not a carnal, man, **J** the scripture, **H** he says, **J** speaks thus: "Open the gates, your rulers [archons], and be you lifted up, you everlasting gates, and the King of glory will come in." This is a wonder of wonders.[65] "For who," **H** he says, **J** "is this King of glory? A worm, and not a man, a disgrace of man, and an outcast of the people. This is the King of glory, who is powerful in war."[66] (19) By war he means the war in the body, because its frame has been made out of hostile elements; as it has been written, **H** he says, **J** "Remember the conflict that exists in the body."[67] Jacob, **H** he says, **J** saw this entrance and this gate in his journey into Mesopotamia, when from a child he was becoming a youth and a man, that is, [the gate] was made known unto him as he journeyed into Mesopotamia. (20) But Mesopotamia, **H** he says, **J** is the current of the great Ocean flowing from the midst of the Perfect Man; and he was astonished at the celestial gate, exclaiming, "How terrible is this place! It is nothing other than the house of God, and this is the gate of heaven."[68] C On account of this, H he says, C Jesus uses the words "I am the true gate."[69] (21) J Now, he who says these things, H he says, J is the Perfect Man that is imaged from the Unportrayable One from above. C Thus, the perfect man cannot, H he says, C be saved, unless he be born again by entering in through this gate.

(22) S But this very one the Phrygians, H he says, S call also Papas, because he brought peace to everything which moved irregularly and discordantly, before his own appearance. The name Papas, H he says, S belongs simultaneously to all creatures—celestial, terrestrial, and sub-terranean—who exclaim: "Calm! Calm!" [Put an end! Put an end!] to the discord of the world, C and make "peace for those who are afar off," that is, with material and earthly men, and "peace for those that are near,"[70] that is, for perfect men who are spiritual and imbued with reason. S But the Phrygians call this same being the "corpse" because he is buried in the body, as if in a mausoleum and tomb. (23) C This, H he says, C is the saying, "You are whitened sepulchers, full," H he says, C "of the bones of the dead,"[71] because the living Man is not in you. And, again, he exclaims, "The dead shall leap out of their graves,"[72] that is, from the earthly bodies, being born again spiritually, not in a carnal manner. (24) For this, H he says, C is the Resurrection that takes place through the gate of heaven, through which, H he says, C all those that do not enter remain dead. S These same Phrygians, however, H he says, S affirm again that this very [man], as a consequence of the change, [becomes] a god. C For, H he says, C he becomes a god when, having risen from the dead, he enters into heaven through a gate of this kind. (25) Paul the apostle, H he says, C knew of this gate, partially opening it in a mystery, and stating "that he was caught up by an angel, and ascended as far as the second and third heaven into paradise itself, and that he beheld sights and heard unspeakable words which it would not be possible for man to declare."[73]

(26) These are, H he says, C the ineffable mysteries declared by everyone [i.e., all traditions], "which [we also speak], not in words taught by human knowledge, but with those taught by the Spirit [i.e., Wisdom], comparing spiritual things with spiritual. But the 'man of

soul' (Ψυχικός)[74] does not accept the things of the Spirit of God, for to him they are foolishness."[75] And these are, **H** he says, **C** the ineffable mysteries of the Spirit, which we alone know. (27) Concerning these, **H** he says, **C** the Savior has declared, "No one can come to me, unless my heavenly Father draws him."[76] For it is very difficult, **H** he says, **C** to accept and receive this great and ineffable mystery. And again, **H** he says, **C** the Savior has declared, "Not every one who says, Lord, Lord, shall enter into the Kingdom of Heaven, but only he who does the will of my Father in heaven."[77] (28) And they must enter the Kingdom by doing this will, not merely by hearing it. And again, **H** he says, **C** the Savior has declared, "The publicans [i.e., tax collectors] and the harlots go into the Kingdom of Heaven before you."[78] For "the publicans," **H** he says, **C** are those who receive the revenues of all things, but we, **H** he says, **C** are the publicans, "unto whom the ends of the ages have come."[79] For "the ends," **H** he says, **C** are the seeds scattered from the Unportrayable One upon the world, through which the whole cosmic system is completed. (29) Through them too it began to exist. And this, **H** he says, **C** is what has been said: "A sower went out to sow. And some seed fell by the wayside, and was trodden down; and some on the rocky places, and sprang up," **H** he says, **C** "and on account of its having no depth [of soil], the seed withered and died; and some," **H** he says, **C** "fell on fair and good ground, and brought forth fruit, some a hundred, some sixty, and some thirty fold. Who has ears," **H** he says, **C** "to hear, let him hear."[80] The meaning of this, **H** he says, **C** is as follows. No one has become a hearer of these mysteries except the perfect Gnostics. (30) This, **H** he says, **C** is the fair and good land that Moses speaks of: "I will bring you into a fair and good land, into a land flowing with milk and honey."[81] This, **H** he says, **C** is the honey and the milk, by the tasting of which those who are perfect become kingless, and share in the Pleroma (πλήρωμά). This, **H** he says, **C** is the Pleroma through which all existent things are begotten by the Unbegotten One, which has come into being and been completed.

(31) **S** This same [one] is also called "unfruitful" by the Phrygians. **C** For he is unfruitful when he is carnal, and carries out the desires of the

flesh. This, **H** he says, **C** is the saying: "Every tree not producing good fruit is cut down and cast into the fire."[82] For these fruits, **H** he says, **C** are only the rational living men who enter [the spiritual realm] through the third gate. (32) **J** Indeed, they say, "If you eat dead things and make of them living ones, what will you make if you eat living things?"[83] For they say that words and minds and men are the living things or pearls that the Unportrayable One has cast into the creature below [the body]. (33) **C** This, **H** he says, **C** is what [Jesus] asserts: "Do not throw that which is holy to the dogs, nor pearls to the swine."[84] **J** For they allege that the work of swine and dogs is the intercourse of man with woman. (34) **S** And the Phrygians, **H** he says, **S** call this very same one "goatherd" (αἰπόλός), not because, **H** he says, **S** he pastures nannies and billy goats, as the "men of soul" (Ψύχίκόί) use the name, but because, **H** he says, **S** he is ἀέιπόλός (Aipolis)—that is, the one who always revolves—and carries the entire cosmic system around by this revolutionary motion. For πόλέίν is turning and changing things, (35) whence, **H** he says, **S** they all call the two centers of the heaven poles. And the poet says:

> *By turns an unerring sea-born sage comes hither,*
> *the immortal Egyptian Proteus?*
> HOMER, *ODYSSEY*, 4.384

He does not say that Proteus is undone, **H** he says, **S** but that he revolves and goes round himself. Moreover, the cities in which we dwell, because we turn and go round in them, are also called πόλέίν. (36) In this manner, **H** he says, **S** the Phrygians call this one αἰπόλόν (Aipolis) inasmuch as he turns all things, everywhere, ceaselessly, and changes them into their own peculiar [functions]. And the Phrygians, **H** he says, **S** style him, "very fruitful." **J** Likewise, **H** says he, **J** "the children of the widow are more numerous than those of the women with a husband,"[85] **C** that is, things become immortal by being born again, and abide for ever in great plenitude, even though their numbers are few; whereas things carnal, **H** he says, **C** remain mortal, even though their numbers are very great. (37) **C** For this reason, **H** he says, **C**

"Rachel wept for her children, and would not," says [the prophet], "be comforted, sorrowing for them; for she knew," **H** says he, **C** "that they are no more"[86] [i.e., gone over to the enemy = the flesh]. **J** But Jeremiah likewise laments for Jerusalem below, not the city in Phoenicia, but the mortal generation below. For Jeremiah likewise knew, **H** he says, **C** the Perfect Man, the one reborn of water and the Spirit,[87] not carnal. (38) Indeed, Jeremiah himself remarked: "Man [Adamas] exists, yet who shall know him?"[88] **C** In this manner, **H** the Naassene says, **C** the knowledge of the Perfect Man is exceedingly profound, and difficult to grasp. For, **H** he says, **C** the beginning of perfection is the knowledge of man, whereas knowledge of God is absolute perfection.

(39) **S** The Phrygians, however, assert, **H** he says, **S** that he is likewise "a harvested green ear of corn." And after the Phrygians, the Athenians, while initiating people into the Eleusinian rites, likewise display to those who are being admitted to the highest grade at these mysteries, the mighty, and marvelous, and most perfect secret suitable for one initiated into the highest mystic truths: a harvested ear of corn. (40) But this ear of corn is also [considered] among the Athenians to constitute the perfect enormous illumination **J** [descended] from the Unportrayable One. **S** Likewise, the Hierophant himself, who, while he is not castrated like Attis, but made a eunuch by means of hemlock, **C** and despising all carnal generation, **S** enacts the great and secret mysteries by night in Eleusis, beneath a huge fire, and shouting in a loud manner, cries, "August Brimo has brought forth a consecrated son, Brimus"; that is, a mighty [mother has delivered] a mighty child. (41) **J** But revered, **H** he says, **J** is the generation that is spiritual, heavenly, from above, and mighty is he who is so born. This is the mystery called "Eleusis" and "Anactorium," "Eleusis," **H** he says, **J** because we are spiritual and come from above, flowing down from Adam; for ἐλεύσεσθαί (eleusesthai), **H** he says, **J** is "to come"; and "Anactorium" also, which means "to ascend." (42) This, **H** he says, **J** is what they affirm who have been initiated in the mysteries of the Eleusinians. **S** It is, however, a regulation of law that those who have been admitted into the lesser [mysteries] should again be initiated into the Great Mysteries. "For greater destinies obtain greater por-

tions."[89] (43) But the inferior mysteries, **H** he says, **S** are those of Persephone below. In regard of these mysteries, and the path which leads thither, which is wide and spacious, and conducts the dying to Persephone, the poet likewise says:

> *But under her a fearful path extends,*
> *Hollow miry, yet best guide to*
> *Highly-honored Aphrodite's lovely grove.*
>
> PARMENIDES

(44) These, **H** he says, are the inferior mysteries, **C** those appertaining to carnal generation. **S** Now, those men who are initiated into these inferior [mysteries] ought to pause, and [then] be admitted into the great **C** and heavenly **S** ones. For they, **H** he says, **S** who obtain their shares [in this Greater Mystery], receive greater portions. **J** For this, **H** he says, **J** is the gate of heaven, and this is the house of God, where the good God alone dwells.[90] And into this [gate], **H** he says, **J** no unclean person shall enter, no "man of soul," or carnal. But it is reserved for the spiritual only. And those who go there must cast off their clothes,[91] and become bridegrooms, made thoroughly male through the virginal Spirit.[92] (45) For this is the virgin[93] who carries in her womb and conceives and brings forth a son, not animal, not corporeal, but blessed for evermore. Concerning these, it is said, the Savior has expressly declared that "straight and narrow is the way that leads to life, and there are very few who find it and enter, whereas broad and spacious is the way that leads to perdition: and there are many who travel this road."[94]

Chapter 4

5.9.1 S The Phrygians, however, further assert that the father of the universe is Amugdalon (Amygdalus = almond), **J** not a tree [of the same name], **H** he says, **J** but Amygdalus in the sense of the Preexisting One, who held within himself the perfect fruit, as it were, throbbing and moving in his depth. He burst his womb, and gave birth to his own son, **C** the invisible, nameless, and ineffable One of whom we speak. (2) S For amuxai (ὠμῶξάί) signifies, as it were, "to burst" and "sever through," as, H he says, S [happens] in the case of inflamed bodies, and in those which have some internal tumor; and when doctors lance them, they call it ἀμύχάς (Amychai). In this way, H he says, S the Phrygians refer to the Preexistent One as "Amygdalus," C who proceeded and gave birth to the Invisible [One], "by whom all things were made, and nothing was made without Him."[95] (3) S The Phrygians say that what was born through him is the piper [or: flute player],[96] J because the Spirit that is born is harmonious. C "For God," he says, "is Spirit; wherefore," he affirms, "true worshipers do not worship him on this mountain, nor in Jerusalem [i.e., not in a physical place only], but in spirit.[97] (4) For the worship of the perfect ones," he says, "is spiritual, not carnal."[98] J And the Spirit, H he says, J exists wherever the Father is named along with the Son who is born from this same Father. This, he says, is the many-named, thousand-eyed Incomprehensible One, of whom every nature—each, however, differently—is desirous. (5) This, he says, is the word (ῥήμά) of God, which, he says, is a word of revelation of the Great Power. Wherefore, it will be sealed, and hid, and concealed, lying in the house where lies the root of the universe: Aeons, Powers, Intelligences, Gods, Angels, delegated Spirits, Entities, Nonentities, Generables, Ingenerables, Incomprehensibles, Comprehensibles, Years, Months, Days, Hours, [and] the Invisible Point from which what is least begins to increase gradually. This, H he says, J which is nothing, and which consists of nothing, inasmuch as it is indivisible—a point—yet becomes through its own reflective power an incomprehensible magnitude. (6) C This, H he says, C is the Kingdom of Heaven, the grain of mustard seed,[99] the point which is indivisible in the body; and, H he says, C no one knows this [point] save the spiritual only. J This, H he says, J is what has been spoken: "No utterance that anyone can hear."[100]

(7) H They rashly improvise in this manner, interpreting what is said and done by all men according to their own particular mental view, alleging that all things become spiritual. Whence they say that even the performers in the theaters neither say nor do anything outside the influ-

ence of divine Providence. S So certainly, H he says, S when the people gather in the theaters, and a man enters wearing a distinctive robe, and carrying a harp on which he plays a tune, even when he sings he speaks the Great Mysteries without knowing what he is doing:

> (8) Whether [you are] the race of Cronus or happy Zeus, or mighty Rhea, Hail, Attis, gloomy mutilation of Rhea. Assyrians style you thrice-longed-for Adonis, and the whole of Egypt [calls you] Osiris, celestial horn of the moon; Greeks denominate [you] Wisdom; Samothracians, venerable Adam; Haemonians, Corybas; and the Phrygians [name you] at one time Papas, at another time Corpse, or God, or Fruitless, or Aipolos, or "harvested green Ear of Corn," or he whom the fertile Amygdalus produced: a man, a musician.

(9) This, H he says, S is multiform Attis, whom they celebrate in a hymn, and utter these words:

> I will sing of Attis, son of Rhea, not with the buzzing sounds of trumpets, or of Idaean pipers, which accord with (the voices of) the Curetes; but I will mingle [my song] with Apollo's music of harps, 'evoe, evan,' inasmuch as you are Pan, as you art Bacchus, as you are the shepherd of brilliant stars.

(10) H On account of these and similar reasons, these constantly attend the mysteries called those of the "Great Mother," supposing especially that they behold by means of the ceremonies performed there the entire mystery. For these have nothing more than the ceremonies that are performed there, except that they are not castrated: they merely behave as if they are castrated. (11) For they enjoin [their votaries] with the utmost severity and vigilance to abstain from sexual intercourse. The rest of these mysteries, however, as we have declared, [they follow]. And they do not worship any other object but Naas, [thence,] are called Naassenes. (12) But Naas is the serpent, i.e., from the word Naas, from

whom, **H** the Naassene says, **J** all that are under heaven are denominated temples [Naous]. And to him alone—that is, Naas—is also dedicated every shrine and every initiatory rite, and every mystery; and, in general, because religious ceremonies always involve a temple [Naous], in which is Naas, this explains how temples came to be so named [i.e., Naous]. **(13) H** And they affirm that **J** the serpent is a fluid substance, **H** just as Thales, the Milesian, also spoke of water as an originating principle,[101] **J** and that nothing of existing things, immortal or mortal, animate or inanimate, could consist at all without him [the waters = Ocean]. **(14)** And that all things are subject unto him, and that he is good, and that he has all things in himself, as in "the horn of the one-horned bull," just as he imparts beauty and bloom to all things that exist according to their own nature and peculiarity, as if passing through all, just as "the river proceeding forth from Eden divides itself into four heads."[102]

(15) H And they assert that Eden is the brain, as it were, bound and tightly fastened in encircling robes, as if [in] heaven. But they suppose that man, as far as the head only, is Paradise, therefore that **J** "this river, which proceeds out of Eden,"[103] that is, from the brain, "is divided into four heads, and that the name of the first of these rivers is called Phison. This encompasses all the land of Havilath, in which there is gold, and the gold of that land is excellent, and also bdellium and the onyx stone." **(16)** This, **H** he says, **J** is the eye, which, by its honor [among the rest of the bodily organs], and its colors, furnishes testimony to what is spoken. "But the name of the second river is Gihon. This is that which compasses the land of Ethiopia." This, **H** he says, **J** is hearing, since Gihon is a tortuous stream, resembling a sort of labyrinth. "And the name of the third is Tigris, which flows over against [the country of] the Assyrians." **(17)** This, **H** he says, **J** is smell, employing the exceedingly rapid current of the stream [as an analogy of this sense]. But it flows over against [the country of) the Assyrians, because in every act of respiration following upon expiration, the breath drawn in from the external atmosphere enters with swifter motion and greater force. For this, **H** he says, **J** is the nature of respiration. "But the fourth river is Euphrates." (**18**) This, **H** they assert, **J** is the mouth, the passage out of which comes prayer, and the passage inwards of nourishment. The mouth makes glad, and nurtures and fashions the spiritually perfect man. This, **H** he says, **J** is "the water that is above the firmament,"[104] **C** concerning which, he says, the Savior has declared, "If you knew who it is that asks, you would have asked from Him, and He would have given you living, bubbling water to drink."[105] (**19**) **J** Into this water, he says, every nature enters, choosing its own substances; and its peculiar quality comes to each nature from this water, **H** he says, **J** more than iron does to the magnet, and the gold to the backbone of the sea falcon, and the chaff to the amber.

(**20**) **C** But if any one, **H** he says, is blind from birth, and has never beheld the true light, "which lights up every man that comes into the world,"[106] by us let him recover his sight, and behold, as it were, through **J** paradise planted with every description of tree, and supplied with abundance of fruits, water coursing its way through all the trees and fruits. And he will see that from one and the same water the olive chooses for itself and draws the oil, and the vine the wine; and [so is it with] the rest of plants, according to each genus. Though that [higher] Man, **H** he says, **J** has no honor in the world, he is of illustrious fame in heaven, being betrayed by those who are ignorant [of his perfections] to those who know him not, being accounted as a drop from a cask.[107] **C** We, however, **H** he says, **C** are spiritual, who, from the life-giving water **J** of Euphrates, which flows through the midst of Babylon, choose our own peculiar quality as we pass through the true gate, **C** which is the blessed Jesus. (**22**) And of all men we alone are Christians, those who in the third gate celebrate the mystery, **J** and are anointed there with the unspeakable chrism from a horn, as David was anointed—not from an earthen vessel,[108] **H** he says, as was Saul, **C** who held converse with the evil demon of carnal lust.[109]

Chapter 5

5.10.1 H The foregoing remarks, then, though few out of many, we have thought proper to bring forward. For innumerable are the silly and crazy notions of fools. But since, to the best of our ability, we have explained the unknown Gnosis, it seems expedient likewise to add the following. It is a psalm of their composition, by which they appear to celebrate all the mysteries of the error [advanced by] them in a single hymn, couched in the following terms:

> J The world's producing law was Primal Mind,
> And next was First-born's outpoured Chaos;
> And third, the soul received its law of toil:
> Encircled, therefore, with an aqueous form,
> With care overpowered it succumbs to death.
> Now holding sway, it eyes the light,
> And now it weeps on misery flung;
> Now it mourns, now it thrills with joy;
> Now it wails, now it hears its doom;
> Now it hears its doom, and dies.
> . . . and, without escape, the wretched soul
> Enters a labyrinth of evils in its wanderings.
> But Jesus said, Father, behold,
> A strife of ills across the earth
> Wanders from thy breath [of wrath];
> But bitter Chaos [man] seeks to shun,
> And knows not how to pass it through.
> On this account, O Father, send me;
> Bearing seals, I shall descend;
> Through ages whole I'll sweep,
> All mysteries I'll unravel,
> And forms of Gods I'll show;
> And secrets of the saintly path,
> Called "Gnosis," I'll impart.

Chapter 6

5.11.1 H These doctrines, then, the Naassenes attempt to establish, calling themselves Gnostics. But since the error is many-headed and diversified, resembling, in truth, the hydra that we read of in history; whence, at one blow, we have struck off the heads of this [delusion] by means of refutation, employing the wand of truth, and shall entirely exterminate the monster. For neither do the remaining heresies present much difference of aspect from theirs, having a mutual connection through [the same] spirit of error. But since, altering the words and the names of the serpent, they wish that there should be many heads of the serpent, neither thus shall we fail to thoroughly refute them.

Glossary to The Refutation of All Heresies Book 5

Achamoth. Aramaic word for Sophia; the Divine Mother. A related word, Echamoth, refers to the death Mother, one of the aspects of the Divine Mother.

Adam. The biblical Adam, the earthly first man.

Adamas. The heavenly Adam; means "the unconquerable one." His other names include: Primal Man, Blessed Man, Higher Man, Perfect Man, Anthropos, Adam Kadmon, the Secret Adam, the Great Man from Above. See Irenaeus, *Against Heresies,* 1 29.3, 19.1.

Adonis. Youthful consort of Aphrodite, the fickle goddess of love. According to myth, Adonis was torn apart by a wild boar. Sometimes identified with the Near Eastern deity Tammuz, or Dumuzi. See also **Attis.**

Aeon (Aion). A link in, or level of, the great chain of being, the sum total of which is the All or the Gnostic Pleroma. In this system the earth is the most gross link, or Aeon. Can also mean a world age.

Aipolis (ἀέίπολός). Means "always turning," According to the text, a Phrygian goatherd; possibly referring to Attis. The word might also refer to the turning of the earth on its axis, but in the context of the Sermon it remains obscure.

Alalcomenes (Alalchomeneus). A native of Boeotia who claimed a special relationship with the goddess Athena.

Alcyoneus. See **Phlegraean Alcyoneus.**

Amychai (ἀμύχάς). According to the text, this refers to a lanced tumor. Obscure.

Amyxia (ἀμύξάί). According to the text, this means "to burst and to sever." Obscure.

Amygdalus (μύγδάλόν). Means "almond shaped." According to Hippolytus, this is the Phrygian equivalent of Amychai (Amyxia). An almond seed was important in the Greek myth of Attis and Cybele. According to legend, the goddess Cybele was born from a rock that Zeus accidentally fertilized while ejaculating on the ground. Initially, the offspring was hermaphroditic. However, on seeing the strange creature, the gods became alarmed by what might happen if this bisexual offspring of Zeus reached maturity. Thus, they excised the male sex organs. The creature grew up to become Cybele, the great goddess of Phrygia, and the severed genitals grew into an almond tree. Attis was later born from the fruit of this same tree. The meaning of Amygdalus in the Sermon is obscure, but from the context it seems to pertain to the Preexistent One and the first throb of Creation. In the Bible the "watchful tree" was the first to flower (Jeremiah 1:11–12).

Anacreon. A famous Greek poet of the fifth and sixth centuries B.C. who authored five known books. Of these, only fragments remain. He was best known for his polished banter and urbane style. Anacreon was said to be fond of wine, women, and boys.

anactorium. Means "leading back," "returning," or "to ascend upwards." The Naassene scribe apparently appropriated the term from the Eleusinian Mysteries. However, it takes on a new meaning in the Sermon. It is hard to imagine how the Naassenes could have known of the word unless one or more members of the sect had participated in the rites at Eleusis. The mysteries were protected by a secrecy oath so solemn that violations were punishable by death. There were no recorded violations—with one possible exception: the case of Alcibiades. For a discussion, see R. Gordon Wasson, Albert Hofman, and Carl A. P. Ruck, *The Road to Eleusis* (New York: Harcourt Brace, 1978), 79. Whether we are witness to a leak in the Naassene Sermon is impossible to determine. Yet there can be no mistake about the word's meaning. In the context of the Sermon, the meaning of *anactorium* is spiritual. It refers to the backward flow. We are explicitly told that it means "to ascend upwards."

Anat (Anath). Canaanite equivalent of the Greek goddess Athene.

Aphrodite. Greek goddess of love and beauty; equivalent to the Babylonian and Assyrian Ishtar, the Canaanite Astarte, the Sumerian Inanna, and the Roman Venus.

apocryphon. A secret book.

Apollo. Greek god of youth, music, prophecy, archery, and healing; son of Zeus and Leto; sponsor of the famous oracle at Delphi.

Arcadia. District of Greece located in the central Peloponnesus.

Archon. (Gr.) Gnostic ruler, sometimes equivalent with the demiurge. These are the world "rulers" mentioned in the Sermon (*Refutation* 5.8.18); synonymous with the "prince of the world" in the Gospel of John.

Attis. Youthful consort of the Phrygian goddess Cybele. According to legend, Attis was driven mad by the goddess, and he castrated himself, though some say he was castrated by Cybele. Comparable to and sometimes synonymous with Adonis.

Bacchus. Synonymous with Dionysus, the orgiastic son of Zeus.

Boeotians. Inhabitants of Boeotia, a region of Greece northwest of Athens.

bridegroom. Birdsall thinks this is a veiled reference to the Gospel of Thomas 21:37. I believe it's more likely a reference to the Gospel of Philip. See James M. Robinson, ed., *The Nag Hammadi Library* (San Francisco: Harper and Row, 1977), 151.

Brimo. The Great Goddess of northern Greece; sometimes equated with Kore (Demeter/Persephone) or with Artemis/Hecate.

Brimus. Son of Brimo.

Cabirus (pl: Cabeiri). Obscure divinities of Phrygia and islands of the northern Aegean, including Samothrace, Imbros, and Lemnos; honored in the Samothracian Mysteries, pagan rites second in importance only to the Eleusinian Mysteries and involving Rhea, Hermes, and Demeter.

Chaldean. Pertaining to lower Mesopotamia, Elam, and possibly Iran.

Cliff of Leucas. In his *Theogony,* Hesiod mentions a cliff in relation to the sacred river Styx (Acheron). According to Robert Graves, the word *leucon* means "white," but Leucas may simply be a name. Birdsall translates the phrase as "white rock."

Caulacau, Saulasau, and Zeesar. These obscure words are drawn from Isaiah 28:10,13. According to G. R. S. Mead, *caulacau* meant "hope on hope," *saulasau* meant "tribulation on tribulation," and *zeesar* meant "as yet very little." In the context of the Sermon, these words refer to the triple structure: heaven (Caulacau), earth (Saulasau), and the link between them—that is, the Jordan (Zeesar).

Condy (Condymium). This refers to the cup mentioned in Genesis 44:2–5. See also chapter 11, The Grail.

Corybas (χόρύφής). Refers to the Primal or Perfect Man in heaven (*Refutation* 5.8.13). Means "crown of the head" (χόρνφής) and from the standpoint of spiritual anatomy may refer to the crown chakra (sahasrara). We know from other sources that the plural, Corybantes, referred to the priests involved in the worship of the goddess Cybele in the Phrygian Mysteries. Apparently the Thracians practiced the same rites.

Cronus. Ruler of the Titans (the giants). Cronus and the Titans were the children of Ge (earth) and Uranus (sky). Cronus was the husband of Rhea and the father of Zeus. He overthrew Uranus by castrating him, then swallowed his own children. Zeus eluded him, however, by successfully hiding out in a cave on Crete until he was old enough to oppose his father. When Zeus came of age, he defeated Cronus, and forced him to vomit forth the other siblings. Cronus and the Titans were then flung into dark Tartarus, the hellish realm beneath Hades. Cronus was equivalent to the Canaanite god El and the Roman Saturn. The theme of one divine generation struggling with the next is very ancient. The cuneiform transcriptions from Mesopotamia have documented the same pattern in ancient Babylon, though it probably traces to Sumer.

Curetes. The mountain nymphs and satyrs who attended to Rhea. The Curetes were diviners, and performed a function similar to the Corybantes, who attended the Phrygian goddess Cybele. See also **Idaean Curetes.**

Cybele. The Phrygian equivalent of the Greek goddess Rhea. Cybele was the Great Mother goddess of Asia Minor and was honored in the Phrygian Mysteries. See also **Amygdalus.**

Cyllenian Hermes. According to legend, Hermes was born on Mount Cyllene in Arcadia, the central region of the Peloponnesus (west of Corinth). See also **Hermes.**

Eleusis. Rural town near Athens that was the site of the Eleusinian Mysteries.

Demeter. One of the divine children of Cronus and Rhea—hence, a sister to Zeus—goddess of grain; mother of Persephone by Zeus. Demeter grieved over the abduction of her daughter by Hades, god of the underworld. Equivalent to Rhea after the fifth century B.C.

Endymion. King of Elis, to whom Selene, his consort and the moon goddess, granted the rare boon of choosing his own fate. Endymion chose never to grow old. Instead, he slept forever.

evil demon. In the context of the Sermon, this refers to the witch of Endor, with whom the biblical Saul consulted (I Samuel 16:14).

Geryon. According to the Naassenes, the Jordan River. Geryon was also a Greek king who had the body of three different men from the waist down. The king owned a large herd of cattle that was stolen by Heracles. Geryon met his end at the river Anthemus. In the Sermon, the king with three bodies is compared to the trinity of the higher Adamas, the lower (mortal) body, and the Jordan (*Refutation* 5.8.4).

Havilah (Havilath). A district in Arabia peopled by Semites and Hamites and noted for its gold, aromatic gems, and precious stones such as those cited in the text: bdellium and the onyx stone.

Haemonians. Thracian residents of Mount Haemus.

heirophant. A pagan priest (*Refutation* 5.8.40).

Hermes. Wing-footed Greek god; messenger of the gods. The name derives from *herma* or *hermaion*, which means "stone heap." A *herm* (Gr.) is therefore a stone. One of Hermes' functions was to assist travelers. For this reason, stone heaps and pillars were erected along roads in his honor. Hermes, the son of Zeus and father of Pan, was the Greek equivalent of the Egyptian god Thoth. He carried a staff known as the caduceus, which later became the symbol for the medical profession. He was also said to be the psychopomp or guide of souls. Hermes enchanted the eyes of the dead and awakened sleepers. He shared some of the characteristics of the Son of Man, for which reason he is identified with the logos in the Naassene Sermon.

Hippocrates. Greek physician who lived in the fifth century B.C. and is considered the father of Greek medicine.

Hype, Cue. According to F. Legge, this expression meaning "Rain! Conceive!" was a famous expression in the Eleusinian Mysteries. Apparently the words were spoken during the Mystery rites in reference, Legge thinks, to "the fecundation or village of the earth." According to Plutarch, the Greeks called Dionysus Hypes, which means "Lord of the moist." G. R. S. Mead agrees, and adds that Hypes and Hype were respectively designations of Dionysus and Semele. Hypes was also a popular epithet of Zeus as god of rain.

Ialdabaoth (Yaldabaoth, Jaldabaoth). The Gnostic demiurge; the demoted Yahweh; the chief Archon (*Refutation* 5.8.18). Scholar Kurt Rudolph claims that the word is Aramaic in origin and probably means "begetter of Sabaoth." In the Bible, Yahweh is occasionally referred to as Yahweh Sabaoth. See Kurt Rudolph, *Gnosis: The Nature and History of Gnosticism* (San Francisco: HarperSan Francisco, 1977), 73. Other scholars translate the name as "child of chaos," which finds support in Gnostic myths from the Nag Hammadi library that tell of Ialdabaoth's birth from the depths of chaos. See John Dart, *The Laughing Savior* (New York: Harper and Row, 1976), 68. Other synonyms are Saklas, meaning "fool" in Aramaic, and Samael, meaning "the blind god" in Aramaic. The Sermon makes several references to the demiurge (*Refutation* 5.7.7, 5.7.30, 5.8.5, 5.8.18).

Iarbas (Garamas). A king of North Africa. Also known as Amphithemis. G. R. S. Mead believed that this figure points to a very ancient connection with the old Minoan civilization of Crete.

Idaean Curetes. The nymphs from Mount Ida, near Troy. See also **Curetes.**

Incomprehensible One. God; Phanes; Protogonos. The phrase is associated with the experience of God as form, as opposed to Sunyata (God without form). Synonymous with the **Preexistent One** and the **Unportrayable One.** See also **Amygdalus.**

indivisible point. The Hindu concept of *bindu* and closely related to the Christian mustard seed; the singularity, jot, or tittle that in spiritual anatomy is associated with the place between the eyebrows; the point where duality begins and ends; the font of logos. In Kashmir Shaivism it is also described as the space between the breaths, or *madhyadasha*. The point of consciousness that gives rise to Supreme Yoga. The disciple must penetrate this point to know the Self, the All (the Pleroma).

Isis. Most important goddess of Egyptian religion; the Great Mother; sister and wife to Osiris.

Jothor (Iothor). See **Miriam.**

Lake Cephisis. A lake in Boeotia. Also, a river by the same name.

Lemnos. Island in the northern Aegean. Site of Samothracian Mysteries. See also **Cabirus.**

logos (λόγος). One of the most commonly used words in Greek. In *The Earlier PreSocratics and the Pythagoreans: A History of Greek Philosophy,* vol. 1 (Cambridge: Cambridge University Press, 1962), W. K. C. Guthrie lists eleven different meanings in use in fifth-century B.C. Greece, some without idiomatic English equivalents: 1) Anything said or written; 2) The idea of worth, reputation, esteem, or fame (e.g., to be of *logos* in someone's eyes); 3) The notion of taking account of things, having a conversation with oneself, or weighing the pros and cons; 4) Cause, reason, or argument (e.g., to keep silent for no *logos*); 5) The truth of the matter; 6) Full or due measure of a thing (e.g., not many of them reached the *logos* of old age; 7) Correspondence, relation, proportion, in accordance with, similar to (e.g., to pay the remaining tax in the *logos* of the original assessment); 8) General principle or rule (e.g., when Aristotle refers to the "right *logos*"; 9) The faculty of reason (e.g., humanity being distinct from beasts due to the possession of *logos*); 10) Formula or essential definition of a thing, its reason for existence; 11) Consent (e.g., to agree by common *logos*). To these definitions we should add another: Creation via the word *(nada)* or throb *(spanda)*.

Mariamne. The Sermon never clarifies her identity. We can't be certain, but she may have been the sister of the apostle Philip. A teacher by this name is mentioned in the Acts of Philip, an apocryphal Christian scripture. In the Acts, Mariamne travels with her brother to the land of the Ophites, presumably for the purpose of proselytizing. Not much background information is available on the Acts of Philip, though the text is available for study. See Montague Rhodes James, *The Apocryphal New Testament* (Oxford: Clarendon Press, 1924). Origen also mentions a teacher named Mariamne in his *Contra Celsum* 5.62. However, he provides no further details.

men of soul (Ψυχίκόί). The phrase probably refers to a certain type of Greek philosopher. Obscure.

Midian. Region east of Sinai peopled by the Midianites. Moses was instructed by the Midianite priest Jethro (Reuel), and he married a Midianite wife named Zipporah (Sephora). The mixed-blood marriage was strongly opposed by Moses' sister, Miriam.

Miriam, Jothor (Iothor = Jethro), and Sephora (Zipporah). The prophetess Miriam was the sister of Moses. See Exodus 15:20. Sephora was Moses' wife and Jothar (Iothor = Jethro) was Sephora's father. Jung adduced the following quaternity in *Aion: Researches into the Phenomenology of the Self*, trans. R. C. F. Hull (Princeton, N.J.: Princeton University Press, 1959), 210: Husband (Moses); Wife (Sephora); Sister (Miriam); Wise Old Man (Jethro). Miriam produced the "Song of Miriam," one of the most archaic fragments in the Bible (Exodus 15, Numbers 12). For a further discussion, see Notes, chapter 8, n. 12.

Moira (Moire). Fate; one of the three sisters of the seasons. (Greece had three seasons, not four).

Mother of the Gods. Probably refers to Cybele.

Mount Haemus. A mountain in Thrace. The Haemonians were the inhabitants of Mount Haemus.

naas. Hippolytus believed this was the Hebrew word for serpent and the root of the name Naassene. The actual Hebrew word for serpent is *nahash*.

nahash. Hebrew word for serpent.

naos. Inner sanctuary of a temple.

naous. The soul.

nous. This word does not appear in the Sermon. *Nous* is closely related to *logos,* and means mind, light, or understanding. See Irenaeus, *Against Heresies,* 2.13.1; see also Kurt Rudolph, *Gnosis: The Nature and History of Gnosticism* (San Francisco: HarperSan Francisco, 1977), 77, 87.

Oannes (Iannes). Fish god that the scholar Robert Eisler traced to ancient Sumer. According to legend, Oannes emerged from the waters of the Persian Gulf and taught the Sumerians the arts of civilization. A parallel figure to the Egyptian Osiris.

Osiris. The first divine king of Egypt, whose tragic death and miraculous resurrection provided the basis for much of Egyptian religion. Osiris was associated with the upper waters, the renewal of life, the Great Pyramid, and the soul of the departed king. Chief centers of his cult were Abydos and the northern delta at Busiris. Abydos became the more important of the two. The reference in the Sermon is taken from Plutarch's account.

Pallene. See **Phlegraean Alcyoneus.**

Pan. Son of Hermes and Penelope. An Arcadian shepherd god who lived in the mountains, where he danced, sang with the nymphs, and played his pipes.

papas. According to Legge, a word for "father" in the Phrygian Mysteries. The word *pope* derives from *papa.*

Pelasgus. Eponym of the Pelasgians, the indigenous inhabitants of several regions of Greece, including Arcadia. According to tradition, Pelasgus was the original or first man of Arcadia.

Penelope. Wife of Odysseus.

Persephone (Kore). Daughter of Demeter who was abducted and taken into the underworld by Hades. Means "maid." Kore was the name used during the Eleusinian Mysteries. The goddess was referred to as Kore only when she was above ground.

Phison, Gihon, Tigris, and Euphrates. The four rivers that flow out of Eden in Genesis 2.

Phlegraean Alcyoneus. Alcyoneus was the oldest of the giants and, along with his brother Porphyrion, the strongest. The reference here is to the ancient battle between the giants and the gods, which occurred at Phlegra. Alcyoneus was invulnerable in battle as long as he stayed within the borders of his homeland, the Thracian peninsula of Pallene. He was killed when Heracles dragged him outside the protected zone.

Phrygian. Pertaining to Phrygia, a region in western Asia Minor. Site of pagan rites known as the Phrygian Mysteries.

Phrygian Corybantes. See **Cabirus.**

Pleroma (πλήρώμά). "Fullness"; the sum total of all levels or Aions; in Gnosticism, the All.

Preexistent One. Synonymous with Incomprehensible One and Unportrayable One. See also **Amygdalus.**

Primal Man. See **Adamas.**

Proteus. King of Egypt during the time of the Trojan War; also a minor sea deity who in the *Odyssey* is referred to as "the Old Man of the Sea."

Rhea. Mother of Zeus; wife of Cronus. Merged with Demeter after the fifth century B.C. Synonymous with the Canaanite goddess Asherah (wife of El).

Samothracians. Inhabitants of Samothrace, an island in the Aegean.

Selene. The moon and the moon goddess; consort of Endymion, king of Elis. Selene offered to grant her lover any wish. Endymion (after siring fifty daughters) chose to sleep forever.

Sephora. See **Miriam.**

spinther. (Gr.) Means "spark." In Gnosticism, the fragments of light cast off from the original Adamas or Perfect Man into the souls of men and women. In the Redeemer myth, the Savior gathers up the shards and returns them to heaven. The Sermon mentions the "seeds scattered by the Unportrayable One" (*Refutation* 5.8.28–29). These are likened to the parable of the sower (Gospel of Thomas 9, Matthew 13:3–9).

Styx. The most important branch of Ocean, it flowed into Hades. Sometimes known as Acheron. Also, a goddess.

Thales. A Greek philosopher from Melitus (hence: the Milesian) who lived in the seventh century B.C. He was reputedly of Phoenician birth and was educated in Egypt and the Near East. A number of firsts are attributed to him: In addition to being the first of the seven sages, according to Strabo, Thales was also the first Greek philosopher to write about the science of nature and the first to use the expression "Know thyself." He is credited with introducing mathematics and astronomy into Greece and is said to have startled Ionia by successfully predicting a solar eclipse for May 28, 585 B.C. Thales calculated the height of the Egyptian pyramids by means of their shadows and believed water was the first and final principle of all things. According to Thales, the world is a hemisphere resting on an endless expanse of water (i.e., the primordial waters). He was the teacher of Anaximander.

theogony. Creation of the gods. Beginning with the first pair, each divine generation gives rise to the next.

theophany. Visitation by God.

Thracians. Inhabitants of Thrace, a province in northwestern Greece, on the Aegean.

Unportrayable One. Synonymous with the Incomprehensible One. See also **Amygdalus** and **Preexistent One.**

Word. See **logos.**

Zeus. A sky (storm) god and the head of the Olympian pantheon. Equivalent to the Canaanite god Baal and the Roman Jupiter. Father of (and sometimes equivalent to) Dionysus.

Notes

Introduction

1. Irenaeus, *Against Heresies*, ed. W. W. Harvey (Ridgewood, N.J.: Cambridge, 1965), 1.1–2.
2. This is close to a verbatim quote from J. Daniélou, *The Theology of Jewish Christianity*, trans. J. H. Baker (London: Darton, Longman and Todd, 1964), 84.
3. G. van Groningen, *First-Century Gnosticism: Its Origin and Motifs* (Leiden: E. J. Brill, 1967), 119.
4. Kurt Rudolph, *Gnosis: The Nature and History of Gnosticism* (San Francisco: HarperSan Francisco, 1977), 55.
5. W. F. Albright, *History, Archaeology, and Christian Humanism* (New York: McGraw Hill, 1964), 41.
6. James M. Robinson, ed., *The Nag Hammadi Library* (New York: Harper and Row, 1977).
7. Cited in John Dart, *The Laughing Savior* (New York: Harper and Row, 1976), xvi.
8. Robinson, *The Nag Hammadi Library*.
9. Hippolytus's derivation of the name Naassene is dubious. Yet, insofar as I am aware, no scholars have proposed an alternative explanation. Thus, it seems reasonable to review some possibilities. The reader should bear in mind that I am not a linguist. One possible origin of the name Naassene might be the Aramaic word *nasi,* meaning "leader," "tribal official," or "prince." Roland de Vaux, *Ancient Israel: Its Life and Institutions,* trans. John McHugh (Grand Rapids, Mich.: William B. Eerdman, 1997), 8. The Book of Esdras uses the word Nasi in reference to Sheshbazzar, the Davidic official who led one of the returning groups of Jews out of Babylonian captivity. The word was also in use among Arabs, and denoted a sheikh. De Vaux, *Ancient Israel: Its Life and Institutions,* 8. Zionists resurrected Nasi after World War I because of its biblical history. The word appeared in a Zionist working paper that proposed a new administration for Palestine. The provisional administration was to be an executive council with similar authority to that of the British High Commissioner. The council was to be headed up by a Jewish

official with the title Nasi. The proposal came to nothing, however. Tom Segev, *One Palestine Complete: Jews and Arabs Under the British Mandate* (New York: Henry Holt, 1999), 59.

Dr. Robert Eisenman, an authority on the Dead Sea Scrolls, proposed Nozrei ha-Brit, which means "keepers of the covenant," as the root of both Nazarene and Nasorean. Robert Eisenman, *James the Just* (New York: Penguin, 1996), 269–70.

According to the Dead Sea Scroll scholar John Allegro, Nasi can also mean "one lifted up," which implies, or could imply, a spiritual dimension. John Allegro, *The Dead Sea Scrolls* (New York: Penguin Books, 1956), 168. Notice that Naassene resonates closely with Nazarene and Nazorean, the latter two being the standard names used in the New Testament for the Jesus movement. The resemblance could be more than superficial. Another closely related word, Nasara, is the Arabic word for Christian, even today. E. S. Drower, *The Secret Adam* (Oxford: Clarendon Press, 1960), i. Further support for this etiology can be found in the Gospel of Philip, one of the Gnostic scriptures discovered in 1945 at Nag Hammadi, Egypt. Philip describes Jesus as "the Nazorean," and even equates Nazorean with Nazarene. Robinson, *The Nag Hammadi Library,* 134. This tallies with the New Testament, where Nazarene occurs four times in Mark and twice in Luke. Nazorean occurs eight times altogether in Luke and the Lukan Acts, three times in John, and twice in Matthew. Raymond E. Brown, *The Birth of the Messiah* (Garden City, N.Y.: Doubleday, 1977), 209. It is of great interest, then, that the Gospel of Philip defines Nazarene as "he who reveals what is hidden," implying secret teachings. Robinson, *The Nag Hammadi Library,* 137.

An early Christian writer, Julius Africanus (170–245 C.E.), proposed a geographical origin for the name Nazarene. Africanus asserted that Jesus and his family lived in two ancestral villages in Judea, one of them called Nazara. Pamphilus Eusebius, *The Ecclesiastical History* (Grand Rapids, Mich.: Baker Book House, 1990), 1.7. The Gospel of Luke 4:16–17 affirms that Jesus "had been brought up" in Nazara, which the late biblical scholar Raymond Brown equated with Nazareth, the traditional home of Jesus. According to Brown, archaeological evidence shows continual occupation of the site since the seventh century B.C.E. Yet Brown conceded that the name Nazareth never appears in any pre-Christian Jewish writing. Brown, *The Birth of the Messiah,* 207. See also Eisenman, *James the Just,* 248–50.

A number of scholars have discussed the phonological problem of equating Nazorean with the third form Nasorean, where the z is replaced by an s. Raymond Brown concluded, however, that the problem is not insuperable. He believed that the s and z could have been interchangeable. Brown, *The Birth of the Messiah,* 212. This was also the view of E. S. Drower, who reported that among the Mandaean Gnostics, a Nasorean was someone who understood the secret doctrine. Drower, *The Secret Adam,* i. The Mandaeans, who later settled in the south of present-day Iraq, were followers of John the Baptist and are known to have practiced purificatory bathing and to have used the name Jordan in a special sense. All of these names appear to have been a family of words. Brown went so far as to suggest that Nazarene,

Nazorean, and Nasorean had several different origins, all of which were (and are) valid. As he put it, "we should recognize that Christians might have been attracted by the wealth of possible allusions in a term applied to Jesus." This explanation is certainly plausible. Might not the name Naassene also have been a part of this word family? Brown, *The Birth of the Messiah,* 212.

Brown considered most of the alternatives—including Nazir, the root of the word Nazirite; Neser, meaning "branch," from Isaiah 11:1 ("There will come forth a shoot from the root of Jesse . . ."); and also Nasar, which means "to measure." Nasar finds support in the Gospel of Philip, which refers to Christians as "those who have been measured." Robinson, *The Nag Hammadi Library,* 137.

10. Richard Reitzenstein and G. R. S. Mead were two early scholars who drew this conclusion. Scott Birdsall and Miroslav Marcovich are recent examples. For a discussion, see R. Scott Birdsall, "The Naassene Sermon and the Allegorical Tradition" (Ph.D. diss., Claremont Graduate University, 1984), 41–42; Hippolytus, *Refutatio Omnium Haeresium,* trans. Miroslav Marcovich (Berlin: Walter de Gruyter, 1986), 32–33.

Chapter 1

1. Flavius Josephus, "Antiquities of the Jews," in *The Life and Works,* trans. William Whiston (New York: Holt, Rinehart, and Winston, 1998), 20.5.1.
2. Ibid., 8.6.
3. Frank Moore Cross, *The Ancient Library of Qumran and Modern Biblical Studies* (Garden City, N.Y.: Doubleday, 1958), 274–89.
4. For a discussion, see Cyrus Gordon, *The Ancient Near East* (New York: W. W. Norton, 1964), 200. The passage reads:

   If a man has two wives, one loved and the other unloved, and the loved one and the unloved one both bear him children, and if the first-born son is of the unloved wife, then when the man comes to bequeath his goods to his sons, he may not treat the son of the wife whom he loves as the first-born. He must acknowledge as first-born the son of the wife he does not love and give to him a double share of his estate, for this son is the first fruit of his strength, and the right of the first-born is his.

5. Ian Wilson, *The Exodus Enigma* (London: Weidenfield and Nicolson, 1985), 128–41.
6. Immanuel Velikovsky, *Worlds in Collision* (New York: Dell, 1950), 63–81.
7. Wilson, *The Exodus Enigma,* 167.
8. Rudolf Otto, *The Idea of the Holy,* trans. John W. Harvey (London: Oxford University Press, 1923).
9. W. F. Albright, *From the Stone Age to Christianity* (Baltimore: Johns Hopkins University Press, 1940), 306–7.
10. Frank Moore Cross, *Canaanite Myth and Hebrew Epic: Essays in the History of the Religion of Israel* (Cambridge: Harvard University Press, 1973), 223.
11. Many more details can be found in the pseudoepigraphic Book of Enoch, which the early fathers of the Church regarded as part of the canon (a status it retains in the Ethiopian Church even today).

Chapter 2

1. Robinson, *The Nag Hammadi Library* (introduction, n. 6).
2. These were the Oxyrhynchus fragments, written in Greek. See Helmut Koester, *History and Literature of Early Christianity* (Philadelphia: Fortress Press, 1982), 76.
3. For sources on this, see Helmut Koester, *Ancient Christian Gospels* (Philadelphia: Trinity Press International, 1990), 85.
4. Koester was a student of Rudolf Bultmann. Koester, *Ancient Christian Gospels,* 75–89.
5. Examples are legion. Name a Christian scholar from the past one hundred years and the chances are that he or she subscribed to this view.
6. George Wesley Buchanan, *Jesus, the King and His Kingdom* (Macon, Ga.: Mercer University Press, 1984), 303–8.
7. Paramahansa Yogananda, *Autobiography of a Yogi* (Los Angeles: Self-Realization Fellowship, 1988), 328.
8. Buchanan, *Jesus, the King and His Kingdom,* 304–5.
9. William Schoedel was the first. William R. Schoedel, "Naassene Themes in the Coptic Gospel of Thomas," *Vigiliae Christianae* 14 (1960); see also Koester, *Ancient Christian Gospels,* 78.
10. Cyrus Gordon, *The Common Background of Greek and Hebrew Civilizations* (New York: W. W. Norton, 1965), 79.
11. Elizabeth Clare Prophet, *Reincarnation: The Missing Link in Christianity* (Livingston, Mont.: Summit University Press, 1997), 221.

Chapter 3

1. Robinson, *The Nag Hammadi Library,* 406–7 (introduction, n. 6).
2. Ibid. For those willing to search, bits of corroborating evidence also turn up in surprising places, for instance in an obscure Scandinavian folk legend describing how Jesus "stopped up the Jordan." Giorgio de Santillana and Hertha von Dechend, *Hamlet's Mill* (Boston: Gambit, 1969), 223.
3. For an excellent discussion, see D. S. Russell, *The Message and Method of Jewish Apocalyptic* (Philadelphia: Westminster Press, 1964), 357.
4. The Noachic fragments are found in the following chapters of Enoch: 6–11, 54–55, 60, 65–69, 106–7. See chapters 4, 7, and 13 for pertinent Babylonian and Sumerian antecedents.
5. The Testimony of Truth expresses a similar idea. Robinson, *The Nag Hammadi Library,* 407 (introduction, n. 6).
6. The word *jordan* (Hebrew: *yardin;* Greek: *iordanes*) is not a proper name. Rather, *jordan* is a generic word for "river." Thus, it could be used in reference to any river. This explains the proliferation of Jordans in the ancient world, each distinguished by a local identifier (e.g., "the Jordan of Jericho" or "the Iardanus of Crete"). Gordon, *The Ancient Near East,* 284–85 (chapter 1, n. 4). The Mandaeans, a sect of Gnostic disciples of John the Baptist who later settled in what is now southern Iraq, took the name Jordan with them. This sect survived into the twentieth century and continued to refer to its local river as the Jordan. Drower, *The Secret Adam,* 13 (introduction, n. 9).

While the historical baptism of Jesus probably occurred along the Jordan River, as tradition holds, it need not have been so. Barbara Thiering, theologian and author, claimed some years ago that she had found the site of John's baptismal mission not in the Jordan valley but in one of the wadis (valleys) of the Judean wilderness east of Jerusalem. According to Thiering, the traditional path of priests and pilgrims from Jerusalem into the wilderness was not via the road to Jericho. Rather, it was down either a path that started at the Essene Gate and followed the Kidron valley downstream into the Wadi Kidron or a path that started on the Mount of Olives and passed through Bethany, then east down into the Wadi Sekhakha, where, Thiering says, the site of John's mission was located. The same wadi leads to Qumran. In fact, according to Thiering, Sekhakha was the ancient name for Qumran! Barbara Thiering, *Jesus the Man* (London: Corgi Books, 1992), 55, 394–95. Thiering might be correct. The generic meaning of the word *jordan* allows for almost any flowing body of water, even an intermittent stream in a wadi.

7. Plato, *The Republic* (New York: Pantheon Books, 1961), 10.621.
8. Robinson, *The Nag Hammadi Library*, 230 (introduction, n. 6).
9. Ibid., 229. See also Koester, *History and Literature of Early Christianity*, 154–55 (chapter 2, n. 2).
10. The account of the death of James in Josephus differs in certain details from that found in Eusebius, but the differences do not cast doubt on Hegesippus's reference to the gate. For a good discussion, see S. G. F. Brandon, *The Fall of Jerusalem and the Christian Church* (London: S.P.C.K., 1951), 95–100; Josephus, "Antiquities of the Jews," Book 20, chapter 9 (chapter 1, n. 1); Pamphilus Eusebius, *The Ecclesiastical History* (Grand Rapids, Mich.: Baker Book House, 1990), 2.23.
11. Maccoby was referring to the evangelist John. Hyam Maccoby, *The Mythmaker: Paul and the Invention of Christianity* (New York: Barnes and Noble, 1986), 44.
12. Yogananda, *Autobiography of a Yogi*, 328 (chapter 2, n. 7).

Chapter 4

1. For an excellent overview of the scholarly debate on the Son of Man from its beginning until the present, see Delbert Burkett, *The Son of Man Debate* (Cambridge: Cambridge University Press, 1999).
2. Elaine Pagels, *Beyond Belief* (New York: Random House, 2003), 41–42.
3. Andrew Harvey, *Son of Man* (New York: Jeremy Tarcher, 1998), 68–78.
4. D. S. Russell's book on the apocalyptic writings is an invaluable resource. Russell, *The Message and Method of Jewish Apocalyptic* (chapter 3, n. 3).
5. Ibid., 332.
6. For a good discussion and sources, see Burkett, *The Son of Man Debate*, 43.
7. Use the index in Robinson, *The Nag Hammadi Library*, 490 (introduction, n. 6).
8. The Gospel of Thomas and the Dialogue of the Savior are in agreement with the Sermon on this. Neither mentions Christ. This provides additional support for Koester's view that Thomas reflects the earliest period of Christianity. The same could be said of the Dialogue. See Robinson, *The Nag Hammadi Library* (introduction, n. 6).

9. For an excellent discussion, see Russell, *The Message and Method of Jewish Apocalyptic,* 327–30 (chapter 3, n. 3).

10. Graham Hancock, *The Sign and the Seal* (New York: Simon and Schuster, 1992), 181–82.

11. J. T. Milik, *Ten Years of Discovery in the Wilderness of Judaea,* trans. J. Strugnell (Naperville, Ill.: Alec R. Allenson, 1959), 89–92.

12. For an excellent discussion, see Russell, *The Message and Method of Jewish Apocalyptic,* 324–27 (chapter 3, n. 3).

13. Pagels, *Beyond Belief,* 43.

14. Albright, *From the Stone Age to Christianity,* 378–80 (chapter 1, n. 9); Russell, *The Message and Method of Jewish Apocalyptic,* 346 (chapter 3, n. 3). See also Robert Eisler, *Orpheus the Fisher* (London: J. M. Watkins, 1921).

15. Russell, *The Message and Method of Jewish Apocalyptic,* 347 (chapter 3, n. 3).

16. The surviving fragments of Berossos's writings are available for study. They have been reproduced in appendix 2 of Robert Temple's remarkable book *The Sirius Mystery* (Rochester, Vt.: Destiny Books, 1987).

17. Carl G. Jung, *Aion: Researches into the Phenomenology of the Self,* trans. R. C. F. Hull (Princeton, N.J.: Princeton University Press, 1959), 115.

18. Eisler, *Orpheus the Fisher,* 71–72.

19. These include the Babylonian Noah, Atra-Hasis, who in the Assyrian recension of the Flood was known as "the Very Wise One," and the figure of Adapa, who is described in the El Amarna Tablets as "the Very Wise." Albright believed that the two were equivalent. Albright, *From the Stone Age to Christianity,* 378–79 (chapter 1, n. 9). The association with the waters is compelling. The legend of Adapa describes how the hero was created in the sea. Stephen Langdon, *The Sumerian Epic of Paradise, the Flood, and the Fall of Man* (Philadelphia: University Museum, 1915), 39.

20. Pagels, *Beyond Belief,* 55.

21. Use the index in Robinson, *The Nag Hammadi Library,* 478 (introduction, n. 6). See also Irenaeus, *Against Heresies,* 1.29.3 (introduction, n. 1).

22. Charles Ponce, *Kabbalah* (Wheaton, Ill.: Theosophical Publishing House, 1973), 44, 80.

23. Drower, *The Secret Adam* (introduction, n. 9).

24. Richard Reitzenstein, *Poimandres: Studien zur griechisch-agyptischen und fruhchristlichen Literatur* (Leipzig: Teubner, 1904), 540. The scholar Hans Jonas agreed. Hans Jonas, *The Gnostic Religion* (Boston: Beacon Press, 1958), 154–55.

25. E. S. Drower found the same to be true of the Secret Adam of the Gnostic Mandaeans, who apparently originated as followers of John the Baptist. Drower, *The Secret Adam,* 96 (introduction, n. 9).

26. Irenaeus, *Against Heresies,* 1.30, pp. 1, 11 (introduction, n. 1); Jonas, *The Gnostic Religion,* 57; Rudolph, *Gnosis: The Nature and History of Gnosticism,* 57 (introduction, n. 4). Richard Reitzenstein was the first to note the parallel with Gayomart, the Iranian Son of Man who was created by Ahura Mazda. In the Iranian text *Bundahishn* Gayomart is fashioned in the sphere of endless light. Carl H. Kraeling, *Anthropos and Son of Man* (New York: AMS Press, 1927), 159. See also the *Bundahishn,* 1, 2.

Chapter 5

1. Cross, *Canaanite Myth and Hebrew Epic: Essays in the History of the Religion of Israel,* 293 (chapter 1, n. 10).
2. Reitzenstein, *Poimandres: Studien zur griechisch-agyptischen und fruhchristlichen Literatur,* 82–83 (chapter 4, n. 24); G. R. S. Mead, *Thrice Greatest Hermes: Studies in Hellenistic Theosophy and Gnosis* (North Beach, Maine: Samuel Weiser, 1992), vol. 1, p. 99.
3. For a good summary of the debate and sources, see Birdsall, "The Naassene Sermon and the Allegorical Tradition," 42 (introduction, n. 10).
4. Ibid., 207–8.
5. M. Simonetti, "Qualche osservatione sulle presunte interpolazioni della Predica dei Naaseni," *Vetera Christianorum* 7 (1970), 119–21.
6. Birdsall, ii, 216.
7. G. Sfameni Gasparro, "Interpretatazioni gnostiche e misteriosofiche del mito di Attis." In Roelof van den Broek and M. J. Vermaseren, eds. *Studies in Gnosticism and Hellenistic Religions: Presented to Gilles Quispel on the Occasion of His 65th Birthday.* (Leiden: E. J. Brill, 1981), 393.
8. Birdsall, 231.
9. Ibid., 232.
10. Ibid., 266.
11. Ibid., 267.

Chapter 6

1. Israel Finkelstein and Neil Asher Silberman's book *The Bible Unearthed* (New York: Free Press, 2001) is recommended in its entirety.
2. The fact is well attested by archaeology. Ibid., 240–42.
3. Ibid., pp. 278–79.
4.   I hate, I despise your feast days,
      and I will not smell in your solemn assemblies.
      Though ye offer me burnt offerings and your meat offerings,
      I will not accept them:
      Neither will I regard the peace offerings of your fat beasts.
      Take away from me the noise of your songs;
      for I will not hear the melody of thy viols.
      But let judgment roll down as waters,
      And righteousness as a mighty stream. (Amos 5:21–24)

      For I desire mercy and not sacrifice;
      and the knowledge of God more than burnt offerings. (Hosea 6:6)

      To what purpose is the multitude of your sacrifices unto me?
      Said the Lord:
      I am full of the burnt offerings of rams,
      And the fat of fed beasts:
      And I delight not in the blood of bullocks or of lambs or of hegoats . . .
      Bring no more vain oblations;

Incense is an abomination unto me;
The new moons and Sabbaths and your appointed feasts my soul hates:
they are a trouble unto me;
I am weary to bear them.
And when ye spread forth your hands,
I will hide mine eyes from you:
Yea, when ye make many prayers, I will not hear:
Your hands are full of blood.
Wash you, make you clean;
Put away the evil of your doings from before mine eyes;
Cease to do evil; learn to do well;
Seek judgment, judge the fatherless, plead for the widow. (Isaiah 1:11–15)

What do I care about incense
imported from Sheba,
or fragrant cane from a distant country?
Your holocausts are not acceptable,
your sacrifices do not please me. (Jeremiah 6:20)

Yahweh Sabaoth, the God of Israel, says this: Add your holocausts to your sacrifices and eat all the meat. For when I brought your ancestors out of the land of Egypt I said nothing to them, gave them no orders, about holocaust and sacrifice. (Jeremiah 7:21–23)

5. Harvey, *Son of Man,* 80–81 (chapter 4, n. 3).
6. From Albright, *History, Archaeology, and Christian Humanism,* 252–53 (introduction, n. 5):

> There are basic fallacies in Toynbee's treatment of Hinduism and Buddhism as though they were on a logical par with Judaism and Christianity—and judging from many statements of his, even superior to them. In the first place, Hinduism is ancient Oriental polytheism and Nature worship, with a philosophical facet which remains far more out of touch with reality (since the phenomenal world is simply *maya,* "illusion") than the Greek philosophical systems which developed in the coil of paganism during the last few centuries B.C. There is indeed a post-Buddhist phase of Hinduism, which Toynbee often stresses, but there is also a post-Christian phase of Hinduism, illustrated on the practical level by Mahatma Gandhi and on the philosophical level by Sir Sarvepalli Radhakrishnan, which Toynbee fails to mention. Buddhism arose in the fifth century B.C. on the soil of Hindu paganism, and turned into pantheism because of the already developed metaphysical pantheism of the Upanishads.
>
> When one thinks of the historical, ethical, and spiritual treasures of the Old and New Testament, and considers the long process by which the ancestral faith of the West developed from ancient Oriental, Hebrew, and Greek sources, and when one then contrasts them with the relative poverty of Hindu and Buddhist scriptures, it scarcely seems

fair to place them on a level. Christianity has developed through the ages in constant interaction with the complex Western civilization which is now sweeping the world, and it stands to reason that it would be better adapted to the new age of technology than the illusionist and escapist faiths of the East.

7. Robinson, *The Nag Hammadi Library,* 235 (introduction, n. 6).

8. Consider also passage 3: ". . . the Kingdom is inside of you, and it is outside of you. When you come to know yourselves, then you will become known, and you will realize that it is you who are the sons of the Living Father."

9. From Clement:

> When Salome inquired when the things concerning which she asked should be known, the Lord said, "when ye have trampled on the garment of shame, and when the two become one, and the male with the female is neither male nor female." In the first place, then, we have not this saying in the four gospels that have been delivered to us, but in that according to the Egyptians.

From *Stromaties (or Miscellanies),* in *Alexandrian Christianity, The Library of Christian Classics,* vol. 2, eds. John Ernest, Leonard Oulton, and Henry Chadwick (Philadelphia: Westminster Press, 1954), 3.3.64. See also Montague Rhodes James, ed., *The Apocryphal New Testament,* (Oxford: Clarendon Press, 1924), 11.

10. This teaching appears to have been standard among Gnostic Christians. See the Gospel of Philip in Robinson, *The Nag Hammadi Library,* 140 (bottom paragraph).

11. For a good discussion, see Russell, *The Message and Method of Jewish Apocalyptic,* 351 (chapter 3, n. 3).

12. The case of the Ebionites is an interesting one because it illustrates just how rapidly Christian teaching devolved. The word Ebionite means "the poor," and was used by orthodox Christians in a pejorative sense. This fact is unabashedly reported by Eusebius in his *Ecclesiastical History,* a quasi-official record of the Church. Eusebius makes no bones about Christian distaste for Jewish Christians. He tells us the Ebionites were so named because they "cherished low and mean opinions of Christ." Eusebius describes what he calls "the poverty of their intellect. For it is thus that the Hebrews call a poor man." Eusebius, *The Ecclesiastical History,* xxvii (introduction, n. 9). Eusebius's original source may have been Origen. Origen, *Contra Celsum,* trans. Henry Chadwick (Cambridge: Cambridge University Press, 1953), 2.1.

Fourth-century bishop Epiphanius of Salamis (on Cyprus) was another Ebionite basher. In his *Panarion* he wrongly attributes the name to a founder, Ebion, who, we are told, "took any item of preaching from every sect if it was dreadful, lethal, and disgusting, if it was ugly and unconvincing, if it was full of contention, and patterned himself after them all. For he [Ebion] has the Samaritans' repulsiveness but the Jews' name . . ." Epiphanius of Salamis, *The Panarion,* trans. Frank Williams (Leiden: E. J. Brill, 1987), 1.30.1,2. Notwithstanding such abuse, the fact is that the Ebionites almost certainly descended from the original Nazarene community in Jerusalem. Irenaeus was the first writer to mention them, late in the second century, by which time the sect was already regarded as heretical. Irenaeus, *Against Heresies,* 1.26.2 (introduction, n. 1).

The word Ebionim (the poor) ought to ring bells, and for good reason. Jesus used the expression in his Sermon on the Mount, although it may have originated in Psalm 109. The first Beatitude, "Blessed are the poor in spirit," puzzled me for many years—"poor in spirit" makes absolutely no sense—until I realized that "the poor" originally stood alone as an identifier. In other words, "the poor" was a self-appellation of the Nazarenes, and may have originated from II Isaiah 55:1. Thus, the Beatitude is rendered: "The poor are blessed in spirit." It was an expression of praise, not derision! The words of Jesus stand in sharp contrast with the ridicule of Eusebius and Epiphanius. And for this reason it behooves us to investigate the expression "the poor" in more detail. It turns up in Paul's Epistle to the Galatians (2:10), but in a somewhat ambiguous context. In Galations we are informed that Paul has just met with James, Peter, and John and is about to depart on one of his missionary journeys. Before he leaves, he is counseled by the three pillars to "help the poor." The orthodox interpretation, of course, is that Paul was advised to give alms to the needy. But the phrase could just as well mean that Paul was urged to support the Jerusalem community—that is, "the poor"—by remaining true to its teaching, and materially by sending home funds. Paul's own words support this interpretation. In I Corinthians 16:2–4 Paul writes to the faithful of Corinth: "Every Sunday, each one of you must put aside what he can afford, so that collections need not be made after I have come. When I am with you I will send your offerings to Jerusalem . . ." The Lukan Acts 24:17–18, 26 also report that sometime later Paul arrived in Jerusalem "to bring alms to my nation and to make offerings." Therefore, it is perfectly clear that the funds gathered by Paul were intended for the Jerusalem Church. A passage in Paul's Epistle to the Romans (15:24–27) also confirms this thesis. In the letter Paul tells the disciples in Rome, "I hope to see you on my way to Spain . . . and to complete the rest of the journey with your good wishes. First, however, I must make a present of money to the saints in Jerusalem, since Macedonia and Achaia have decided to send a generous contribution to the poor . . ." Here, Paul explicitly refers to the Nazarenes as "the poor." Further proof can be found in the Gospel of Thomas. Saying 54 reiterates the first Beatitude, and in a wholly unambiguous context: "Blessed are the poor, for yours is the kingdom of heaven." Here, the pronoun *yours* confirms beyond the shadow of a doubt that "the poor" was an appellation and referred to the Nazarenes. This sort of detail has established the tremendous importance of the Gospel of Thomas and the Nag Hammadi library as a whole.

The name Ebionite, then, traces to the Nazarenes. Is it not likely that the sect that borrowed its name from the parent community also shared in the parent community's core beliefs? We are on firm ground to make such an inference. Yet, insofar as I am aware, no Christian scholar has done so. The record shows that by the close of the second century C.E., if not before, the

Church had condemned the Ebionites as heretical. According to Irenaeus, they were considered so for not subscribing to the doctrine of the virgin birth. In other words, the Ebionites affirmed Jesus' full humanity, believing he had been born in a normal manner. Irenaeus, *Against Heresies,* 5.1.3 and 3.21.1 (introduction, n. 1). Who, then, were the true Christians? In my view, it is much more likely that the Ebionites, rather than the Church of Rome, preserved the original Nazarene teachings. If this is true, it shows just how rapidly the orthodox Church slid into error and doctrinal rigidity. Within the short space of less than two hundred years, a living spiritual tradition began to devour and debase itself.

13. In chapter 4 of his *Address to the Greeks,* Tatian wrote: "God is spirit, not pervading matter; He is invisible, impalpable, being Himself the Father of both visible and invisible things." In chapter 13 he wrote:

> The soul is not in itself immortal, O Greeks, but mortal. Yet it is possible for it not to die. If, indeed, it knows not the truth, it dies, and is dissolved with the body, but rises again at last at the end of the world with the body, receiving death by punishment in immortality. But, again, if it acquires the knowledge of God, it dies not, although for a time it is dissolved. In itself it is darkness, and there is nothing luminous in it. And this is the meaning of the saying, "The darkness comprehendeth not the light." For the soul does not preserve the spirit but is preserved by it, and the light comprehends the darkness. The Logos, in truth, is the light of God, but the ignorant soul is darkness. On this account, if it continues solitary, it tends downward toward matter, and dies with the flesh; but, if it enters into union with the Divine Spirit, it is no longer helpless, but ascends to the regions whither the spirit guides it . . .

14. Gregory of Nyssa, *The Creation of Man,* 29.3, cited in Claude Tresmontant, *The Origins of Christian Philosophy,* trans. by Mark Pontifex, in *Twentieth Century Encyclopedia of Catholocism,* vol. 2 (New York: Hawthorne Books, 1963), 88.

15. Gregory of Nyssa expressed similar ideas. For a discussion see Elizabeth Clare Prophet, *Reincarnation: The Missing Link in Christianity* (Livingston, Mont.: Summit University Press, 1997), 195.

16. A fine presentation of the Greek idea of the immortality of the soul can be found in the *Phaedo,* which recounts the poignant last conversation of Socrates. Immediately prior to taking the lethal dose of hemlock, the great philosopher waxes eloquent on the nature of the soul. *The Collected Dialogues of Plato,* ed. Edith Hamilton (New York: Pantheon Books, 1961). It is important to remember, however, that according to Herodotus the belief in the immortality of the soul did not originate with the Greeks, but was an Egyptian innovation. Herodotus. *The Histories,* trans. Aubrey de Selincourt (New York: Penguin, 1988), Book 2, 178. Even Plato reminds us in his *Timaeus* (22) that, according to Solon, one of the seven sages, the Greeks knew nearly nothing about "the times of old" compared with the Egyptians.

17. Today, we know that the first twelve chapters of Genesis, including the story of the Garden of Eden (Genesis 3:1–23), did not originate with the Hebrews

but instead was a part of the Hebrews' Semitic heritage. In 1966 W. F. Albright commented that "nearly all biblical scholars are coming to recognize that the stories of Genesis [including the story of Eden] go back to very ancient oral traditions." Albright, *New Horizons in Biblical Research* (London: Oxford University Press, 1966), 10; *Yahweh and the Gods of Canaan* (Garden City, N.Y.: Doubleday, 1968), 91; *From the Stone Age to Christianity*, 238 (chapter 1, n. 9).

No doubt the story was handed down from an older Mesopotamian account, now lost. In the biblical version there are even clues that the story had been reworked better to reflect Hebrew beliefs, though exactly how this was done cannot be determined until a copy of the Mesopotamian original turns up. Even so, it is obvious that the so-called fall from grace was not originally part of the story. In the ancient world the phrase *good and evil* did not have today's moral connotation. According to the linguist Cyrus Gordon, the ancients often used the phrase *good and evil* as an antonym, that is, a kind of shorthand expression. *Good and evil* simply meant "everything." Thus, in the context of the Eden story the meaning was: "the knowledge of everything." Other examples of antonyms can be found in Genesis 24:50, Zephaniah 1:12, and Proverbs 15:3. Gordon, *The Ancient Near East,* 36, 109 (chapter 1, n. 4).

The Garden of Eden story has close affinities with the epic of Gilgamesh, in which the hero searches for the secret of immortality. The influence of Gilgamesh is clearly detectable in the Adam and Eve story, which may even be a continuation of the same quest. The theme of immortality recurs and is accompanied by the same gloomy outcome. When Adam and Eve disobey the command not to eat of the forbidden fruit, Yahweh replies: "See, the man has become like one of us, with his knowledge of good and evil. He must not be allowed to stretch his hand out next and pick from the tree of life also, and eat some and live forever." Just as in Gilgamesh, the gods deny the boon of immortality, which remains their exclusive prerogative. The text refers to physical immortality, but the "knowledge of everything" surely hints at wisdom or spiritual knowledge. We can note that the expression "like one of us" is unmistakably polytheistic, which shows that the story did not originate within a monotheistic framework. The original god of Eden was a pagan deity, not the universal Godhead of Moses, though his identity remains unknown. The Hebrew scribe obviously inherited the story and merely inserted Yahweh in place of the god's name. Even this renaming points to polytheistic origins. In the King James edition, the name Lord God, which appears numerous times, is, in fact, a mistranslation of the text. The actual Hebrew reads "Yahweh God (El)." Here, the name Yahweh serves to denote which of many gods the story is referring to. The fact that the Hebrew scribe allowed traces of polytheism to remain indicates that the Hebrews were henotheistic at the time Genesis was compiled. In other words, they worshipped Yahweh, but they also recognized the existence of other gods worshipped by other peoples. Yahweh was simply the favored deity of the Hebrews, just as other nations had their favored gods. The pessimistic outcome again shows the strange negative reaction of the gods, including

Yahweh, to the human quest for knowledge. It is as if the deities feel threatened. Unlike the cunning serpent of the Gilgamesh epic, however, the wily serpent in the Garden story is a willing helper. Certainly this was the Gnostic interpretation.

If Augustine had been familiar with the Hebrews' Semitic background, he would have been compelled to draw very different conclusions rather than cooking up his cockamamie theory of Original Sin. But Augustine labored under a number of illusions, including the belief that the Garden story had been revealed directly by Yahweh to Moses. Augustine did not have the benefit of archaeology. For a thorough discussion of Augustine's ideas, see Henry Chadwick, *Heresy and Orthodoxy in the Early Church* (Aldershot, Hampshire, UK: Variorum, 1991), 221–22.

18. Only three letters and the fragment of a long rhapsody of verse and prose remain. See J. G. Davies, *The Early Christian Church* (New York: Holt, Rinehart, and Winston, 1965), 169.

19. Prophet, *Reincarnation: The Missing Link in Christianity,* 198 (chapter 2, n. 11).

20. See Davies, *The Early Christian Church,* 192.

21. *New Catholic Encyclopedia,* s.v. "Creation."

22. Notice the striking similarity between John 3:14 and the following passage from the Naassene hymn (*Refutation* 5.10.1). The Naassenes believed that Jesus (Yeshua = the second Joshua) had descended through the Aeons to reveal, again, the original state of perfection:

> On this account, Father, send me;
> Bearing seals, I shall descend;
> Through ages (Aeons) whole I'll sweep,
> All mysteries I'll unravel,
> And forms of Gods I'll show;
> And secrets of the saintly path,
> Styled Gnosis, I'll impart.

John's fourth gospel establishes the mystical significance of the Son of Man. The word for "man" in Aramaic, Bar-Nasha, has no such mystical connotation. See Maccoby, *The Mythmaker: Paul and the Invention of Christianity,* 77 (chapter 3, n. 11); G. R. S. Mead, *The Hymn of the Robe of Glory* (Kila, Mont.: Kessinger Publishing, n.d.), 42.

We also note that the Son of Man is closely connected to the serpent and, with the phrase "must be lifted up," to ideas that recur in the Naassene Sermon. No wonder that some bishops of the Church rejected John's Gospel as "too Gnostic."

23. Robert M. Grant, *Gnosticism and Early Christianity* (New York: Columbia University Press, 1966), 173.

24. Davies, *The Early Christian Church,* 159.

25. Luciano Canfora, *The Vanished Library* (Berkeley: University of California Press, 1989), 86–92.

Chapter 7

1. James B. Pritchard, *Archaeology and the Old Testament* (Princeton, N.J.: Princeton University Press, 1958), 110.
2. H. L. Ginsberg, *Kitvei Ugarit* [Hebrew] (Jerusalem: Bialik Foundation, 1936); also see J. W. Jack, *The Ras Shamra Tablets: Their Bearing on the Old Testament* (Edinburgh: T. and T. Clark, 1935), 8.
3. Claude F. A. Schaeffer, "The Last Days of Ugarit," *Biblical Archaeology Review* (September–October 1983), 75.
4. Albright, *History, Archaeology, and Christian Humanism,* 34 (introduction, n. 5); W. F. Albright, *The Biblical Period from Abraham to Ezra* (New York: Harper and Row, 1949), 197, 230.
5. The exception may be Elephantine, located on the Nile in southern Egypt, where the site of a Hebrew temple has been confirmed. Excavations at Elephantine have shown that the Hebrews in Egypt practiced polytheism. In his 1992 book *The Sign and the Seal,* Graham Hancock traced the lost Ark of the Covenant to Elephantine, and from there to Ethiopia. See also Albright, *History, Archaeology, and Christian Humanism,* 153 (introduction, n. 5).
6. Frank Moore Cross, *From Epic to Canon: History and Literature in Ancient Israel* (Baltimore: Johns Hopkins University Press, 1998), 87–91.
7. In their 1996 book about the origins of Freemasonry, Christopher Knight and Robert Lomas argue that various architectural features of the famous temple, such as the pillars of Jachin and Boaz, were Egyptian in origin and, along with other mysteries, were passed to the Hebrews through Moses. Even if the dubious authenticity of Egyptian origins is assumed, however, it is much more likely that the transmission occurred via the Canaanite city-states of Phoenicia, which were former Egyptian vassals. We can recall that in the story of Osiris, the body of the god landed in Byblos, on the coast of Canaan. The epochal 1929 find at Ra's Shamra and much archaeological evidence from other coastal sites confirms strong links between the coastal cities of Canaan and Egypt during the second millennium. Knight and Lomas, 1996.
8. Albright, *From the Stone Age to Christianity,* 294 (chapter 1, n. 9).
9. Jack, *The Ras Shamra Tablets: Their Bearing on the Old Testament,* 31.
10. Cited in Cross, *Canaanite Myth and Hebrew Epic: Essays in the History of the Religion of Israel,* 152 (chapter 1, n. 10).
11. H. L. Ginsberg, "The Rebellion and Death of Ba'lu," *Orientalia* 5 (1936), 180f.
12. Cross, *Canaanite Myth and Hebrew Epic: Essays in the History of the Religion of Israel,* 91–97 (chapter 1, n. 10).
13. Jack, *The Ras Shamra Tablets: Their Bearing on the Old Testament,* 28–29.
14. Ibid., 21.
15. Aharon Wiener, *The Prophet Elijah in the Development of Judaism* (London: Routledge and Kegan Paul, 1978), 12.
16. Finkelstein and Silberman, *The Bible Unearthed,* 31 (chapter 6, n.1).
17. Cross, *Canaanite Myth and Hebrew Epic: Essays in the History of the Religion of Israel,* 229–73 (chapter 1, n. 10).
18. Another Israeli archaeologist, Amihai Mazar, has taken issue with some of Finkelstein and Silberman's minimalist conclusions. Mazar agrees with them

that the biblical narrative exaggerates the accomplishments of David's united monarchy; however, Mazar thinks that they take their case too far. Mazar attributes some of the monumental structures at Megiddo, Hazor, and Gezer mentioned in I Kings 9:15 to Solomon. "Does Amihai Mazar Agree with Finkelstein's Low Chronology?" an interview, *Biblical Archaeology Review,* March–April 2003, pp. 60–61. All the same, Finkelstein and Silberman's book is a must-read. It's a riveting summation of fifty years of archaeology. Finkelstein and Silberman, *The Bible Unearthed* (chapter 6, n. 1).

19. James B. Pritchard, ed., *The Ancient Near East: An Anthology of Texts and Pictures,* vol. 1. (Princeton, N.J.: Princeton University Press, 1958), 96; IIIABA, lines 5–6.

20. Ibid., 106.

21. Albright, *Yahweh and the Gods of Canaan,* 124–25 (chapter 6, n. 17).

22. Ibid., 183–85. Rudolf Bultmann coined the term.

23. Albright's comment, made in reference to the Hebrews, is eerily similar to a remark by Jessie Weston, an Arthurian scholar whose investigation of the Grail Legend is discussed in chapter 13. Weston's remark pertained to the Adonis-Attis cult, which she referred to as the "the disjecta membra of a vanished civilization." How strange and ironic. Ibid., 183–85; Jessie L. Weston, *From Ritual to Romance* (Garden City, N.Y.: Doubleday, 1920), 7.

24. Ibid., 183–86.

25. Cross, *Canaanite Myth and Hebrew Epic: Essays in the History of the Religion of Israel,* 58 (chapter 1, n. 10).

26. Scholars believe the name Yahweh (YHWH) was in use from a very early date. The name derived from the Canaanite/proto-Hebrew verb "to be." The usual rendering is: "I am who am." Ibid., 65.

27. Ibid., 26.

28. Ibid., 123.

29. Pritchard, *Archaeology and the Old Testament,* 186–93 (chapter 7, n. 1).

30. Hermann Gunkel, *Schöpfung und Chaos in Urzeit und Endzeit* (Göttiingen: Vandenhoeck und Ruprecht, 1895).

31. For a discussion, see Cross, *Canaanite Myth and Hebrew Epic: Essays in the History of the Religion of Israel,* 106–7.

32. Ibid., 113.

33. Gordon, *The Common Background of Greek and Hebrew Civilizations,* 178–79, 189, 236 (chapter 2, n. 10).

Chapter 8

1. For a detailed study of the various Greek theophanies see M. L. West's brilliant book, *The Orphic Poems* (Oxford: Clarendon Press, 1983). For a look at Egyptian theophany, see Robert Bauval and Adrian Gilbert, *The Orion Mystery* (New York: Crown Books, 1994). For a discussion of the Sumerian gods, see Samuel Noah Kramer, *The Sumerians* (Chicago: University of Chicago Press, 1963), chapter 4.

2. Most scholars have followed Hans Jonas, *The Gnostic Religion* (Boston: Beacon Press, 1958), 92–93.

3. For a good discussion, see Yehoshafat Harkabi, *The Bar Kokhba Syndrome* (Chappaqua, N.Y.: Rossel Books, 1983).

4. See also Albright, *Yahweh and the Gods of Canaan,* 168 (chapter 6, n. 17), and Cross, *Canaanite Myth and Hebrew Epic: Essays in the History of the Religion of Israel,* 3–75 (chapter 1, n. 10).

5. For example, see Michael Grant, *The History of Ancient Israel* (New York: Scribners, 1984), 175.

6. W. F. Albright noted the absence of references in Job to any of the prophetic books and cited this as evidence that Job was composed before these books—that is, in the seventh century B.C. or even earlier. He drew the same conclusion based on allusions in Job to Chaldea. But I take a very different view: While Jeremiah criticizes king and nation, the Book of Job goes further and critiques God himself—the male God concept pervasive even in the Books of Jeremiah and Isaiah. There was good reason for Job to stand apart! Allusions to Chaldea also point to a late (post-exilic) rather than an early date for Job. The presence of the Son of Man in Ezekiel, II Isaiah, and Job points to a common Eastern source for the three. Albright, *Yahweh and the Gods of Canaan,* 260–61 (chapter 6, n. 17).

7. Carl G. Jung, *Answer to Job,* trans. R. C. F. Hull (Princeton, N.J.: Princeton University Press, 1958), 23.

8. Robinson, *The Nag Hammadi Library* (introduction, n. 6).

9. Irenaeus, *Against Heresies,* 1.29.4, 30.6 (introduction, n. 1).

10. Jung, *Answer to Job,* 13.

11. R. Gordon Wasson, Albert Hofman, and Carl A. P. Ruck, *The Road to Eleusis* (New York: Harcourt Brace, 1978), 59.

12. Ibid., 67.

13. Twentieth-century archaeology established the prevalence of goddess worship in ancient Israeli folk religion. This stood in sharp contrast to the official state religion: the pure Yahwism of the temple priesthood. For some reason, although Yahweh acquired the various epithets and qualities of all-male Canaanite gods such as Baal and El, the same did not happen with the pagan goddess. Ephraim Stern, "Pagan Yahwism," *Biblical Archaeology Review* (May–June 2001): 21. See also Finkelstein and Silberman, *The Bible Unearthed,* 241 (chapter 6, n. 1).

14. According to W. F. Albright, the eighth Proverb is filled with Canaanite words and expressions that refer to the pagan goddess. He dated it to as early as the seventh century B.C. Yet, as Albright notes, paeans to Wisdom can be found in the literature from Ugarit dating back well into the second millennium B.C. Albright, *From the Stone Age to Christianity,* 368. But if Wisdom entered Judaism as early as Albright asserts, how, then, do we explain the all-male character of Yahweh? Albright never explained this. The fact is that Yahweh did not assimilate aspects of Wisdom until very late.

15. If the late Israeli archaeologist Yigael Yadin is correct, the village of Bethany was a leper's colony in the first century. Hershel Shanks, ed., *Understanding the Dead Sea Scrolls* (New York: Random House, 1992), 104. If this is the case, Jesus surely defiled himself in the eyes of the Essenes and other strict Jews by spending time there. Matthew 21:17, 26:6; Mark 11:11, 14:3; Luke

24:50; John 11:1, 12:1. His visits were probably meant as a strong protest against the extremism of Jewish purity laws. That the Jews were a superstitious people is evidenced by the Old Testament passages indicating that they believed leprosy was a curse visited upon the wicked. II Kings 5:7, II Chronicles 26:20.

Consider the case of Miriam, sister of Moses, who, we are told, was stricken with leprosy because she opposed her brother's leadership during the wanderings in the wilderness. Numbers 12:9–10. That the incident is an obvious scribal attempt to inflate the image of the patriarch Moses is attested to by the Book of Jasher, which describes the same events in a very different light. Jasher is mentioned in Joshua 10:12–13 and II Samuel 1:18–27, but the text was regarded as a lost book until a copy turned up in England in 1721. It was first published in 1829. Albinus Flaccus Alcuinus, *The Book of Jasher* (Kila, Mont.: Kessinger Publishing, 1997). The contrast with the version of events in Numbers is remarkable: In Jasher 12–15 Miriam's stature as a prophetess is so great that she overshadows even her brother. For instance, it is Miriam, not Moses, who finds water in the desert. Miriam's importance is affirmed in the Talmud, which assigns her a status equal with that of Abraham, Isaac, Jacob, Aaron, and even Moses, the only woman so named. Raphael Patai, *The Hebrew Goddess* (New York: Avon Books, 1978), 117. In Numbers 12:9–10, Miriam's sudden attack of leprosy is portrayed as an angry intervention by Yahweh, but in Jasher leprosy is never mentioned; the punishment meted out to Miriam is instead more credible: Moses places his sister under house arrest for reasons of political expedience. Moreover, he is forced to release her when Miriam's many supporters flock to her defense. She is even credited with an important oral relic, the "Song of the Sea" (also known as the "Song of Miriam"), which establishes her unique place in Hebrew history. The archaic song, one of the oldest fragments of oral tradition in the Bible, celebrates the Red Sea crossing. (See chapter 7.) All of this appears to have been understood by the Naassenes. The Sermon mentions Miriam and describes her as "the one who is sought after" (*Refutation* 5.8.2).

King Uzziah was another Old Testament figure cursed by leprosy, stricken for entering (and thus defiling) the temple sanctuary. II Chronicles 26:19–21. It is curious that no such fate was visited upon Pompey, the Roman general who was despised for a similar offense.

16. The hymn refers to the hermaphroditic Primal Man. Clearly, his androgynous nature mirrors the Godhead. The very next line even states that "the knowledge of him [Primal Man] is the originating principle of the capacity for knowledge of God."

17. Montague Rhodes James, *The Apocryphal New Testament* (chapter 6, n. 11), 1–2.

18. Robinson, *The Nag Hammadi Library*, 128–29 (introduction, n. 9).

19. Cited in Robert M. Grant, *Gnosticism and Early Christianity*, (chapter 6, n. 23), 33.

20. Grant, *Gnosticism and Early Christianity*, 35 (chapter 5, n. 23).

21. Brandon, *The Fall of Jerusalem and the Christian Church*, chapter 9 (chapter 3, n. 10).

22. In his history, Eusebius reports that the Romans pursued the family of David for many years. The successor of James the Just was finally hunted down and executed during the reign of Trajan. Eusebius, *The Ecclesiastical History*, 11, 12, 32 (introduction, n. 9).
23. Irenaeus, *Against Heresies*, 4.4 (introduction, n. 1).
24. For an abundance of detail, see the Secret Book (Apocryphon) of John in Robinson, *The Nag Hammadi Library*, 98 (introduction, n. 6).
25. Ibid., 158.

Chapter 9

1. See chapter 8, n. 15.
2. Elaine Pagels, *The Gnostic Gospels* (New York: Random House, 1979), 41–43.
3. Will Durant, *Caesar and Christ* (New York: Simon and Schuster, 1944), 616.
4. Ibid., 746.
5. Hermas, vision 3.11, line 2. Eds. J. B. Lightfoot, J. R. Harmer, and Michael W. Holmes, *The Apostolic Fathers, Greek Texts and English Translations of Their Writings* (Grand Rapids, Mich.: Baker Book House, 1992), 351.
6. Ibid., vision 3.11, line 3.
7. Ibid., 2.8, line 1.
8. Ibid., mandate 11, line 20.
9. Ibid., vision 2.8, line 1.
10. Cited in Davies, *The Early Christian Church*, 144 (chapter 6, n. 18). See also Cyprian's Epistles 37.2 and 75.2–3. Regarding the case of Tertullian, see Eusebius, *The Ecclesiastical History*, 6.43.11 (introduction, n. 9).
11. Fifty years ago, the able Cambridge scholar Henry Chadwick first suggested that the Mariamne mentioned in the apocryphal Acts of Philip might be the very same woman who, according to the Naassene Sermon, had passed on the Nazarene teachings from James the Just. Origen, *Contra Celsum*, 312, note 9 (chapter 6, n. 12). According to the Acts of Philip, Mariamne, the sister of the apostle Philip, is described as a spiritually advanced teacher. James, *The Apocryphal New Testament*, 446 (chapter 6, n. 9). For this reason, it is extremely interesting that Origen also mentions a woman teacher named Mariamne. Is this the same woman mentioned in the Naassene Sermon? Origen provides no further details, but the very fact that he mentions her name lends credence to her historicity. Origen, *Contra Celsum*, 5 (chapter 6, n. 12).
12. Irenaeus, *Against Heresies*, fragment 29 (introduction, n. 1).
13. Jerome, Papias, and Epiphanius all confirm that Matthew was written in Hebrew. James, *The Apocryphal New Testament*, 3, 5 (chapter 6, n. 9). Contemporary scholars dispute this, however. Helmut Koester thinks the early testimony "is extraordinary because it is certain there never was a Semitic (Hebrew or Aramaic) original of the Gospel of Matthew. The Greek literary style of the Gospel of Matthew and its use of Greek sources (Mark and 'Q') and materials exclude this." This disparity has never been satisfactorily explained by scholarship. It remains one of the outstanding mysteries of Christian tradition. Koester, *Ancient Christian Gospels*, 314–17 (chapter 2, n. 3).
14. Brandon, *The Fall of Jerusalem and the Christian Church*, 237 (chapter 8, n. 21).

15. I tallied up the scriptural references in the Naassene Sermon: Matthew, 18; John, 15; Mark, 7; Luke, 9; Paul, 14; Thomas, 9; Acts, 2.
16. Irenaeus, *Against Heresies*, 1.26.2 (introduction, n. 1).
17. The evidence is found in an early document known as the *Didascalia*. See R. H. Connelly, *Didascalia Apostolorum* (Oxford: Clarendon Press, 1929).
18. Paul wrote in Galatians 1:15–16: "Then God, who had specially chosen me while I was still in my mother's womb, called me through his grace and chose to reveal his Son in me, so that I might preach the good news about him to the pagans."
19. Form criticism is an analytical method used to investigate scripture. Bultmann's first step was to reconstruct the context of the early Church—that is, the methods of preaching and evangelizing of the day. He then reconstructed the evolution of doctrine. A scriptural phrase or verse would be subjected to exhaustive linguistic and contextual analysis to determine its value—for example, whether it was original or had been adapted or even invented in light of later conditions.

   Form critical methodology, requiring command of Greek, Hebrew, and Aramaic, has proved to be a valuable tool, but there have been critics. MIT scholar Giorgio de Santillana took a derisive swipe when he referred to Bultmann as a "hyperscholar." The barb was aimed at Bultmann's arid style, especially his lack of "feel" for mythological language. Bultmann certainly did employ a dry methodology, his ostensible purpose being to demythologize the New Testament. W. F. Albright acknowledged the contributions of form critical scholars, but also observed that the results were often subjective given the short supply of substance regarding historical context. Archaeological evidence has sometimes conflicted with form critical conclusions. Giorgio de Santillana and Hertha von Dechend, *Hamlet's Mill* (Boston: Gambit, 1969), 226; Albright, *From the Stone Age to Christianity*, 380–81 (chapter 1, n. 9), *The Biblical Period from Abraham to Ezra*, 242–43 (chapter 7, n. 4).
20. Rudolf Bultmann, *Primitive Christianity in Its Contemporary Setting* (New York: Meridian Books, 1957), 140.
21. Ibid., 20.
22. Koester, *Ancient Christian Gospels*, 314 (chapter 2, n. 3).

Chapter 10

1. The two names are explained in the following way: The first and fourth chapters of the work deal with the Greek philosophers—hence, the name *Philosophumena*. The rest of the extant work is a polemic against heresy; hence, the second and more common title, the *Refutation*.
2. Cited in Birdsall, "The Naassene Sermon and the Allegorical Tradition," 41 (introduction, n. 10).
3. Mead, *Thrice Greatest Hermes: Studies in Hellenistic Theosophy and Gnosis*, 97 (chapter 5, n. 2).
4. Maccoby, *The Mythmaker: Paul and the Invention of Christianity* (chapter 3, n. 11).

5. Ibid. and Eisenman, *James the Just* (introduction, n. 9). See also Christopher Knight and Robert Lomas, *The Hiram Key.*

6. By my count, the number of references are as follows: Matthew, 18; John, 15; Paul, 14; Luke, 9; Thomas, 9; Mark, 7; Acts, 2.

7. Koester, *History and Literature of Early Christianity,* 222 (chapter 2, n. 2).

8. G. R. S. Mead, *Pistis Sophia: A Gnostic Gospel* (Blauvelt, N.Y.: Spiritual Science Library, 1921), xxi.

9. Hippolytus, *Refutatio Omnium Haeresium,* 32 (introduction, n. 10).

10. Ibid., 37.

11. Irenaeus, *Against Heresies,* 1.23.1–2.

12. Ibid., 1.30.14–15.

13. Ibid., 1.30.15.

Chapter 11

1. Will Durant, *The Story of Civilization: The Life of Greece* (New York: Simon and Schuster, 1939), 148–49.

2. Birdsall, "The Naassene Sermon and the Allegorical Tradition," 42, note 118 (introduction, n. 10); see also R. P. Casey, "Naassenes and Ophites," *Journal of Theological Studies* 27 (1926).

3. In those versions that connect the Grail with Joseph of Arimathea, the Grail King is traced either from Joseph or from Nicodemus, and the hero must show that he is descended from this family. Weston, *From Ritual to Romance,* 2 (chapter 7, n. 23).

4. Ibid., 5.

5. Ibid., 7.

6. Karl Kerényi, *Hermes: Guide of Souls* (Woodstock, Conn.: Spring Publications, 1976), 132–33.

7. Garth Fowden, *The Egyptian Hermes* (Cambridge: Cambridge University Press, 1978).

8. Erich Neumann, *The Great Mother: Analysis of the Architect,* trans. Ralph Manheim (Princeton, N.J.: Princeton University Press, 1955), 116.

9. Michael Baigent, Richard Leigh, and Henry Lincoln, *Holy Blood, Holy Grail* (New York: Dell Books, 1982); see also Laurence Gardner, *Bloodline of the Holy Grail* (New York: Barnes and Noble, 1996).

10. Rudolf Otto coined the word. Otto, *The Idea of the Holy* (chapter 1, n. 8).

11. Jung, *Aion: Researches into the Phenomenology of the Self,* 223 (chapter 4, n. 17).

12. Carl G. Jung, *The Archetypes and the Collective Unconscious* (Princeton, N.J.: Princeton University Press, 1959), 121.

13. Carl G. Jung, *Two Essays on Analytical Psychology* (New York: Meridian Books, World Publishing Co., 1956), 81.

14. Carl G. Jung, *The Secret of the Golden Flower: A Chinese Book of Life* (New York: Harcourt, Brace, and World, 1931), 128–29.

15. Carl G. Jung, *Memories, Dreams, and Reflections* (New York: Vintage, 1965), 288.

16. For a detailed discussion with primary sources, see Immanuel Velikovsky, *Worlds in Collision* (New York: Dell, 1950), 198–99.
17. Emma Jung and Marie-Louise von Franz, *The Grail Legend* (Baltimore: Sigo Press, 1980), 19.
18. Ibid., 159.
19. Will Durant, *The Age of Faith* (New York: Simon and Schuster, 1950), 588.
20. Ibid., 785–818.
21. Ean Begg, *The Cult of the Black Madonna* (New York: Penguin Books, 1985).
22. Jung, *Aion,* 150.
23. Will Durant is an excellent source on this. Durant, *The Age of Faith,* 863–94.
24. Jung and von Franz, *The Grail Legend,* 100.
25. In 1542, the Inquisition was euphemistically renamed the Holy Office.

Chapter 12

1. See the introduction of H. McLachlin, ed., *Sir Isaac Newton: Theological Manuscripts* (Liverpool: University Press, 1950).
2. Betty Jo Teeter Dobbs, *The Foundations of Newton's Alchemy* (Cambridge: Cambridge University Press, 1975).
3. Jung and von Franz, *The Grail Legend,* 142 (chapter 11, n. 17).
4. Ibid., 138.
5. Matthew 23 and Luke 11:40 make allusion to this saying of Jesus from the Gospel of Thomas, although in a context that does not hint at its mystical significance: a vitriolic diatribe against the Pharisees. Note that the related passage in Mark 12:38 is much milder, although the cup is not mentioned. If Helmut Koester is correct, the Gospel of Thomas preceded the other accounts, in which case the mystical variant was the original. Mark came later, and last of all came the heavily rewritten episodes in Matthew and Luke as the anti-Pharisee rhetoric heated up after the Jewish War. Robinson, *The Nag Hammadi Library,* 127 (introduction, n. 6).
6. Cited in Jung and von Franz, *The Grail Legend,* 143 (chapter 11, n. 17).
7. Elisabeth Kübler-Ross, *The Wheel of Life* (New York: Scribner, 1997), 220–21.
8. This cultic bowl remains enigmatic. In a 1939 paper, "The Mystery of the Serpent," Hans Leisegang subjected the carvings on the bowl to exhaustive investigation. He also analyzed the Greek inscription on the outside (not visible in fig. 12.1). Leisegang convincingly showed that the inscription and all or most of the symbolism were Orphic in origin. He thereby cast serious doubt on a Christian provenance. Leisegang's paper was later included in an important collection of essays published by the Jung Institute. See Joseph Campbell, ed., *The Mysteries: Papers from the Eranos Yearbooks* (Princeton, N.J.: Princeton University Press, 1955), 194.

I recall the first time I read Leisegang's paper—and the disconcerting effect it had on me. The paper was generally persuasive. However, I did not wish to be persuaded that pagans had produced the bowl. I was already convinced that the Ophite bowl was an artistic representation of the mystical Grail. To me, the object suggested the open heart center; I did not wish to believe otherwise. After further investigation, however, I discovered the answer: The bowl is *both* Christian and Orphic. Before Ivan Linforth's brilliant 1941 book about Orpheus, most scholars believed that the many surviving pseudonymous poems from the ancient world attributed to Orpheus documented the existence of an Orphic religious community dating to pre-Homeric times. Linforth was the first scholar to put this assumption to the test. In a remarkable book, he analyzed every single reference to Orpheus in classical and preclassical literature, including both primary and secondary sources—a prodigious effort. Try as he might, however, he was unable to find in the literature a scintilla of evidence indicating that an Orphic religious tradition had ever existed. Ivan M. Linforth, *The Arts of Orpheus* (New York: Arno Press, 1973).

How, then, to explain Orphism? The probable answer is that it was a tendency, not a religion. That is, Orphism was a progressive current within Greek culture and religion as a whole, but not a separate tradition. Greeks who regarded themselves as followers of Orpheus tended to be vegetarians, who often believed in the soul, a monotheistic God, and reincarnation. At the same time, they often participated in various pagan rites, which they attempted to reconcile with Orphic philosophy, probably succeeding most of the time. Thus, Orphism was a positive force and a civilizing influence within Greek society. This continued to be the case over many centuries, but when Christianity appeared on the scene, it became an irresistible attraction to Orphics. In fact, there is powerful evidence suggesting that Orphics were among the first Gentile converts. Robert Eisler showed that many of the paintings that still adorn the walls of the catacombs of Rome were Orphic images. Indeed, the first artistic Christian impressions of Jesus were probably borrowed from Orphism. Today, most paintings of Jesus resemble the image on the Shroud of Turin, but this depiction did not gain prominence until the sixth century C.E. Copies of several of the older Orphic illustrations from the catacombs appear at the back of Eisler's book. Eisler, *Orpheus the Fisher* (chapter 4, n. 14).

In short, a melding of Orphic ideas and Christian teachings seems to have occurred in the early period of Christianity. Because Orphics were especially attracted by the Gnostic element, we should not be surprised to find this reflected in the Ophite bowl. I have not found any convincing evidence that the cultic bowl was indigenous to pagan Greece. The famous krater mentioned by Plato in his *Timaeus* has sometimes been cited, but the krater was neither a cup nor a chalice, nor did it resemble the Ophite bowl. Instead, it was an amphora, a large, widemouthed jug commonly used for mixing wine. (In Greece it was customary to dilute the infamously potent concoctions that passed for table wine with water in order to achieve the desired level of inebriation.) It seems, then, that Weston was basically on the right path but did not pursue her investigation far enough. The Grail was an invention of Gnostic Christianity. R. Gordon Wasson, Albert Hofmann, and Carl A. P. Ruck, *The Road to Eleusis* (New York: Harcourt Brace, 1978); M. L. West, *The Orphic Poems,* (chapter 8, n. 1); W. K. C. Guthrie, *Orpheus and Greek Religion* (London: Methuen, 1935).

9. Swami Rama, "The Awakening of Kundalini," in John White, ed., *Kundalini, Evolution, and Enlightenment* (Garden City, N.Y.: Doubleday, 1979), 27.

10. Swami Kripananda, *The Sacred Power: A Seeker's Guide to Kundalini* (South Fallsburg, N.Y.: SYDA Foundation, 1995), 9.

11. The place between the eyes is the focus of concentration, but the actual point is probably deep in the head, coextensive with the brain.

12. Jung refused to accept the existence of the seventh chakra, the sahasrara, because of its location outside the head. We may wonder if Jung knew about Kirlian photography, which clearly demonstrates that the life field extends beyond the skin. J. Marvin Spiegelman and Arwind U. Vasavada, *Hinduism and Jungian Psychology* (Phoenix, Ariz.: Falcon Press, 1987), 56, 63.

13. The Gnostic Monoimus had a similar teaching that also involved immanence. Hippolytus describes Monoimus as an Arab and allocates four chapters to his teaching. Hippolytus writes: "This . . . single monad . . . is uncompounded and indivisible, [and yet at the same time] compounded and divisible . . . This [is] Mother, this [is] Father—two immortal names." This point or jot contains all and is found within, for Hippolytus goes on, quoting Monoimus: " . . . seek for Him from [out of] thyself, and learn who it is that absolutely appropriates [unto Himself] all things in thee . . ." Hippolytus continues: "[I]f, he says, you actively investigate these [points], you will discover [God] Himself, unity and plurality, in thyself . . ." *Refutation* 8.11–14.

14. Shyam Sundar Goswami, *Layayoga* (London: Routledge and Kegan Paul, 1980), 156.

15. "For the dwelling place of our heart, my brothers, is a holy temple dedicated to the Lord." Epistle of Barnabas, 6.15; see also 16. 7–10 in J. B. Lightfoot and J. R. Harmer, eds., *The Apostolic Fathers* (Grand Rapids, Mich.: Baker Book House, 1992).

16. Goswami, *Layayoga,* 152.

17. Ibid., 212–15.

18. See K. [T. V. Kapali Sastry], *Sat-Darshana Bhashya and Talks with Maharshi with Forty Verses in Praise of Sri Ramana,* 5th edition (Tiruvannamalai, India: Sri Ramanasramam, 1968), xv, xvii; see also Da Avabhasa, *The Knee of Listening* (Clear Lake, Calif.: Dawn Horse Press, 1992), 255–63.

19. Sri Ramana Maharshi, *Talks with Sri Ramana Maharshi* (Tiruvannamalai, India: Sri Ramanasramam, 1972), 55, 92–93.

20. Goswami, *Layayoga,* 16–17.

21. Ibid., 152–53.

22. Kripananda, *The Sacred Power: A Seeker's Guide to Kundalini,* 88.

23. Swami Vivekananda, *Raja Yoga* (New York: Brentano, 1929), 51, 59.

24. Christopher Isherwood, *Ramakrishna and His Disciples* (New York: Simon and Schuster, 1959) , 318–21.

25. Kripananda, *The Sacred Power: A Seeker's Guide to Kundalini,* 82.

26. Dialogue of the Savior in Robinson, *The Nag Hammadi Library,* 229–30 (introduction, n. 6). See also Koester, *History and Literature of Early Christianity,* 154–55 (chapter 2, n. 2).

27. Geshe Kelsang Gyatso, *Heart of Wisdom* (London: Tharpa Publications, 1986), 13–14.

28. Joshu Sasaki Roshi, *Buddha Is the Center of Gravity,* trans. Fusako Akino (San Cristobal, N.M.: Lama Foundation, 1974), 24.

29. John of the Cross, *Collected Works,* trans. by Kieran Kavanaugh (Washington, D.C.: ICS Publications, 1973), 43.

30. Ibid., 15–26.

31. Joan Carroll Cruz, *The Incorruptibles* (Rockford, Ill.: Tan Books, 1977), 199–201; see also Yogananda, *Autobiography of a Yogi,* 85 (chapter 2, n. 7).

32. Yogananda, *Autobiography of a Yogi,* 315.

33. Ibid., 498.

34. Carl Jung, "The Process of Individuation," in *Modern Psychology* 3 (1959): 17.

35. Ibid. p. 71.

36. Carl Jung, "Yoga and the West," in *Collected Works,* vol. 11 (Princeton: Princeton University Press, 1958), 876.

37. Albright wrote: "Confrontation of all the evidence now available [from Nag Hammadi] for the origin of Gnosticism confirms the accounts of the Church Fathers . . ." Again: "There is no reason to doubt the essential correctness of the tradition of Irenaeus and Hippolytus . . ." And again, from *History, Archaeology, and Christian Humanism,* 40, 41, 295 (introduction, n. 5):

> . . . their belief in salvation from the power of archontic determinism through knowledge (gnosis) of all cosmic mysteries, stands in direct opposition to the Gospel. No wonder that the Orthodox, whether New Testament writers, or Church Fathers, reacted violently against the radical ideas of the Gnostics, who tended to express themselves either in extreme asceticism and rejection of the world or in equally excessive libertinism.

38. Ibid., 46; Albright, *New Horizons in Biblical Research,* 42 (chapter 6, n. 17).

39. Albright, *History, Archaeology, and Christian Humanism,* 40, 253 (introduction, n. 5).

40. Albright, *From the Stone Age to Christianity,* 23 (chapter 1, n. 9).

41. Jung's concluding comments in his discussion of Gnosticism show that even though he was not a rationalist like Albright, in the end he embraced the same belief in a transcendent deity. Jung believed that the growth of the human personality and the development of consciousness were ". . . gravely threatened in our anti-Christian age, not only by the sociopolitical delusional systems, but above all by the rationalistic hubris which is tearing our consciousness from its transcendent roots and holding before it immanent goals." Jung, *Aion,* 221 (chapter 4, n. 17).

42. Weston, *From Ritual to Romance,* 188 (chapter 7, n. 23).

Chapter 13

1. Pritchard, *The Ancient Near East: An Anthology of Texts and Pictures,* vol. 1, 28–30 (chapter 7, n. 19).

2. Nicholas Roerich, *Shambala: In Search of the New Era* (New York: Nicholas Roerich Museum, 1990), 20.

3. Pritchard, *The Ancient Near East: An Anthology of Texts and Pictures,* vol. 1, 102.

4. Robert K. G. Temple, *The Sirius Mystery* (Rochester, Vt.: Destiny Books, 1987), 138, 142.

5. Plato, *Timaeus* (New York: Pantheon Books, 1961) 21–26.

6. The Mesha Stone is on display in the Louvre. Jack Finegan, *Light from the Ancient Past* (Princeton, N.J.: Princeton University Press, 1959), 188; see also Pritchard, *Archaeology and the Old Testament,* 103 (chapter 7, n. 1).

7. Joyce Milton, Robert A. Orsi, and Norman Harrison, *The Feathered Serpent and the Cross: The Pre-Columbian God-Kings and the Papal States* (London: Cassell, 1980), 64.

8. Ibid., 55.

9. Peter Tompkins, *Mysteries of the Mexican Pyramids* (New York: Harper and Row, 1976), 355–63.

10. Ibid.

11. Cross, *Canaanite Myth and Hebrew Epic: Essays in the History of the Religion of Israel,* 36 (chapter 1, n. 10).

12. Langdon, *The Sumerian Epic of Paradise, the Flood, and the Fall of Man,* 11 (chapter 4, n. 19).

13. Homer, *Iliad,* Book 18, trans. Alston Hurd Chase and William G. Perry (New York: Bantam Books, 1950).

14. The shield of Heracles is described in Hesiod's *Theogony,* trans. Apostolos N. Athanassakis (Baltimore: Johns Hopkins University Press, 1983), 138.

15. Homer, *Iliad,* Book 14.

16. Herodotus, *The Histories,* Book 4 (chapter 6, n. 16).

17. The seven sages included Thales, Solon, Plato, Pythagoras, Eudoxus, Socrates, and Lycurgus.

18. R. T. Rundle Clark, *Myth and Symbol in Ancient Egypt* (London: Thames and Hudson, 1995), 36.

19. R. O. Faulkner, *The Ancient Egyptian Pyramid Texts* (Oxford: Oxford University Press, 1969), Utterance 600, 246–47.

20. Thorkild Jacobsen, *The Treasures of Darkness: A History of Mesopotamian Religion* (New Haven, Conn.: Yale University Press, 1976), 181.

21. Ibid., 167.

22. Ibid., 173.

23. Eisler, *Orpheus the Fisher,* 169 (chapter 4, n. 14).

24. Louis Ginzberg, *The Legends of the Jews,* vols. 1 and 4 (Philadelphia: The Jewish Publication Society of America, 1941), 96.

25. The line is from the Atra-Hasis, the Babylonian story of the Flood. W. G. Lambert and A. R. Millard, *Atra-hasis: The Babylonian Story of the Flood* (Oxford: Clarendon Press, 1969), 43.

26. Kramer, *The Sumerians,* 151–52 (chapter 8, n. 1).

27. Eisler, *Orpheus the Fisher,* 177.

28. Graham Hancock and Robert Bauval, *The Message of the Sphinx* (New York: Three Rivers Press, 1996), 140–44.

29. Plutarch, "The Mysteries of Isis and Osiris," in Mead, *Thrice Greatest Hermes: Studies in Hellenistic Theosophy and Gnosis,* 178 (chapter 5, n. 2).

30. Strabo, *The Geography,* vol. 8, 111–13, cited in Graham Hancock, *Fingerprints of the Gods* (New York: Crown Trade Paperbacks, 1995), 399.

31. Margaret Murray, *The Splendour That Was Egypt* (London: Sidgwick and Jackson, 1963), 160–61:

> It [the Osireion] was made for the celebration of the mysteries of Osiris, and so far is unique among all the surviving buildings of Egypt. It is clearly early, for the great blocks of which it is built are of the style of the Old Kingdom; the simplicity of the actual building also points to it being of that early date. The decoration was added by Seti I, who in that way laid claim to the building, but seeing how often a Pharaoh claimed the work of his predecessors by putting his name on it, this fact does not carry much weight. It is the style of the building, the type of the masonry, the tooling of the stone, and not the name of a king, which date buildings in Egypt.

32. Frankfort found several cartouches of Seti I, which led him to date the temple to the time of Seti. Henri Frankfort, *The Cenotaph of Seti I at Abydos* (London: Kegan Paul, Trench, Trubner, and Co., 1933), 4.
33. Ibid., 21.
34. For an excellent discussion, see Graham Hancock, *Fingerprints of the Gods* (New York: Crown, 1995), chapter 45.
35. Edouard Naville, "Excavation at Abydos," *Journal of Egyptian Archaeology* 1 (July 1914): 159–67.
36. Strabo, *The Geography*, Volume 8, 111–13.
37. Margaret Murray, *The Osireion at Abydos* (London: Barnard Quaritch, 1904), 2.
38. H. F. Ferrar, "The Movements of the Sub-soil Water in Upper Egypt," paper no. 19 of the Survey Department of the Ministry of Finance, Cairo, 1911. Also cited in Frankfort, *The Cenotaph of Seti I at Abydos.*
39. Frankfort, *The Cenotaph of Seti I at Abydos,* 19.
40. Naville, "Excavation at Abydos," 159–67.
41. Ibid.
42. Albright, *From the Stone Age to Christianity,* 376 (chapter 1, n. 9).
43. My primary sources on Osiris are: Clark, *Myth and Symbol in Ancient Egypt,* 124–25; Plutarch, "The Mysteries of Isis and Osiris," in Mead, *Thrice Greatest Hermes: Studies in Hellenistic Theosophy and Gnosis,* 178–256; Murray, *The Osireion at Abydos;* and Frankfort, *The Cenotaph of Seti I at Abydos.*
44. Bauval and Gilbert, *The Orion Mystery.*
45. Faulkner, *The Ancient Egyptian Pyramid Texts,* 285.
46. Utterance 366, cited in Clark, *Myth and Symbol in Ancient Egypt,* 117.
47. The passage, from Mead, *Thrice Greatest Hermes: Studies in Hellenistic Theosophy and Gnosis,* 215, reads:

> Moreover, they say that sun and moon do not use chariots for vehicles, but sail around in boats . . . [thus] riddling their being nourished by and being born by in the "moist." And they think that Homer also, like Thales, set down Water as source and birth of all things, after learning [it] from the Egyptians; for [the Greek god] Ocean is Oriris . . .

48. Murray, *The Osireion at Abydos,* 11 and plate 13; Frankfort, *The Cenotaph of Seti I at Abydos,* 29.

49. Homer, *Iliad,* Book 21.

50. Clark, *Myth and Symbol in Ancient Egypt,* 129–30.

51. Cited in Frankfort, *The Cenotaph of Seti I at Abydos,* 32.

52. K. A. Kitchen, *Pharaoh Triumphant: The Life and Times of Ramses II* (Warminster, England: Aris and Phillips, 1983), 45; see also maps on 114 and 117.

53. E. A. Wallis Budge, trans., *The Book of the Dead: The Hieroglyphic Transcript of the Papyrus of Ani* (New Hyde Park, N.Y.: University Books, 1960), 197.

54. In the earliest period of Egyptian civilization, there were apparently two separate deities with the name Horus. One was Horus the sun god (Ra or Re). The other was Horus the son of Osiris. At some point the two fused into a single deity. This probably explains why in hieroglyphic language the falcon is the symbol of both the sun god, Re, and the son of Osiris. It also explains why Horus-as-sun-god is sometimes distinguished by a double symbol: the sun disk above the falcon's head. The identification of Horus the sun with the earthly Horus (son of Osiris) added an element of confusing complexity to a mythology that was already complex. This confusion marred an otherwise fascinating study by Hancock and Bauval, *The Message of the Sphinx.*

55. For a discussion, see Clark, *Myth and Symbol in Ancient Egypt,* 50–67. Rundle Clark does a nice job of describing the various stories, but, surprisingly, fails to recognize that the issue of the fight is order versus chaos.

56. Budge, *The Book of the Dead: The Hieroglyphic Transcript of the Papyrus of Ani,* 166, 179.

57. William Irwin Thompson, *The Time Falling Bodies Take to Light* (New York: St. Martin's Press, 1981), chapter 5.

58. Faulkner, *The Ancient Egyptian Pyramid Texts,* 200, lines 1259–61.

59. Ibid., 253, lines 1716–17.

60. Hesiod, *Theogony,* 32–33, lines 775–79.

61. Ibid., lines 360–63.

62. Virgil, *The Aeneid,* Book 6, lines 439–40.

63. West, *The Orphic Poems* (chapter 8, n. 1).

64. Eisler, *Orpheus the Fisher,* 169–81.

65. Langdon, *The Sumerian Epic of Paradise, the Flood, and the Fall of Man,* 68.

66. According to Wallis Budge, one of the most ancient symbols associated with the worship of Osiris was known as the Tet, which he interpreted as the sacrum of Osiris. The Egyptians believed that the Tet had been preserved from very ancient times in the northern center. The cult city also shared the name Tet, which the Greeks translated as Busiris. According to Budge, from a very early time "Osiris was assimilated to the Tet, and the ceremony of 'setting up the Tet' became the equivalent of the reconstitution of the backbone and the body of Osiris." Budge, trans., *The Book of the Dead: The Hieroglyphic Transcript of the Papyrus of Ani,* 48–52. For a good discussion about the sacred basin, see Ida Rolf, *Rolfing: The Integration of Human Structures* (San Francisco: Harper and Row, 1977), chapter 5.

67. Marie-Louise von Franz and Emma Jung thoroughly analyze both symbols in *The Grail Legend*. They inform us that the Grail as vessel represents the fruition of spiritual development in wholeness and unity, while the Grail as stone represents the divine presence in matter. Both symbols have to do with God's immanence, but the vessel stands for the realization of this truth in a more personal way, while the stone simply refers to the fact. The stone, in other words, conveys the same truth, but in the raw. It implies no awareness. A stone, after all, is something underfoot, ordinary, worthless; we step over stones and walk upon them every day without paying them any thought. The same is true of the divine presence. We are enfolded in God. God is around us and within us every second of every hour of every day. No matter where we turn, no matter where we go, the face of the divinity greets us. Yet we fail to recognize this great truth. We are like sleepwalkers caught up in the illusions and delusions of life, and so we squander the greatest part of our lives in mundane and trivial pursuits. Perhaps this is why in stories from the various spiritual traditions the guru often comes to test the disciple in the guise of a lowly beggar, cripple, or leper. The object of scorn or ridicule, that which is undervalued or outcast, often holds the key to the divine mystery. In Isaiah 28:16 the cornerstone is the precious stone, the foundational stone. Yet according to Psalm 118, the builders rejected this same stone. The question is why? Jung and von Franz, *The Grail Legend,* 157 (chapter 11, n. 17).

Chapter 14

1. Gershom G. Scholem, *Jewish Gnosticism, Merkabah Mysticism, and Talmudic Tradition* (New York: Jewish Theological Seminary of America, 1960), 35.
2. The reader is referred to the index of Robinson, *The Nag Hammadi Library,* 484, 488, and 492 (introduction, n. 6).
3. Budge, trans., *The Book of the Dead: The Hieroglyphic Transcript of the Papyrus of Ani,* 111–13 (chapter 13, n. 53).
4. Swami Muktananda, *Play of Consciousness* (South Fallsburg, N.Y.: SYDA Foundation, 1971), 101–3.
5. Swami Muktananda, *Secrets of the Siddhas* (South Fallsburg, N.Y.: SYDA Foundation, 1980), 21.
6. Muktananda, *Play of Consciousness,* 168–71.

Appendix 1

1. Rev. MacMahon points out that the actual word is Nahash. The meaning of Naassene has never been definitively explained.
2. Origen mentions a woman teacher named Mariamne in his *Contra Celsum* 5.62 (chapter 6, n. 12). However, he provides no further details. An apocryphal Christian scripture known as the Acts of Philip also mentions a woman named Mariamne. In it she travels with her brother, the apostle Philip, to the land of the Ophites, presumably for the purpose of proselytizing. I was unable to discover much background information about the gospel. The text is available for study. See James, *The Apocryphal New Testament* (chapter 6, n. 9). See also chapter 9, n. 11.

3. This is Hippolytus speaking, not the Naassene scribe.

4. Isaiah 53:8.

5. Birdsall attributes this to Apollodorus, *The Library,* 1.6.1.

6. According to Legge, this passage is a lost Pindaric ode. Mead agrees and identifies it as the Hymn to Jupiter Ammon, which, he says, shows the heavy influence of the Egyptians.

7. Ephesians 3:15. This section (5.7.6–8) is one of the strangest and most obscure parts of the Naassene Sermon. As early as 1927 the scholar Carl Kraeling referred to it as the Chaldean Tale. Kraeling followed Reitzenstein's view that it is based on very ancient material that probably originated in Iran. In the Iranian account, Primal Man is known as Gayomart. He contends with hostile powers and is overcome after a long struggle. Humanity is born in the moment of his defeat. Carl H. Kraeling, *Anthropos and Son of Man* (New York: AMS Press, 1927), 51, 115, 120.

8. Birdsall attributes this line to Plutarch. Birdsall, "The Naassene Sermon and the Allegorical Tradition," 261 (introduction, n. 10).

9. Birdsall attributes this to Apollodorus, *The Library,* 3.14.4.

10. Galatians 3:28.

11. 2 Corinthians 5:17, Galatians 6:15–16.

12. Romans 1:20–27.

13. Thomas 3, Luke 17:21.

14. Thomas 4.

15. This is Hippolytus speaking, not the Naassene scribe.

16. This is Hippolytus speaking.

17. This was Rev. McMahon's translation. Birdsall omitted the word *logos* from his rendering, which was: "This is their unspeakable and secret doctrine." F. Legge's 1921 translation was as follows: "This is their ineffable and mystical saying . . ." But there is no question that in this passage the word *logos* is linked with the phrase "fourteenth age" in the previous line. This was confirmed by Dr. Jorge Bravo, a professor of Greek at the University of California, Berkeley, which establishes an incontrovertible link between Jesus and Elisha.

18. Herodotus 2.2, 5.

19. Plutarch, "The Mysteries of Isis and Osiris," in Mead, *Thrice Greatest Hermes: Studies in Hellenistic Theosophy and Gnosis,* chapter 34 (chapter 5, n. 2).

20. Proverbs 24:16, Luke 17:4.

21. Exodus 3:14.

22. Birdsall believes that he found a source for this in Aristotle, *Metaphysics,* 12.71072b8.

23. Matthew 19:17, Mark 10:18, Luke 18:19.

24. Matthew 5:45.

25. Thomas 33, Mark 4:21.

26. Matthew 5:15, 10:27.

27. The demiurge Ialdabaoth. Mead thinks this was a mistranslation from the Greek, and prefers Esaddaios, which he calls "the transliteration of *El Shaddai.*"

28. Psalm 2:9.
29. Ephesians 5:14.
30. Compare to Psalm 8:6, 1 Corinthians 15:27.
31. Romans 10:18. Unsubstantiated. This is a passage from Exodus 9:16—hence, it cannot be attributed to Paul with certainty. See also Psalm 19:4.
32. The theme of the cornerstone. Psalm 118:22, Isaiah 28:16, 1 Peter 2:7.
33. Ephesians 3:15, Thomas 66, Matthew 21:42, Mark 12:10–11, Luke 20:17, Acts 4:11–12.
34. Homer, *Iliad* 4:350.
35. Daniel 2:45.
36. Notice, Hermes is associated with the logos principle no less than Jesus because he has some of the characteristics of the Son of Man.
37. Homer, *Iliad* 14:201, 246.
38. Psalm 82:6, John 10:34.
39. Galatians 4:26.
40. After the fall of Jerusalem in 586–587 B.C., Jeremiah warned the survivors that if they took flight into Egypt, they would be killed. His prophecy was realized when the Babylonians later invaded the delta. Jeremiah 42:42, Psalm 82:7. See also Philo, *De Agricult. lib.* i.
41. John 3:3.
42. John 3:6.
43. Joshua 3:7–17.
44. In his 1921 translation, F. Legge interprets the word as Joshua. Birdsall translates it as Jesus/Joshua. Birdsall, "The Naassene Sermon and the Allegorical Tradition" (introduction, n. 10). Rev. MacMahon (1868) got it right.
45. This phrase, "the one who was much sought after," seems to refer to chapter 15 of the Book of Jasher, one of the lost books, a copy of which turned up in the early eighteenth century in England. Jasher 12–15 presents an alternative history of the wanderings in the desert. In the traditional account (Exodus 15 and Numbers 12) Miriam is stricken with leprosy, a punishment inflicted by Yahweh for inciting the people against her brother Moses. In Jasher, however, there is no heavenly intervention. Moses puts Miriam under house arrest for opposing him. Subsequently, however, he is compelled to release her because of Miriam's great popularity—the people demand it. Thus, the Naassene Sermon appears to confirm this alternative version of events recounted in Jasher. For an extended discussion, see also chapter 8, n. 15.
46. Matthew 13:13–14, Luke 8:10. The original source is Isaiah 6:9.
47. Isaiah 28:10–13.
48. John 1:3–4.
49. Genesis 44:2–5.
50. John 2:1–11.
51. Thomas 3, Luke 17:21.
52. Matthew 13:33.
53. John 6:53, Mark 10:38.
54. Matthew 20:22, Mark 10:38.
55. John 8:21, 13:33.
56. Deuteronomy 4:12, John 5:37.

57. Psalm 29:3,10.
58. Psalm 22:20–21, 35:17.
59. Compare to Isaiah 41:8.
60. Isaiah 43:1. Here again we see the equivalence of sea and river; both = the waters.
61. Isaiah 41:8, 43:1–2.
62. Isaiah 43:1.
63. Isaiah 49:15.
64. Paraphrase of Isaiah 49:15.
65. Psalm 24:7–9.
66. Psalm 22:6, Psalm 24:8.
67. Job 40:32.
68. Jacob's ladder. Genesis 28:7–17.
69. John 10:9, Matthew 7:13.
70. Ephesians 2:17, Isaiah 57:19.
71. Matthew 23:27, Luke 11:44, Acts 23:3.
72. Matthew 27:52–53.
73. 2 Corinthians 12:2.
74. This expression "man of soul" was idiomatic. The meaning is never clarified in the Sermon. It remains obscure.
75. 1 Corinthians 2:13–14.
76. John 6:44.
77. Matthew 7:21.
78. Matthew 21:31.
79. 1 Corinthians 10:11.
80. Thomas 9, Matthew 13:3–9, Mark 4:3–9, Luke 8:5–8.
81. Deuteronomy 31:20.
82. Matthew 3:10, Luke 3:9.
83. Thomas 11.
84. Matthew 7:6.
85. Isaiah 54:1, Galatians 4:27.
86. Jeremiah 31:15, Matthew 2:18.
87. John 3:5.
88. Jeremiah 17:5–9.
89. Birdsall attributes this line to Heraclitus.
90. Again, this refers to the story of Jacob. Genesis 28:17.
91. Thomas 37.
92. Thomas 114.
93. According to Rev. MacMahon, this refers to Isaiah 7:14, the key passage cited by Matthew in his infancy gospel. If this is true, the passage must be based on the Septuagint in which *alma*, the Hebrew word for "a young woman," was rendered as "virgin." I disagree with Rev. MacMahon on this, however. I believe that the Naassene reference to virginal Spirit simply means the feminine nature of the Holy Spirit. The Naassenes, in my view, did not ascribe to the virgin birth doctrine. They believed Jesus had been born in the normal manner.

94. Matthew 7:13–14.
95. John 1:3.
96. Possibly alludes to Matthew 11:17.
97. A conflation of John 4:21 and 23.
98. John 4:21.
99. Matthew 13:31–32, Mark 4:31–32, Luke 13:19.
100. The full quote is: "The heavens declare the glory of God, the vault of heaven proclaims his handiwork, day discourses of it to day, night to night hands on the knowledge, [yet] no utterance at all, no speech, no sound that anyone can hear . . ." Psalm 19:3.
101. This equivalance of serpent (or dragon) and water finds its basis in ancient Near Eastern mythology. See chapters 7 and 13.
102. Genesis 2:10.
103. Genesis 2:11–14.
104. The upper waters. Genesis 1:7.
105. John 4:10.
106. John 1:9, 9:1.
107. Isaiah 40:15.
108. 1 Samuel 10:1, 16:13.
109. The witch of Endor. See 1 Samuel 16:14.

Bibliography

Albright, W. F. *From the Stone Age to Christianity*. Baltimore: Johns Hopkins University Press, 1940.

———. *The Archaeology of Palestine*. Baltimore: Penguin, 1949.

———. *The Biblical Period from Abraham to Ezra*. New York: Harper and Row, 1949.

———. *History, Archaeology, and Christian Humanism*. New York: McGraw Hill, 1964.

———. *New Horizons in Biblical Research*. London: Oxford University Press, 1966.

———. *Yahweh and the Gods of Canaan*. Garden City, N.Y.: Doubleday, 1968.

Alcuinus, Albinus Flaccus, trans. *The Book of Jasher*. Whitefish, Mont.: Kessinger Publishing, 1997.

Allegro, John. *The Dead Sea Scrolls*. New York: Penguin Books, 1956.

———. *The Treasure of the Copper Scroll*. Garden City, N. Y.: Doubleday, 1964.

Alt, Albrecht. *Essays on Old Testament History and Religion*. Garden City, N.Y.: Doubleday, 1967.

Armstrong, Karen. *A History of God*. New York: Ballantine Books, 1993.

Athanassakis, Apostolos N. *The Orphic Hymns*. Missoula, Mont.: Scholars Press, 1977.

Baigent, Michael, Richard Leigh, and Henry Lincoln. *Holy Blood, Holy Grail*. New York: Dell Books, 1982.

Baigent, Michael, and Richard Leigh. *The Dead Sea Scroll Deception*. New York: Simon and Schuster, 1991.

Barnstone, Willis, ed. *The Other Bible*. New York: Harper and Row, 1971.

Bauer, Walter. *Orthodoxy and Heresy in Earliest Christianity*. Edited by Robert Kraft and Gerhard Krodel. Philadelphia: Fortress Press, 1971.

Bauval, Robert. "Investigation on the Origin of the BenBen Stone." In *Discussions in Egyptology* 14 (1989).

Bauval, Robert, and Adrian Gilbert. *The Orion Mystery*. New York: Crown Books, 1994.

Begg, Ean. *The Cult of the Black Madonna*. New York: Penguin Books, 1985.

Bibby, Geoffrey. *Looking for Dilmun*. New York: Alfred A. Knopf, 1969.

Birdsall, R. Scott. "The Naassene Sermon and the Allegorical Tradition." Ph.D. dissertation, Claremont Graduate University, 1984.

Black, Matthew, ed. *Peake's Commentary on the Bible.* London: Thomas Nelson and Sons, 1962.

Brandon, S. G. F. *The Fall of Jerusalem and the Christian Church.* London: S.P.C.K., 1951.

Brown, Raymond E. *The Churches the Apostles Left Behind.* New York: Paulist Press, 1984.

————. *The Birth of the Messiah.* Garden City, N.Y.: Doubleday, 1977.

Buchanan, George Wesley. *Jesus, the King and His Kingdom.* Macon, Ga.: Mercer University Press, 1984.

Budge, E. A. Wallis. *Osiris and the Egyptian Resurrection,* vol. 1. New York: Dover, 1973.

————, trans. *The Book of the Dead: The Hieroglyphic Transcript of the Papyrus of Ani.* New Hyde Park, N.Y.: University Books, 1960.

Bultmann, Rudolf. *The History of the Synoptic Tradition.* Translated by John Marsh. New York: Harper and Row, 1963.

————. *Primitive Christianity in Its Contemporary Setting.* New York: Meridian Books, 1957.

Burkett, Delbert. *The Son of Man Debate.* Cambridge: Cambridge University Press, 1999.

Campbell, Joseph, ed. *The Mysteries: Papers from the Eranos Yearbooks.* Princeton, N.J.: Princeton University Press, 1955.

Canfora, Luciano. *The Vanished Library.* Berkeley: University of California Press, 1989.

Casey, R. P. "Naassenes and Ophites," In *Journal of Theological Studies* 27 (1926).

Ceram, C. W. *The Secret of the Hittites.* Translated by Richard and Clara Winston. New York: Alfred A. Knopf, 1956.

Chadwick, Henry. *Heresy and Orthodoxy in the Early Church.* Aldershot, Hampshire, UK: Variorum 1991.

Charles, R. H., trans. *The Book of Enoch.* Whitefish, Mont.: Kessinger Publishing, 1912.

Chiera, Edward. *They Wrote on Clay.* Chicago: University of Chicago Press, 1938.

Chrétien de Troyes. *Arthurian Romances.* Translated by D. D. R. Owen. London: Dent, 1987.

Clark, R. T. Rundle. *Myth and Symbol in Ancient Egypt.* London: Thames and Hudson, 1995.

Clement of Alexandria. *The Exhortation to the Greeks.* Translated by G. W. Butterworth. Cambridge: Harvard University Press, 1960.

Coogan, Michael David, ed. *Stories from Ancient Canaan.* Philadelphia: Westminster, 1978.

————, ed. *Oxford History of the Biblical World.* Oxford: Oxford University Press, 1998.

Cornwell, John. *Hitler's Pope.* New York: Penguin Books, 1999.

Cross, Frank Moore. *The Ancient Library of Qumran and Modern Biblical Studies.* Garden City, N.Y.: Doubleday, 1958.

————. *Canaanite Myth and Hebrew Epic: Essays in the History of the Religion of Israel.* Cambridge: Harvard University Press, 1973.

———. *From Epic to Canon: History and Literature in Ancient Israel*. Baltimore: Johns Hopkins University Press, 1998.

Cruz, Joan Carroll. *The Incorruptibles*. Rockford, Ill.: Tan Books, 1977.

Dart, John. *The Laughing Savior*. New York: Harper and Row, 1976.

Davies, J. G. *The Early Christian Church*. New York: Holt, Rinehart, and Winston, 1965.

Davies, William D. "The Jewish State in the Hellenistic World." In *Peake's Commentary on the Bible*. Edited by Matthew Black. Surrey, England: Thomas Nelson, 1980.

de Santillana, Giorgio, and Hertha von Dechend. *Hamlet's Mill*. Boston: Gambit, 1969.

Drower, E. S. *The Secret Adam*. Oxford: Clarendon Press, 1960.

Durant, Will. *The Story of Civilization: The Life of Greece*. New York: Simon and Schuster, 1939.

———. *The Story of Civilization: Caesar and Christ*. New York: Simon and Schuster, 1944.

———. *The Story of Civilization: The Age of Faith*. New York. Simon and Schuster, 1950.

Edwards, I. E. S. *The Pyramids of Egypt*. New York: Penguin, 1988.

Eisenman, Robert. *James the Just*. New York: Penguin, 1996.

Eisenman, Robert, and Michael Wise. *Dead Sea Scrolls Uncovered*. New York: Penguin, 1992.

Eisler, Robert. *Orpheus the Fisher*. London: J. M. Watkins, 1921.

Emerton, J. A. "The Origin of the Son of Man Imagery." In *Journal of Theological Studies* 9 (1958).

Epiphanius of Salamis. *The Panarion of Epiphanius of Salamis*. Translated by Frank Williams. Leiden: E. J. Brill, 1987.

Eschenbach, Wolfram von. *Parzival*. Translated by Helen M. Mustard. New York: Vintage Books, 1961.

Eusebius, Pamphilus. *The Ecclesiastical History*. Grand Rapids, Mich.: Baker Book House, 1990.

Fagan, Brian M. *Return to Babylon*. Boston: Little, Brown, and Co., 1979.

Faulkner, R. O. *The Ancient Egyptian Pyramid Texts*. Oxford: Oxford University Press, 1969.

Finegan, Jack. *Light from the Ancient Past*. Princeton, N.J.: Princeton University Press, 1959.

Finkelstein, Israel. "The Date of the Settlement of the Philistines in Canaan." In *Tel Aviv* 22 (1995).

———. "Interview with Israel Finkelstein." In *Biblical Archaeology Review* (November–December 2002).

Finkelstein, Israel, and Neil Asher Silberman. *The Bible Unearthed*. New York: Free Press, 2001.

Fitzmyer, Joseph A. "The Qumran Scrolls, the Ebionites, and Their Literature." In Krister Stendahl, *The Scrolls and the New Testament*. New York: Harper and Brothers, 1958.

———. *Essays on the Semitic Background of the New Testament*. London: Geoffrey Chapman, 1971.

Foerster, Werner. *Gnosis: A Selection of Gnostic Texts*. Edited by R. McL. Wilson. Oxford: Clarendon Press, 1972.

Fowden, Garth. *The Egyptian Hermes*. Cambridge: Cambridge University Press, 1978.

Fraser, P. M. *Ptolemaic Alexandria*. Oxford: Clarendon Press, 1972.

Frankfort, Henri. *The Cenotaph of Seti I at Abydos*. London: Kegan Paul, Trench, Trubner, and Co., 1933.

Gardner, Laurence. *Bloodline of the Holy Grail*. New York: Barnes and Noble, 1996.

Gasparro, G. Sfameni. "Interpretatazioni gnostiche e misteriosofiche del mito di Attis." In Roelof van den Broek and M. J. Vermaseren, eds. "Studies in Gnosticism and Hellenistic Religion: Presented to Gilles Quispel on the Occasion of His 65th Birthday." Leiden: E.J. Brill, 1981.

Ginzberg, Louis. *The Legends of the Jews,* vols. 1 and 4. Philadelphia: The Jewish Publication Society of America, 1941.

Glueck, Nelson. *The River Jordan*. Philadelphia: Jewish Publication Society of America, 1946.

———. *Rivers in the Desert*. New York: Farrar, Straus, and Cudahy, 1959.

Gordon, Cyrus. *The Living Past*. New York: John Day, 1941.

———. *The Ancient Near East*. New York: W. W. Norton, 1964.

———. *The Common Background of Greek and Hebrew Civilizations*. New York: W. W. Norton, 1965.

———. "Against the Tide: An Interview with Maverick Scholar Cyrus Gordon." In *Biblical Archaeology Review* (November–December 2000).

Goswami, Shyam Sundar. *Layayoga*. London: Routledge and Kegan Paul, 1980.

Grant, Michael. *The History of Ancient Israel*. New York: Scribners, 1984.

———. *Constantine the Great*. New York: History Book Club, 1993.

Grant, Robert M. *Gnosticism and Early Christianity*. New York: Columbia University Press, 1966.

Guillamont, A., et al. *The Gospel According to Thomas*. New York: Harper, 1959.

Guthrie, W. K. C. *Orpheus and Greek Religion*. London: Methuen, 1935.

———. *The Earlier PreSocratics and the Pythagoreans. A History of Greek Philosophy,* vol. 1. Cambridge: Cambridge University Press, 1962.

Gyatso, Geshe Kelsang. *Heart of Wisdom*. London: Tharpa Publications, 1986.

Habibi, Labib. *The Obelisks of Egypt*. New York: Scribners, 1977.

Hancock, Graham. *The Sign and the Seal*. New York: Simon and Schuster, 1992.

———. *Fingerprints of the Gods*. New York: Crown, 1995.

Hancock, Graham, and Robert Bauval. *The Message of the Sphinx*. New York: Three Rivers Press, 1996.

Harkabi, Yehoshafat. *The Bar Kokhba Syndrome*. Chappaqua, N.Y.: Rossel Books, 1983.

Harvey, Andrew. *Son of Man*. New York: Jeremy Tarcher, 1998.

Herodotus. *The Histories*. Translated by Aubrey de Selincourt. New York: Penguin, 1988.

Hesiod. *Theogony, Works and Days, Shield*. Translated by Apostolos N. Athanassakis. Baltimore: Johns Hopkins University Press, 1983.

Hinz, Walther. *The Lost World of Elam: Re-creation of a Vanished Civilization.* Translated by Jennifer Barnes. New York: New York University Press, 1973.

Hippolytus. *The Refutation of All Heresies.* Translated by Rev. J. H. MacMahon. Edinburgh: T. and T. Clark, 1868.

———. *The Philosophumena.* Translated by F. Legge. London: Society for Promoting Christian Knowledge, 1921.

———. *Refutatio Omnium Haeresium.* Translated by Miroslav Marcovich. Berlin: Walter de Gruyter, 1986.

Irenaeus. *Adversus Haereses* (Against Heresies). Edited by W. W. Harvey. Ridgewood, N.J.: Cambridge, 1965.

Isherwood, Christopher. *Ramakrishna and His Disciples.* New York: Simon and Schuster, 1959.

Jack, J. W. *The Ras Shamra Tablets: Their Bearing on the Old Testament.* Edinburgh: T. and T. Clark, 1935.

Jacobsen, Thorkild. *The Treasures of Darkness: A History of Mesopotamian Religion.* New Haven: Yale University Press, 1976.

James, Montague Rhodes. *The Apocryphal New Testament.* Oxford: Clarendon Press, 1924.

John of the Cross. *Collected Works.* Translated by Kieran Kavanaugh. Washington, D.C.: ICS Publications, 1973.

Johnson, Paul. *A History of Christianity.* New York: Atheneum, 1976.

Jonas, Hans. *The Gnostic Religion.* Boston: Beacon Press, 1958.

Josephus, Flavius. *The Life and Works.* Translated by William Whiston. New York: Holt, Rinehart, and Winston, 1998.

Jung, Carl G. *The Secret of the Golden Flower: A Chinese Book of Life.* New York: Harcourt, Brace, and World, 1931.

———. *Psychology and Alchemy.* Translated by R. C. F. Hull. Princeton, N.J.: Princeton University Press, 1953.

———. *Two Essays on Analytical Psychology.* New York: Meridian Books, World Publishing Co., 1956.

———. *Answer to Job.* Translated by R. C. F. Hull. Princeton, N.J.: Princeton University Press, 1958.

———. *Aion: Researches into the Phenomenology of the Self.* Translated by R. C. F. Hull. Princeton, N.J.: Princeton University Press, 1959.

———. *The Archetypes and the Collective Unconscious.* Princeton, N.J.: Princeton University Press, 1959.

———. *Memories, Dreams, and Reflections.* New York: Vintage, 1965.

———. *Alchemical Studies.* Translated by R. C. F. Hull. Princeton, N.J.: Princeton University Press, 1967.

———. *The Psychology of Kundalini Yoga.* Edited by Sonu Shamdasani. Princeton, N.J.: Princeton University Press, 1996.

Jung, Emma, and Marie-Louise von Franz. *The Grail Legend.* Baltimore: Sigo Press, 1980.

Kenyon, Kathleen M. *Archaeology in the Holy Land.* New York: W. W. Norton, 1979.

———. *Digging Up Jericho.* New York: Praeger, 1957.

Kerényi, Karl. *Hermes: Guide of Souls.* Woodstock, Conn.: Spring Publications, 1976.

Kersten, Holger, and Elmar R. Gruber. *The Jesus Conspiracy.* Rockport, Mass.: Element Books, 1992.

Kitchen, K. A. *Pharaoh Triumphant: The Life and Times of Ramses II.* Warminster, England: Aris and Phillips, 1983.

Knight, Christopher, and Robert Lomas. *The Hiram Key.* New York: Barnes and Noble, 1996.

Koester, Helmut. *History and Literature of Early Christianity.* Philadelphia: Fortress Press, 1982.

———. *Ancient Christian Gospels.* Philadelphia: Trinity Press International, 1990.

Kraeling, Carl H. *Anthropos and Son of Man.* New York: AMS Press, 1927.

Kramer, Samuel Noah. *The Sumerians.* Chicago: University of Chicago Press, 1963.

Kripananda, Swami. *The Sacred Power: A Seeker's Guide to Kundalini.* South Fallsburg, N.Y.: SYDA Foundation, 1995.

Kübler-Ross, Elisabeth. *The Wheel of Life.* New York: Scribner, 1997.

Lambert, W. G., and A. R. Millard. *Atra-hasis: The Babylonian Story of the Flood.* Oxford: Clarendon Press, 1969.

Langdon, Stephen. *The Sumerian Epic of Paradise, the Flood, and the Fall of Man.* Philadelphia: University Museum, 1915.

Linforth, Ivan M. *The Arts of Orpheus.* New York: Arno Press, 1973.

Lockyer, J. Norman. *The Dawn of Astronomy.* Whitefish, Mont.: Kessinger Publishing, 1894.

Maccoby, Hyam. *The Mythmaker: Paul and the Invention of Christianity.* New York: Barnes and Noble, 1986.

Mack, Burton L. *The Lost Gospel: The Book of Q and Christian Origins.* San Francisco: HarperSan Francisco, 1993.

Maharshi, Sri Ramana. *Talks with Sri Ramana Maharshi.* Tiruvannamalai, India: Sri Ramanasramam, 1972.

Marmorstein, A. *The Old Rabbinic Doctrine of God.* London: Oxford University Press, 1927.

Mazar, Amihai. *Archaeology of the Land of the Bible.* New York: Doubleday, 1990.

McLachlin, H., ed. *Sir Isaac Newton: Theological Manuscripts.* Liverpool: University Press, 1950.

Mead, G. R. S. *Pistis Sophia: A Gnostic Gospel.* Blauvelt, N.Y.: Spiritual Science Library, 1921.

———. *The Gnostic John the Baptizer.* London: John M. Watkins, 1924.

———. *Thrice Greatest Hermes: Studies in Hellenistic Theosophy and Gnosis.* North Beach, Maine: Samuel Weiser, 1992.

Milik, J. T. *Ten Years of Discovery in the Wilderness of Judaea.* Translated by J. Strugnell. Naperville, Ill.: Alec R. Allenson, 1959.

———. *The Books of Enoch: Aramaic Fragments of Qumran Cave 4.* Oxford: Clarendon Press, 1976.

Milton, Joyce, Robert A. Orsi, and Norman Harrison. *The Feathered Serpent and the Cross: The Pre-Columbian God-Kings and the Papal States.* London: Cassell, 1980.

Muktananda, Swami. *Play of Consciousness*. South Fallsburg, N.Y.: SYDA Foundation, 1971.

———. *Secrets of the Siddhas*. South Fallsburg, N.Y.: SYDA Foundation, 1980.

Murray, Margaret A. *The Osireion at Abydos*. London: Barnard Quaritch, 1904.

———. *The Splendour That Was Egypt*. London: Sidgwick and Jackson, 1963.

Naville, Edouard. "Excavation at Abydos." In *Journal of Egyptian Archaeology* 1 (July 1914).

Neumann, Erich. *The Great Mother: Analysis of the Architect*. Translated by Ralph Manheim. Princeton, N.J.: Princeton University Press, 1963.

Nigg, Walter G. *The Heretics*. New York: Alfred A. Knopf, 1962.

Oldfather, C. H., trans. *Diodorus Siculus*. Cambridge: Harvard University Press, 1989.

Oppenheim, A. Leo. *Ancient Mesopotamia: Portrait of a Dead Civilization*. Chicago: University of Chicago Press, 1964.

———. *Letters from Mesopotamia*. Chicago: University of Chicago Press, 1967.

Origen. *Contra Celsum*. Translated by Henry Chadwick. Cambridge: Cambridge University Press, 1953.

Orlinsky, Harry M. *Ancient Israel*. Ithaca, N.Y.: Cornell University Press, 1960.

Otto, Rudolf. *The Idea of the Holy*. Trans. John W. Harvey. London: Oxford University Press, 1923.

Oulton, John Ernest Leonard, and Henry Chadwick. *Alexandrian Christianity: Selected Translations of Clement and Origen*. Philadelphia: Westminster Press, 1954.

Pagels, Elaine. "The Demiurge and His Archons." In *Harvard Theological Review* (1971).

———. *The Gnostic Paul*. Philadelphia: Fortress Press, 1975.

———. *The Gnostic Gospels*. New York: Random House, 1979.

———. *Adam, Eve, and the Serpent*. New York: Random House, 1988.

———. *The Origin of Satan*. New York: Random House, 1995.

———. *Beyond Belief*. New York: Random House, 2003.

Parke, H. W. *Greek Oracles*. London: Hutchinson, 1967.

Patai, Raphael. *The Hebrew Goddess*. New York: Avon Books, 1978.

Patai, Raphael, and Robert Graves. *Hebrew Myths*. New York: Doubleday, 1964.

Pines, Shlomo. "The Jewish Christians of the Early Centuries of Christianity According to a New Source." In *Israel Academy of Sciences* 2, no. 13 (1966).

Ponce, Charles. *Kabbalah*. Wheaton, Ill.: Theosophical Publishing House, 1973.

Pritchard, James B., ed. *Archaeology and the Old Testament*. Princeton, N.J.: Princeton University Press, 1958.

———. *The Ancient Near East: An Anthology of Texts and Pictures*, vol. 1. Princeton, N.J.: Princeton University Press, 1958.

Prophet, Elizabeth Clare. *The Lost Years of Jesus*. Livingston, Mont.: Summit University Press, 1987.

———. *Reincarnation: The Missing Link in Christianity*. Livingston, Mont.: Summit University Press, 1997.

———. *Fallen Angels and the Origins of Evil*. Livingston, Mont.: Summit University Press, 2000.

Quispel, Gilles. "The Origins of the Gnostic Demiurge." In *Kyriakon, Festschrift Johannes Questen,* vol. 1. Edited by Patrick Granfield and Josef A. Jungmann. Munster Westf: Verlag Aschendorff, 1970.

Raban, Avner, and Robert R. Stieglitz. "The Sea Peoples and Their Contributions to Civilization." In *Archaeology Review* (November–December 1991).

Rama, Swami. "The Awakening of Kundalini." In *Kundalini, Evolution, and Enlightenment.* Ed. John White. Garden City, N.Y.: Doubleday, 1979.

Reitzenstein, Richard. *Poimandres: Studien zur griechisch-agyptischen und fruhchristlichen Literatur.* Leipzig: Teubner, 1904.

———. *Hellenistic Mystery-Religions.* Trans. John Steely. Pittsburgh, Pa.: Pickwick Press, 1978.

Reymond, E. A. E. *The Mythical Origin of the Egyptian Temple.* New York: Manchester University Press, 1969.

Robinson, James M., ed. *The Nag Hammadi Library.* San Francisco: Harper and Row, 1977.

Roerich, Nicholas. *Shambala: In Search of the New Era.* New York: Nicholas Roerich Museum, 1990.

Rohl, David M. *Pharaohs and Kings: A Biblical Quest.* New York: Crown, 1995.

Roland de Vaux. *Ancient Israel: Its Life and Institutions.* Translated by John McHugh. Grand Rapids, Mich.: William B. Eerdman, 1997.

Rolf, Ida. *Rolfing: The Integration of Human Structures.* San Francisco: Harper and Row, 1977.

Roshi, Joshu Sasaki. *Buddha Is the Center of Gravity.* Translated by Fusako Akino. San Cristobal, N.M.: Lama Foundation, 1974.

Rudolph, Kurt. *Gnosis: The Nature and History of Gnosticism.* San Francisco: HarperSan Francisco, 1977.

Russell, D. S. *The Message and Method of Jewish Apocalyptic.* Philadelphia: Westminster Press, 1964.

Russell, J. Stuart. *The Parousia: The New Testament Doctrine of Our Lord's Second Coming.* Grand Rapids, Mich.: Baker Books, 1983.

Schaeffer, Claude F. A. "The Last Days of Ugarit." In *Biblical Archaeology Review* (September–October 1983).

Schiffman, Lawrence, ed. "Archaeology and History in the Dead Sea Scrolls." In *Journal for the Study of Pseudepigrapha,* Supplement Series 8 (1990).

Schoedel, William R. "Naassene Themes in the Coptic Gospel of Thomas." In *Vigiliae Christianae* 14 (1960).

Scholem, Gershom G. *Jewish Gnosticism, Merkabah Mysticism, and Talmudic Tradition.* New York: Jewish Theological Seminary of America, 1960.

Schonfield, Hugh J. *Those Incredible Christians.* New York: Bernard Geis, 1991.

Segal, Alan F. *Two Powers in Heaven.* Leiden: E. J. Brill, 1977.

———. *Rebecca's Children.* Cambridge, Mass.: Harvard University Press, 1986.

———. "Judaism, Christianity, and Gnosticism." In *Anti-Judaism in Early Christianity,* vol. 2. Edited by Stephen G. Wilson. Waterloo, Ontario: Wilfred Laurier University Press, 1986.

Segev, Tom. *One Palestine Complete: Jews and Arabs Under the British Mandate.* New York: Henry Holt, 1999.

Shanks, Hershel, ed. *Understanding the Dead Sea Scrolls.* New York: Random House, 1992.

———. "The Enigma of Qumran." In *Biblical Archaeology Review* (January–February 1998).

Simonetti, M. "Qualche osservatione sulle presunte interpolazioni della Predica dei Naaseni." In *Vetera Christianorum* 7 (1970).

Sitchin, Zecharia. *The Wars of Gods and Men.* Rochester, Vt.: Bear and Co., 1992.

Smith, Morton. *Clement of Alexandria and a Secret Gospel of Mark.* Cambridge, Mass.: Harvard University Press, 1973.

———. *The Secret Gospel.* New York: Harper and Row, 1973.

Smyth, Piazzi. *The Great Pyramid.* New York: Random House, 1978.

Sollberger, Edmond. *The Babylonian Legend of the Flood.* London: British Museum, 1971.

Spiegelman, J. Marvin, and Arwind U. Vasavada. *Hinduism and Jungian Psychology.* Phoenix, Ariz.: Falcon Press, 1987.

Stager, Lawrence E. "When Canaanites and Philistines Ruled Ashkelon." In *Biblical Archaeology Review* (March–April 1991).

Stendahl, Krister, ed. *The Scrolls and the New Testament.* New York: Harper and Brothers, 1958.

Stern, Ephraim. "Pagan Yahwism." In *Biblical Archaeology Review* (May–June 2001).

Strabo. *The Geography,* vol. 8. Translated by Horace Leonard Jones. London: G. P. Putnam's Sons, 1933.

Sullivan, William. *The Secret of the Incas.* New York: Three Rivers Press, 1996.

Tatian. "Address to the Greeks." In *The Ante-Nicene Fathers.* Edited by Rev. Alexander Roberts. Grand Rapids, Mich.: Eerdman, 1956.

Teeter Dobbs, Betty Jo. *The Foundations of Newton's Alchemy.* Cambridge: Cambridge University Press, 1975.

Temple, Robert K. G. *The Sirius Mystery.* Rochester, Vt.: Destiny Books, 1987.

Thiering, Barbara. *Jesus the Man.* London: Corgi Books, 1992.

Thompson, William Irwin. *The Time Falling Bodies Take to Light.* New York: St. Martin's Press, 1981.

Tompkins, Peter. *Secrets of the Great Pyramid.* New York: Galahad Books, 1971.

———. *Mysteries of the Mexican Pyramids.* New York: Harper and Row, 1976.

van den Broek, Roelof. *Studies in Gnosticism and Alexandrian Christianity.* Leiden: E. J. Brill, 1996.

van Groningen, G. *First-Century Gnosticism: Its Origin and Motifs.* Leiden: E. J. Brill, 1967.

Velikovsky, Immanuel. *Worlds in Collision.* New York: Dell, 1950.

———. *Ages in Chaos.* Garden City, N.Y.: 1952.

———. *Oedipus and Akhnaton.* Garden City, N.Y.: Doubleday, 1960.

Vermes, Geza. *The Complete Dead Sea Scrolls in English.* Harmondsworth, Middlesex, UK: Penguin Books, 1998.

Virgil. *The Aeneid of Virgil.* Translated by C. Day Lewis. New York: Doubleday, 1952.

Vivekananda, Swami. *Raja Yoga.* New York: Brentano, 1929.

Wasson, R. Gordon, Albert Hofman, and Carl A. P. Ruck. *The Road to Eleusis.* New York: Harcourt Brace, 1978.

Watts, Alan. *The Way of Zen.* New York: Vintage, 1957.

Webster, T. B. L. *From Mycenae to Homer.* New York: Praeger, 1959.

West, M. L. *The Orphic Poems.* Oxford: Clarendon Press, 1983.

Weston, Jessie L. *From Ritual to Romance.* Garden City, N.Y.: Doubleday, 1920.

White, John, ed. *Kundalini, Evolution, and Enlightenment.* Garden City, N.Y.: Doubleday, 1979.

Wiener, Aharon. *The Prophet Elijah in the Development of Judaism.* London: Routledge and Kegan Paul, 1978.

Williams, Jay G. *Understanding the Old Testament.* New York: Barron's, 1972.

Williams, Michael Allen. *Rethinking Gnosticism.* Princeton, N.J.: Princeton University Press, 1996.

Wilson, Edmund. *The Dead Sea Scrolls.* New York: Oxford University Press, 1969.

Wilson, Ian. *The Exodus Enigma.* London: Weidenfield and Nicolson, 1985.

Wood, Bryant G. "The Sea Peoples Enter Canaan." In *Biblical Archaeology Review* (November–December 1991).

Woolley, C. Leonard. *Ur of the Chaldees.* New York: Charles Scribners Sons, 1930.

Woolley, C. Leonard, and T. E. Lawrence. *Carchemish.* London: British Museum, 1914.

Wordsworth, C. H. R. *St. Hippolytus and the Church of Rome in the Earlier Part of the Third Century.* London: Oxford and Cambridge, F. and J. Rivington, 1853.

Yamauchi, Edwin M. *Gnostic Ethics and Mandaean Origins.* Cambridge, Mass.: Harvard University Press, 1970.

———. *The Stones and the Scriptures.* New York: J. B. Lippincott, 1972.

Yogananda, Paramahansa. *Autobiography of a Yogi.* Los Angeles: Self-Realization Fellowship, 1988.

Index